Infrastructures of Caring Citizenship

Infrastructures of Caring Citizenship

COMMONING SOCIAL REPRODUCTION IN
CRISIS-RIDDEN ATHENS, GREECE

ISABEL GUTIÉRREZ SÁNCHEZ

THE UNIVERSITY OF GEORGIA PRESS
Athens

Segments of chapter 2 appeared in "Informal Structures of Welfare: Emerging Spaces of Social Reproduction in Athens," in *Urban Informality and the Built Environment: Infrastructure, Exchange and Image*, edited by Nerea Amorós Elorduy, Nikhilesh Sinha, and Colin Marx (London: UCL Press, 2024), 107–124; "Care Commons: Infrastructural (Re)compositions for Life Sustenance through yet against Regimes of Chronic Crisis," *Urban Studies* 60, no. 12 (2023): 2456–2473; "Infrastructures from Below: Self-Reproduction and Common Struggle in and beyond Athens in Crisis," in *Care and the City: Encounters with Urban Studies*, edited by A. Gabauer, S. Knierbein, N. Cohen, H. Lebuhn, K. Trogal, T. Viderman, and T. Haas, 151–161 (New York: Routledge, 2022), 151–161. Segments of chapter 3 appeared in "Dwelling as Politics: An Emancipatory Praxis of/ through Care and Space in Everyday Life," *Environment and Planning D: Society and Space* 40, no. 3 (2022): 549–566.

Most University of Georgia Press titles are available from popular e-book vendors.

Printed digitally

EU Authorized Representative Easy Access System Europe—Mustamäe tee 50, 10621 Tallinn, Estonia, gpsr.requests@easproject.com

Library of Congress Cataloging-in-Publication Data
Names: Gutiérrez Sánchez, Isabel, 1986– author
Title: Infrastructures of caring citizenship : commoning social reproduction in crisis-ridden Athens, Greece / Isabel Gutiérrez Sánchez.
Description: Athens : The University of Georgia Press, 2025. | Series: Geographies of justice and social transformation; 70 | Includes bibliographical references and index.
Identifiers: LCCN 2025020538 | ISBN 9780820375052 hardback | ISBN 9780820375069 paperback | ISBN 9780820375076 epub | ISBN 9780820375083 pdf
Subjects: LCSH: Social service—Greece—Athens—Citizen participation | Community organization—Greece—Athens | Social change—Greece—Athens | Athens (Greece)—Social conditions—21st century | Greece—Economic conditions—2009–
Classification: LCC HV375.5.Z9 A887 2025
LC record available at https://lccn.loc.gov/2025020538

CONTENTS

ILLUSTRATIONS

ACRONYMS

15M	15th May movement (Spain)
AIDA	Asylum Information Database
ANEL	Anexartitoi Ellines (Independent Greeks—National Patriotic Alliance)
COVID-19	Coronavirus disease 2019
EC	European Commission
ECB	European Central Bank
ECRE	European Council on Refugees and Exiles
EKKA	Ethnikó Kéntro Koivonikís Allileggís (National Center for Social Solidarity)
EL.STAT	Elliniki Statistiki Archi (Greek Statistical Authority)
ESSPROS	European System of Integrated Social Protection Statistics
EU	European Union
FEANTSA	European Federation of National Organisations Working with the Homeless
FIDH	International Federation for Human Rights
GDP	gross domestic product
HLHR	Hellenic League for Human Rights
ICCs	infrastructures of caring citizenship
IMF	International Monetary Fund
ISEPR	Initiative of Solidarity to Economic and Political Refugees
MoU	memorandum of understanding
ND	Néa Dimokratía (New Democracy)
NGO	nongovernmental organization
NHS	National Health System
OECD	Organisation for Economic Co-operation and Development

OEK	Orgánosi Ergatikís Katoikíes (Workers Housing Organisation)
PASOK	Panellinio Sosialistikó Kínima (Panhellenic Socialist Movement)
SYRIZA	Synaspismós Rizospastikis Aristerás (Coalition of the Radical Left)
TCATC	The City at a Time of Crisis Project
TINA	There Is No Alternative
UNHCR	United Nations High Commissioner for Refugees

ACKNOWLEDGMENTS

A book is a challenging and transformative personal endeavor. Yet, in my view, it is collective at the core for, on the one hand, the production of knowledge is necessarily a dialogic process that feeds on past and living sources and, on the other, any author themselves could rarely sustain the work it entails without the support of others. In my case, this work is indebted to a large number of people who have inspired me with their own work, their practice, their struggle, and their commitment to social justice and life sustenance, as well as to many others who have trusted me, supported me, and encouraged me along the way. This book started as a doctoral dissertation, during which I was supervised by Professor Peter Bishop, Professor Claire Colomb, and Professor Yeoryia Manopoulou. I am thankful for their guidance, support, and trust. I am very grateful to Dimitris Soudias, who gave me the push I needed to transform that doctoral thesis into a book. I want to thank University of Georgia Press executive editor Mick Gusinde-Duffy and the series editors Mathew Coleman and Ishan Ashutosh, as well as my anonymous reviewers for their insightful feedback. Thanks also to production editor Mary C. Ribesky and to copy editor Michael Durnin for the work they have put into this project. I also want to kindly thank the artist Emeka Ogboh for generously letting me use his own image of his artwork.

I want to express my thankfulness and solidarity to the people engaged in the self-organized initiatives that in this book I call "infrastructures of caring citizenship," for their work and commitment to building and sustaining worlds in common despite and beyond crisis. Deep thanks to those who kindly and generously accepted my questions and shared with me their stories and thoughts. My most profound gratitude goes to Eirini Konstantopoulou. I especially thank her for her accompaniment during the solitary months of writing. Similarly, my friend Jorge Martín García, whose critical and always well-grounded arguments in our multiple conversations have been of paramount importance during the years that have elapsed while I completed this work. My gratitude also goes to Inés Morales-Bernardos, whose critical insights into the complexities of the Athenian political landscapes as well as her affection and trust have all been of inestimable value to me. Thanks to Candela Morado Castresana for helping me review some chapters with the thorough gaze of the ethnographer. I am deeply grateful for her collaboration throughout the journey into the field of anthropology, which we started together years ago. This journey would not have been the same without Matilde Córdoba Azcárate, who guided us through our first steps into the discipline and encouraged us. To Moustafa Rashid, Salah Rashid, Fatima Rashid, and Joan Hamkalino, I owe an intimate process of learning and transformation, through which I eventually found myself displaced to a new position from which to look at and experience the world. Our friendship tells the story of an encounter, of the kind I reflect on throughout this book. I know I will always find solace and strength in Fatima's memory and the days we spent together, beautiful and hard at the same time. Thanks to Esra Dogan, one of the first to introduce me to the feminist movement(s) in Athens, for welcoming and hosting me; to Doxia Theodorou, also for her affection; and to Electre Mouche, whose honest intelligence and personal integrity continue to challenge me profoundly and have influenced my view and understanding of important aspects of the Solidarity Movement in the Greek capital. My gratitude also goes to Mar López, whose committed and generous work in support of migrant women is to me a source of learning and a call to action; to Christina Darzanou, who not only helped me with my Greek but also gave me her trust and support. I am also immensely grateful to Miguel Carvajal for the conversations, the multiple stories he has shared with me, his kindness and patience, and whose selflessness and commitment have left their mark on my conscience. Thank you also to Alfonso Rengifo Cavestany for being there despite the distance.

Not least, I want to warmly thank my family in Athens—Thaleia Dimitropoulou, Eliana Otta, Vasiliki Sifostratoudaki, Sanem Su Avci, and Mariana Juliana Byck—for making our Mouries Collective a site of shared inspiration and mutual support, as well as Panagiotis Tsintavís and Giorgos Charitakis for their warmth, care, and generosity. My profound gratitude goes to my parents, José Gutiérrez Macías and Maria Cruz Sánchez Castañares, for having accepted so many of my personal choices that were far from their expectations and having eventually supported me in spite of everything. To my sister, María

Gutiérrez Sánchez, for her trust and determination. I know the three of you love me and miss me deeply in the distance. My thanks also go to Carmen Sánchez de las Heras for her encouragement and complicity; and to Martín, Nicolás, and Rocío, my beloved nephews and niece, to whom I dedicate this work in search of existing instances in which a better world, a world in common and grounded in care, is being imagined and created.

Infrastructures of Caring Citizenship

Introduction

The City in Crisis: Enclosures of the Future from Above and Grassroots Radical Imaginations

In the art exhibition Documenta 14, held in Athens in 2017, the artist Emeka Ogboh (2017) presented the work *The Way Earthly Things Are Going* (see figure 0.1).[1] The piece comprises a LED ticker tape featuring livestream stock-exchange data from around the world and a sound installation playing the lamentation song *Αλησμονώ και χαίρομαι* (When I forget, I rejoice) by the female vocal group Pleiades.[2] The song, traditionally from the Epirus region in northwestern Greece, features stories of forced displacement, leaving the past behind, and the quest for hopeful futures. Standing in the middle of that raw concrete room of the amphitheater of the Athens Conservatoire,[3] sensing and trying to make sense of those two distant representations of the relentless crisis in Greece—and beyond—for a moment, I felt reassured in my ongoing research endeavor. Ogboh's (2017) artwork beautifully and eloquently reminded me of the multiscalar, multidimensional, and polyphonic nature of contemporary crises. The Greek crisis was interwoven with multiple other crises intersecting at multiple scales. The voices, languages, platforms, and forms of narrating those intertwined crises were also manifold, ranging from stock-exchange figures to the lived stories of migrants in search of a better life.

In 2008, the collapse of major international banking institutions triggered the unfolding of multiple crises across the world. In Europe, it put an end to decades of economic growth and relative social stability, particularly in southern regions. The aspirations of a bright future linked to ideals of progress and continuous modernization faded away quite suddenly. Austerity, consisting of a wide range of structural adjustment policies and measures, was imposed on national governments as a condition of receiving bailout loans. It was

FIGURE 0.1. *The Way Earthly Things Are Going*, by Emeka Ogboh, from the art exhibition Documenta 14, Athens (2017).

extensively presented as the only possibility to regain good economic performance and was eventually delivered across countries including the United Kingdom, Ireland, Portugal, Italy, Spain, and Greece. Over a decade on, the accelerated retrenchment of the welfare system, the rising deterioration of the living conditions, and the increasing impoverishment, exclusion, and violence that ensued from the global banking collapse and the following austerity regimes still pervade and constrict the lives of millions of people in Europe.

I arrived in Athens for the first time in May 2016 to start fieldwork as part of my doctoral research work. The economic crisis and austerity regime in my home country, Spain, had drastically affected my career path and expectations for the future, as it had for many other young people. My involvement in the occupation of Puerta del Sol in my home town of Madrid and the 15M movement in 2011 also shifted my political practice and commitment.[4] Four years later, I got the opportunity to pursue a PhD at a university in London. My research proposal was about Greece though—Athens in particular. I had been following with interest the developments in the country, especially since the occupation of Syntagma Square was twinned with the one in Madrid.[5] How was the crisis affecting people's lives in the country said to be the most stricken by the economic recession? What would crisis mean for them? What had happened with the transformative energy generated in the squares? Would the collective responses produced there have anything to do with the ones I witnessed in Madrid? Could they learn from each other? I had the intuition that attending to these questions in the Greek reality would provide me with a deeper understanding of the crisis in my own country but also of a phenomenon taking on a global scale and an expanding temporality.

At the time of my arrival, the word "crisis" (κρίση in Greek) was all around. It populated the news and everyday conversations, and appeared on walls and banners across the city. Following the official declaration of the national debt crisis in 2010, "The Crisis" became the new national commonplace, used by the media, politicians, and citizens alike.[6] Some of its effects were apparent at first sight: people sleeping rough and looking for food inside garbage containers, empty stores and abandoned buildings, litter-strewn streets and parks. Beyond these manifestations, I wanted to learn about people's own experiences and meanings generated by The Crisis—individual and collective. I engaged in conversations whenever I felt that that was appropriate and welcomed, always aware that the topic could well be triggering or especially sensitive for some people. I quickly realized, however, that many were willing to share and elaborate on their experiences. The following are excerpts of conversations with Maria, an actress and activist, Christina, a university teacher and artist, and Elina, a young architect and volunteer in a self-organized kitchen at the time. My encounters and exchanges with them provoked lingering thoughts that came to provide me with a basis for how I elaborate and articulate crisis in this book.

I met Maria at Korai Square, where there is an entrance to the Panepistimiou metro station. The flow of people is constant at this central spot of the city.

> People here run. They are deep in their thoughts. It seems they don't care much about how they look. After 2010 the bodies have changed. For me, the first sign of The Crisis was what it did to people's bodies. The body behavior, the body language is not the same. It's more closed, more abandoned, angrier. I think people are more afraid of touching each other. More aggressive. . . . Old people are very angry and scared. These people that worked so much and saved everything for their children, now they have to pay a lot of taxes, they have to pay for their medicines. Most of them invested their money in properties, but now they can't rent them because rents are very cheap. They can't sell them either. The hospitals are really crowded. The generation now in their thirties grew in prosperity. They based their hopes on some standards that are now gone. Teenagers, however, nowadays are different. They share more things. They accompany each other more. They don't judge people for their money. I think there is a different value system. Despite all the hardships and disillusionment, there is a transformation in values and ways of seeing life, which is also politics, that I think can grow and make a change. (Maria, June 9, 2017)

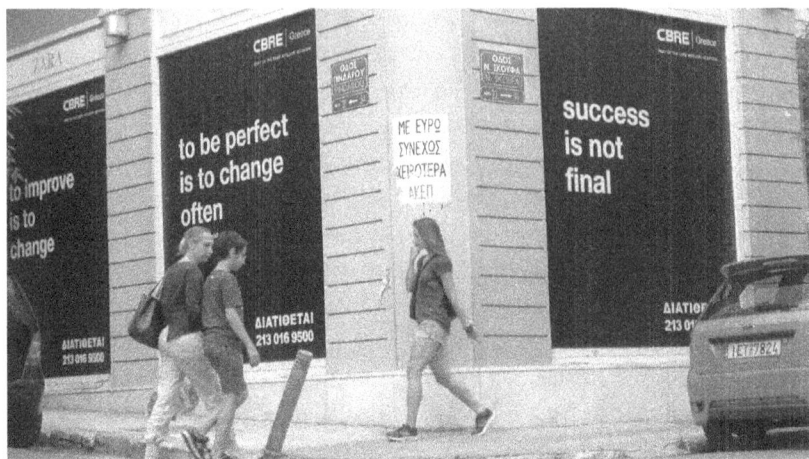

FIGURE 0.2. Corner between Skoufa and Pindarou Streets in the neighborhood of Kolonaki, Athens (2018). Photo by Isabel Gutiérrez Sánchez.

Christina brought me to a corner between Skoufa and Pindarou Streets in the neighborhood of Kolonaki, a high-income area in central Athens. I had told her that I would like to talk with her about the meanings of The Crisis and she chose that paradigmatic location to share her thoughts with me.

> In this corner, there was a Zara store. The multinational companies that were here decided that it was not profitable enough for them, so they abandoned it. Then, a new company, which is driving gentrification in the center of Athens, took over the building and chose, instead of advertising the name of the property company, to put—let's say—some guidelines for life. One of them is: "Success is not final," which basically means for me that whatever you do is not enough. You need to be in a constant struggle for development, moving forward, battling. On the other side of the corner, we have: "To be perfect is to change often," which basically means the same: You should not be yourself, you should change all the time and adjust to the environment and the new conditions. On the contrary, we have this handmade poster from an autonomous political party, which is basically resisting everything, that says: "With Euro [which has two meanings: Euro as a currency but also Euro as Europe] constantly worse." This is a very funny corner for me because we have messages in English, which is maybe the European language, that are directing us to change constantly. And then we have the one in Greek, which says: "But constantly it will be worse." . . .

The Crisis is being a dramatic experience. But I think it is being used in a kind of manipulative way. I think we are misled by the official voices. I like this corner because it's challenging these official tales. We don't want their solutions anymore. (Christina, June 13, 2017)

Elina suggested that we meet at a cooperative-run coffee shop (καφενείο) in the neighborhood of Kypseli, a host area for diverse migrant communities since the 1990s.[7] She told me it was one of her reference sites in the city since she moved to Athens to start her university studies.

I had finished my degree, found a relatively good job and even bought a car. I saw The Crisis on TV. It was there all the time. And the truth is that I also saw it unfolding around me. . . . Still, I guess I thought it would pass, that it wouldn't touch me. It did. First, it hit my parents who went unemployed one after the other. Then it was me. We had never had serious economic issues. I was optimistic at the beginning, but then months and months went by and I started to feel more and more stuck. I also felt very tired and started cancelling plans with friends, isolating myself. I guess I wasn't prepared for it. It was my dear friend Katerina who dragged me out of this. She convinced me to start lending a hand in a social kitchen. . . . I met a lot of new people. . . . They helped me realize that The Crisis is not our fault and that we shouldn't take it for granted anymore. Our future is not lost, we can do something about it. Then, Syntagma came. It shook me. . . . After, I got active in my neighborhood committee and joined neighbors in the construction of a new park on a former parking site. . . . Politics became a new thing for me. Now it's central to my life. I know I can choose my position in this chaos. We can open windows in this crisis and show them [governments] that we are not *gonna* be passive puppets in their show while they squeeze us more and more. (Elina, August 27, 2016)

I have chosen these excerpts of conversations because they reflect different relevant dimensions of The Crisis: from how it affected the very bodies of people to the different messages behind crisis narratives, to distrust and rejection of governments' discourses and policies, to collective solidarity responses. They also reveal stories of transformation and political maturation through crisis, many times leading to the very rejection of it based on a new understanding, that of a "show" orchestrated from above for the powerful and the wealthy. These interpretations of The Crisis, on the one hand, as an external, political instrument intervening and interrupting people's everyday lives in the interest of the established powers, and, on the other, as a personal transformative and politicizing experience, would come up in similar ways in conversations with many others of my research interlocutors. They would make it clear to me that our present is undoubtedly one in crisis, yet also in dispute.

On a broader level, this book is an attempt to critically address The Crisis with this hypothesis: that it is a condition of manifold, interrelated dimensions marked by tense power dialectics between dominant instituted forces and defiant instituting instances. The key driving questions place the focus on this aspect inherent to all crises, meaning critique and resistance. The situated context that grounds this inquiry is Athens, the Greek capital, in the time span from 2010, when the national debt crisis was officially declared by the government of George Papandreou (leader of Panellinio Sosialistikó Kínima [Panhellenic socialist movement], PASOK), to the officially announced completion of the bailout programmes by the president, Alexis Tsipras (leader of Synaspismós Rizospastikis Aristerás [Coalition of the radical left], SYRIZA) in 2018. The four instances of collective struggle that comprise the main field of this investigation are examples of critical responses to The Crisis from below. Crisis is the condition that determines and threatens their existence. Yet, at the same time, it is also the very condition that enabled their formation.

That noted, I deem it important to make a cautionary note regarding this perspective. I want to acknowledge some risks associated with the analyses of crises that focus on bottom-up responses to them. Not all of these responses defy the orderings and workings of the status quo. Not all strive to advance radical alternatives, and not all of those are new. Those that endeavor to do so are among the many and diverse social realities of a crisis. Uncritical accounts may contribute to feeding stereotypical representations of contemporary crises or problematic, romantic imaginaries of resistance and subversion. Both historical processes relevant to the crisis and people's coping responses in everyday life risk being overlooked (Kalantzis 2016). As Ogboh's artwork reminds us, crises constitute polyphonic narratives emerging from and producing multiple and diverse experiences, some of which can collide in space and time. Crisis can be experienced as an imposition, an interruption, an impasse, and a condition of possibility at the same time. The tasks of critical researchers are to lay bare the diversity of processes of crisis formation, the different forms and experiences crisis takes, and to challenge generalized assumptions about what that crisis is and what it does. In the last section of this introduction, I dwell on how I have strived in my analysis to do so, as well as on some limitations of this attempt.

For the remainder of this introductory section, I would like to provide an overarching theoretical conceptualization of the notion of crisis, which will be dissected into four main dimensions. I will refer to them as *the empirical-*

experiential, the imaginary, the governmental, and *the critical-insurgent.* This conceptual distinction emerges in the first place from my encounters and own experience in the city, which I nurture with theoretical and scholarly readings. With it, I seek to assist the reflection about and articulation of the lived experiences of The Crisis that were shared with me and that I myself witnessed. Therefore, I want to highlight that, far from being a theoretical problem, crisis in this book is engaged and elaborated first and foremost from the lived realities I learned about and experienced in Athens during the years of research work.

This theoretical elaboration of crisis also informs a key concept of the book, namely the "city in crisis," which is introduced at the end. Through this notion, crisis takes on an urban form. Space becomes a prominent category in the analysis of crisis as a key element that is materially transformed, as much as it is constitutive of emerging social imaginaries, practices, relationships, and subjectivities. As such, space will cut across the said dimensions.

CRISIS: THE EMPIRICAL-EXPERIENTIAL, THE IMAGINARY, THE GOVERNMENTAL, AND THE CRITICAL-INSURGENT

The crisis of the financial system, the crisis of capitalism, the crisis of the contemporary subject, the crisis of housing markets, the debt crisis, the ecological crisis, the crisis of representative democracy, the crisis of care, the refugee crisis, and more recently, the pandemic crisis, the infrastructure crisis, the energy crisis and the cost of living crisis; they all speak of the multifaceted and multiscalar character of a key condition that defines and determines our contemporary world. As crisis grows, tearing down structures that seemed solid, making precarious livelihoods and everyday lives, the vision of a future beyond permanent breakdown appears increasingly blurred and unattainable. Loss, fear, anxiety, and resignation seem to have captured our subjectivities and collective imaginations, seemingly trapping us in an impasse. No longer a sudden rupture of passing nature, crisis at present is experienced as an enduring condition for many (Roitman 2013), allowing us to speak of a state of chronic crisis (Athanasiou 2018; Athanasiou and Butler 2013).

This condition takes shape in different dimensions and forms, in ways both visible and (quite) invisible (Roitman 2013). Crises have material and experiential forms, which are perhaps their initial indicators. Normally, crisis manifests in the form of a sudden deterioration in living conditions, downward social trajectories, and social unrest, and its primary experiences are those of rupture, loss, and trauma (Athanasiou 2018; Athanasiou and Butler 2013;

Boano and Gyftopoulou 2016). Certainly, the effects of the financial crisis in southern Europe can be traced through an enormous amount of economic data and social indicators produced over the last decade, as well as through the lived experiences of many of those whose lives have been struck, which have been documented in a wide range of ethnographic studies. These diverse sources attest to the dramatic social transformations that this multifaceted crisis has brought about, both at the structural level and in everyday life (Dalakoglou, Agelopoulos, and Poulimenakos 2018).

Yet, crisis has also an imaginary dimension constructed from a multiplicity of images, discourses, and stories (Roitman 2013). In their manifold versions, they all compose a social imaginary, namely a fabric of interwoven images, symbols, narratives, conceptualizations, and values, which societies articulate to represent and recognize themselves and to give sense to their forms of organizing their collective life. According to the philosopher Cornelius Castoriadis ([1975] 1987), in each historical period, social imaginaries give meaning and actually define a social reality, that is, a common understanding of the state of things, which is fundamental for the creation and establishment of the different social institutions and the norms that regulate those. Social imaginaries in this sense work as devices of vision, interpretation, and narration of the world that inform and organize a common perception of reality, (seemingly) fixing it. In this view, social imaginaries would undermine societies' capacity to see themselves as permanently in-the-making, namely as always *instituting* rather than already *instituted*. Crisis as a social imaginary would in this light refer to a social construct by which the concept of *crisis* has become— or has been instituted—as a new truth, a new way of seeing and living. In other words, a new normality. It is in this sense that the anthropologist Janet Roitman (2013) urges us to question the *essentialization* of crisis—which does not mean to deny the existence of crises and their effects—so as to be able to understand it also as a normative mechanism that determines and controls what can be seen, defined, and spoken of, and ultimately what can be done in response. How was the crisis (that particular narrative of crisis) built? By whom? To serve what and whose purposes? Whose crisis is it signalling?

Following Roitman (2013), the scholars Judith Butler and Athina Athanasiou (2013) contend that crisis discourses are in themselves a form of managing crisis. They refer to the contemporary state of enduring crisis as a "perennial state of exception that turns into a rule and common sense" (2013, 149). Athanasiou (2018) explains that certain discourses—like those of the "there is no alternative" type—contribute to instituting crisis as a "truth regime" through which the same crisis is governed. Namely, the ruling powers capitalize on the "crisis imaginary," ultimately turning crisis into a form of governmentality (Athanasiou 2018; Athanasiou and Butler 2013; Boano and Gyftopoulou 2016; Koutrolikou 2016; Roitman 2013; Tsilimpounidi 2017).[8] An overview of the policies and measures rolled out in countless countries across the globe over the last decade makes this argument difficult to contest. The "crisis politics" enforced from above since 2008 has enabled the imposition of states of emergency across the world, through which liberties and rights have been suspended. It has forced citizens to bear the burden of the crash of the financial sector, seriously undermining national sovereignties and condemning populations and entire countries to indefinite indebtedness. It has torn apart public welfare systems through austerity reforms as the condition imposed by international creditors to receive bailout loans. It has shut down borders, incarcerating thousands of migrants and asylum seekers and letting many die. Certainly, years of crisis politics have done nothing but expand the processes of exclusion and dispossession already stretching for decades across the capitalist world. The crisis imaginary has largely served the purposes of the dominant economic and political powers and their institutions. As it settled, it has become a machinery of production of "enclosures of the future"—as the scholar Aris Komporozos-Athanasiou (2015) put it—masking ever-renewing processes of capital extraction and growing inequalities.

The imaginary and the governmental dimensions of crisis in turn inform personal perceptions, sensibilities, meanings, behaviors, practices, and relationships. In involving and deploying knowledge and power, crisis shapes subjects—or subjectivities.[9] According to Athanasiou (2018), the pervading conditions of dispossession, precariousness, and vulnerability, which characterize—and in fact enable—the contemporary regime of chronic crisis, are central to contemporary processes of subjectivation that shape the subject along class, gender, ethnicity, and citizenship lines. Nevertheless, how individuals assimilate and relate to these factors ranges from passive submission to the oppression and alienation that those entail, to resistance and construction of a different subjectivity. As Foucault ([1969] 2002, 2008, 2017) argued, crises constitute liminal fields in which the established premises that shape subjectivities are challenged. Thus, they often provide the conditions for the prefiguration of new subjectivities that seek emancipation from the prevailing order and powers.

In line with this argument, Roitman (2013) reminds us of the paradox of the very necessity of crisis in order to narrate a future without crisis. Inherent to crisis is critique and judgment—as per its Greek etymological root (κρίνειν)—hence the power to give birth to different realities. In our contemporary world, claims of crisis can serve to ground the critique of capitalism, imperialism, colonization, extractivism, globalization, and so on, as well as the very politics of crisis itself. Crisis is therefore an epistemological instrument to deconstruct the crisis imaginary, and in so doing, understand its politics. It is a starting point to break with the cycle of crisis production, a tool to open up the possible, to activate the radical imagination, which as Castoriadis ([1975] 1987) elaborates, is an intrinsic element of the social imaginary.[10] The social imaginary is in fact simultaneously instituted and instituting. It is informed by the very possibility of being broken down, reconfigured, and reestablished. Herein lies its most political power. The efforts from above to cancel the future via crisis regimes are unceasingly met with resisting and generative forces that challenge and reclaim the crisis imaginary and its politics, turning them into ambivalent and conflicting terrains.

THE CITY IN CRISIS

Cities, where more than half of the planet's population lives, are often the sites where crises become more visibly patent. The accelerated frequency and growing magnitude of contemporary crises are triggering rapid urban transformations worldwide. Conversely, cities are recurrently being used for the very production of these crises. In both the academic and the political realms, the "city in crisis" has become a recurrent theme. On the one hand, it has become a common framework of analysis and critique of the impacts of contemporary crises on the urban environment and urban life. On the other, it has served diverse political actors to justify new policies and measures. In this book, far from a mere defining category, the city in crisis will be treated as both an empirical and conceptual site for interrogation and examination of Athens, where the crisis starting in the aftermath of the international banking collapse overlapped with existing urban crises and other emerging ones, continuing into the present. How does The Crisis manifest in Athens? How is it experienced by its dwellers? How is it spoken of? How is it explained? How is it governed and managed? How does it register in the urban environment and the city's social fabric? Athens-in-crisis will be treated as a backdrop as much as a medium of many of the transformations that took place in the city during the aforementioned time span, from the structural to the everyday life, from the collective to the individual. As a prolegomenon to the elaboration and study of Athens-in-crisis, in the following lines, I outline the conceptual framework of the city in crisis that will serve to articulate the analysis. I start with the imaginary dimension, which has received less attention in the scholarship, though that doesn't mean it lacks crucial importance.

Cities are prominent sites of organization and crystallization of social practices, including imagination. At the same time, they are sites in incessant transformation and constant production of new imaginaries. Thus, they can be viewed as simultaneously instituted and instituting, using Castoriadis's terms. Those social imaginaries produced through the urban and manifested specifically in cities are often referred to as urban imaginaries. Urban experiences, spaces, and processes play today a paramount role in the production, institution, contestation, and reinvention of the interwoven fabrics of images, discourses, meanings and values that social imaginaries are (Hiernaux and Lindón 2012; Lindón 2012). In turn, these social imaginaries constructed through the city shape the same urban experiences, spaces and processes. Today, given the role of cities in the production of contemporary crises, we could actually think of crisis as a key urban imaginary. Which are the specific characteristics and implications of crisis as an urban imaginary? How does the city-in-crisis imaginary shape urban life and city space?

To a great extent, as Giorgio Agamben (2003) argues, crisis comes across as an urgent and exceptional matter, predominantly in economic and security terms. The city-in-crisis imaginary is engendered by the perception—whether empirically grounded or socially constructed—of a deterioration of living conditions, usually coupled with a sentiment of increasing insecurity. Images and stories of people falling into poverty or exclusion—like images of people queuing for food at the door of charities or searching for it in garbage containers, rough sleepers on the streets, drug consumption in the squares—and stories of acts of despair, such as public suicides or immolations, all feed the big image of the city as a site of humanitarian emergency. On the other hand, images of riots and violent protests coupled with images of increasing police presence contribute to propagating a climate of rising insecurity and fear, and the normalization of violence. All these phenomena—which have both imaginary and factual components—have an impact on the built environment, which in turn becomes also a showcase of the crisis. Through images of closed-down businesses, abandoned buildings, dirty public spaces, graffiti, and messages—often of criticism and vindication—that are left registered on street walls, the city's space and materiality serve as a canvas of the crisis.

As it consolidates, the city-in-crisis imaginary settles a frame of vision through which urban dwellers see and identify themselves. The city in crisis then becomes a reality, a truth. This truth in turn becomes a mechanism for managing and governing the crisis or multiple crises that manifest in the urban. In other words, the production of images, representations, and narratives of crisis of the city contribute to the emergence of new urban governmentalities, which in turn feed and sustain the imaginary of the city in crisis. Ultimately, this circular process leads to the transformation and configuration of new geographies—human, cultural, territorial—and spatialities in and of the urban. At times, these emerging geographies are the result of processes of construction of "public enemies"—often immigrants and dissidents. The representation of some areas as ghettos and their subsequent criminalization paves the ground either for the justification of exceptional measures of social control—like raids and evictions—or for the neglect of the area and the withdrawal of public services (Athanasiou 2018; Boano and Gyftopoulou 2016; Koutrolikou 2016; Lafazani 2018). The imaginary aspects of these processes of dispossession and exclusion are key for their very emergence and development. Thus, the examination of the city in crisis as a contemporary urban imaginary enables a deeper understanding of specific aspects and forms in which that imaginary crystallizes.

The imaginary components of crisis, as it has been argued, serve the purpose of extraordinary modes of governance, which induce rapid transformations. Yet, as Boano and Gyftopoulou (2016) note, the acknowledgment of "crisis as a rhetoric" does not deny the existence of "crisis as an event." The social changes that crises produce are evident and can be traced both at the structural level and in everyday life, where they are directly experienced socially and individually. Crisis is today a specifically urban phenomenon. Unemployment, poverty, violence, and homelessness manifest in urban contexts with marked harshness. Yet, is there anything particular and common across contemporary cities that can explain today's state of chronic crisis? Are there any processes that can be traced back in search for explanations for the present widespread state of crisis in and through cities?

Much of the urban scholarship has addressed these questions from a critique of neoliberalization and particularly, "urban neoliberalism"—or "urban neoliberalization."[11] Although the concept of neoliberalization cannot be used to explain the entirety of the processes of transformation that cities have undergone in the last decades, the analytical framework is useful still to understand at least some.[12] Largely driven by heavily market-led political agendas, which pushed for the deregulation of urban public planning since the 1990s, many cities experienced a great economic boost and/or territorial growth. The market-driven agenda for urban development—programs of city marketing to attract tourists and investors, projects of "urban revitalization" geared toward the "creative and entrepreneurial classes," public-private partnerships for city infrastructures, flexible zoning, privatization of the public space, and liberalization of housing markets, among others—paved the way for increasing privatization and intensive financial speculation on urban assets. In some cases, those processes have translated into the spatial fragmentation of the urban fabric—with increasing problems of mobility and pollution—and the polarization of uses and rents in the territory. The increasing trend of privatization of public spaces—usually coupled with increasing policing and surveillance—has contributed to removing socialization from those and restricting protests and mobilizations. Additionally, growing numbers of so-called revitalization projects have triggered processes of gentrification and "touristification" that have forced the displacement of long-established residents to other areas. The state of chronic crisis in which many cities seem to be stuck at present has stretched the inequalities derived from the neoliberal model of city making, leading to more inequalities. Cities across the globe are being used as laboratories in which reworked policies and projects of urban neoliberalization are being rolled out. They have become key sites and actors in the ongoing processes of (neoliberal) governance via crisis.

The devastating effects of the international financial crisis on the processes of social and urban reproduction in many cities are easily traceable in their shifting social fabric and urban space. The main urban transformations can be understood in terms of exclusion and dispossession, which have been arranged at several levels and occurred within all the spaces of social life. From expulsion from the labor market to removal from public social services, to housing evictions, to the very exclusion from some public spaces, all these processes have resulted in the increase of inequality. Urban space has been fundamental in the creation of these new social and "urban enclosures."[13] Processes of exclusion and dispossession have therefore severely impacted the livelihoods and everyday lives of large segments of the urban populations. They have adversely affected long-held social structures as well as traditional social safety nets. Great numbers of people have been left at risk of social exclusion with very few means to meet their daily needs. The ongoing crisis regimes have brought about a general devaluation of the living standards for many, as well as a dramatic increase in poverty rates. Yet, it is important to highlight that these processes have affected people unevenly. Women and migrant groups have usually been the most damaged. In general terms, though, in today's extended state of crisis, social reproduction—in its various forms and institutions—is seriously at risk for a large majority. Additionally, following the loss of access to the labor market, social services, housing, and public spaces, many people have found themselves deprived of their rights and status as full citizens. These exclusions and dispossessions, which constitute serious restrictions and/or directly violations of fundamental socioeconomic and democratic rights—such as the very right to healthcare, housing, electricity and water supply, or the right to pacific protest—have been legitimized in many cases by the institution of so-called states of exception.[14] Far from temporary, however, these extraordinary states of affairs appear to be here to stay.

Nevertheless, the politics of governing (the urban) via crisis has not gone without contestation by multiple actors. The city in crisis brings about dispossession and exclusion as much as resistance and insurgency, which also translate into new geographies and spatialities. As a terrain in turmoil in which normalcies are exposed and new truths flourish, the city-in-crisis bears a strong potential to activate major movements and struggles of counter-power that can challenge socioeconomic injustices which play out through the urban space. In our contemporary global impasse of chronic crisis, the acts of "reclaiming and organising" the city (Harvey 2012) hold the capacity to overthrow the crisis imaginary from above and to open up the present and future to alternative imaginations and transformations at the service of the many.

Seeking to tackle the impasse brought about at the end of the twentieth century by the "TINA doctrine" (Athanasiou 2018), Harvey (2000) proposed what he called "dialectical utopianism," namely a sort of utopian imagination that is neither a fixed spatial form nor a predetermined emancipatory process, but a spatiotemporal dialogue. This utopian imagination would be rooted in the present conditions and its possible *becomings*, which are latent in every moment. Arguably, Harvey's dialectical utopianism can be viewed as a kind of radical imagination in Castoriadis's ([1975] 1987) terms, for both are meant to open up the possible to a "plurality of alternatives" (Harvey 2000, 197) by breaking away with the established social imaginaries, which foreclose both present(s) and future(s). However, implicit in Harvey's utopian conception is an understanding and integration of space as a constitutive component, which is not present in Castoriadis's. This spatialized conceptualization of the imagination would be further elaborated by the geographer Doreen Massey (2005, 9) some years later. She describes space as a "simultaneity of stories-so-far," acknowledging the existence of a complex of trajectories concurrent in time and space that are always open to the possibility of potential links or disconnections. She referred to the unexpected inherent in the spatial as the "chance of space." The social therefore is spatial and temporal alike, that is, it occurs at a multiplicity of spatiotemporal scales. Therefore, "real political change arises out of simultaneous and loosely coordinated shifts in both thinking and action across several scales" (Harvey 2000, 234).

Harvey (2000, 233) claims the figure of the "insurgent architect," calling on progressive minds to "build a different sense of possibilities." At the end of *Spaces of Hope*, he himself outlines a personal utopian vision called *Edilia*, where he attempts to depict a "geography of hope" through different yet inter-related spatiotemporal scales of social and ecological life. However, as per his self-critique, his dream fails to be dialectical enough. How to become architects of "spaces of hope" articulated across different scales remains indeed a hard challenge. In a similar vein, the anthropologist James Holston (1998, 166) makes a call on architects and urban planners to keep imagining alternative worlds, but to do it through an ethnographic conception of the social, namely the "ethnographic present," which he defines as "the possibilities for change encountered in existing social conditions." In his view, the paradigm of modernity did affirm the possibility of alternative futures; however, those idealist visions were produced based on an abstract conceptualization of society completely decontextualized from the existing reality. As a result, the modernist projects became totalizing utopias disconnected from the conditions that could generate the climate of desirability for them. In his view, the process of relearning to read society—and its normativity—needs to be grounded in both a spatial and an ethnographic conception of it.

Both Harvey's (2000) and Holston's (1998) claims were posed at a time when the imaginary of globalization had started to fissure. Despite its alluring promises, at a close range, the situated reality of globalization materialized in the form of growing inequality, precariousness, and social unrest. The crash of the international financial system would come to inaugurate a time of even deeper malaise, which—as argued—manifests most prominently in cities. Thus, in our current critical conjuncture, Harvey's and Holston's calls for new imaginations not only remain valid but have become all the more pressing. The latter invites us to look at what he calls "spaces of insurgent citizenship," which "constitute new metropolitan forms of the social not yet liquidated by or absorbed into the old" (Holston 1998, 158). He explains that the spaces of insurgent citizenship have the capacity to disturb established stories, holding therefore a strong transformative potentiality. They constitute sites of enactment of radical imaginations, which emerge embedded in affects and embodied in the very acts of the people they bring together. If as insurgent architects we are to envision ethnographically possible futures that can intervene dominant established imaginaries, we should start from the insurgent spaces in each society.

Thinking through Care, Citizenship, and Infrastructure

Following Holston's (1998) intuitions and drawing on his concept of spaces of insurgent citizenship, I propose the notion of "infrastructures of caring citizenship" (ICCs) to designate bottom-up urban initiatives that articulate and integrate the provision of care and social protection at the local level in broader struggles against processes of dispossession of the means of subsistence and deprivation of rights. The elaboration of the concept will unfold throughout the chapters of this book. Stemming primarily from the ethnographic analysis, it will be grounded on a theoretical articulation of the three categories included in the notion of ICCs, namely care, citizenship, and infrastructure. This framework will serve a twofold purpose. On the one hand, it will provide an analytical lens for the examination of the four instances of ICCs that compose the field of this research—which I will introduce in the following section of this introduction. On the other, it will help frame The Crisis in relation to the field. Namely, the three categories will be used as interconnected theoretical tools to look more closely at particular aspects of The Crisis in which the ICCs are embedded. I argue that care, citizenship, and infrastructure constitute contemporary sites of social struggle, subjectivation, and (contested) production of space. In this light, the three of them will be presented as disputed arenas both in scholarly debates and on the ground.

In what follows, I provide an introduction to these categories as conceptual sites, elaborating on current debates around each one and drawing connections between the three. I will start with care, which is the central concept of this work. In replacing "insurgent" in Holston's (1998) concept for "caring" in the proposed concept of ICCs, I do not mean to erase the subversive character of the urban instances it designates. On the contrary, with this semantic operation, I endeavor to reclaim care as a site of struggle. The conception of care as a form of collective resistance, assertion of rights, and pathway toward social justice is what gives the ICCs their specificity within the great variety of people-driven collectivities that provide care nowadays. Next, I will discuss citizenship, whose centrality in Holston's concept is displaced in the notion of ICCs and which will be elaborated placing the focus on its connection to care. Lastly, I will elaborate on the category of infrastructure, whose substitution for "spaces" seeks to emphasize the sociomaterial composition of the ICCs, their operation as "network" in the urban territories, and their open-oriented nature.

CARE

The present multifaceted crisis can be viewed as a manifestation of what within feminist theory has been called "the crisis of care," which broadly refers to the increasing gaps in care provision in a world that paradoxically requires more care than ever to assure and sustain life (Dowling 2021). Care has historically been undervalued largely for its connection with women and unproductivity (Chatzidakis et al. 2020; Federici 2012; Pérez Orozco 2014). Yet, over the last forty years, the lack of care has become particularly acute, ultimately turning into a systemic crisis. Contributing factors include the massive incorporation of women in the West into the labor market, the progressive rise of job insecurity and low wages—which prevent the demand for conciliation measures—the gradual dismantling of unions, and the cutback on state social services (Chatzidakis et al. 2020; Dowling 2021; Pérez Orozco 2014).

The scholars and activists Silvia Federici (2019) and Raquel Gutiérrez Aguilar (2017, 2018) have located the epicenter of this structural crisis in the realm of everyday life. Decades of economic and social neoliberalization have translated into the gradual emptying of everyday social space. Everyday life's relationships have become depersonalized, while many communal experiences and traditional safety nets have been destroyed. Yet, parallel to this far-reaching scenario of ongoing retrenchment of social rights and welfare and growing precariousness, during the last decade, there has been an emergence of new movements in defense of life and livelihoods, as well as diverse experiences of reorganization of care in the everyday. Both scholars acknowledge and highlight these initiatives, to which they often refer as "struggles over reproduction." Federici (2019, 184) notes in this regard that they "are a sign of a growing realisation that to face the crisis alone is a path to defeat, for in a social system committed to the devaluation of our lives the only possibility of economic and psychological survival resides in our capacity to transform everyday practices into a terrain of collective struggle." Similarly, Gutiérrez Aguilar (2018, 11) observes that "the immense constellation of struggles has again illuminated and nourished horizons of social communitarian and popular transformation."

This juncture has prompted the reopening of debates around the notion of *care*, its social and spatial organization, and, most importantly, the possibility of a new social imagination able to radically challenge the fierce attack on life—its sustenance, maintenance, and reproduction—inherent in capitalism. Claims to revalue care practices, reorganize structures, reconfigure spaces, and put care at the center of politics have recently grown within both academic and activist settings, and are actually being put into practice by many groups in struggle. The topic of care is certainly manifold. Generally, care comes associated with a wide range of practices and relationships intimately related to life—its sustenance, reproduction, and limits: practices and relationships that hold, sustain, and bear, that assist, support, and encourage, that repair and nourish, but which nonetheless are imbued with ambivalent meanings and affections. One of the most frequently cited definitions has been by

Joan C. Tronto and Berenice Fisher (1990, 10), who described care as "a species activity that includes everything that we do to maintain, continue and repair our world so that we can live in it as well as possible." Nevertheless, the concept has been defined in different manners. In fact, it remains unsettled, and present debates constitute contested arenas.

Today, feminist theories on care span multiple fields including economics, ethics and politics, geography, science studies, and environmental humanities, to note but a few, as well as diverse epistemological traditions coming from different contexts. Thus, care is widely regarded as a cross-disciplinary concept that helps expand conceptual, analytical and political boundaries. Yet, the extensive use of care at present endangers its capacity as a critical or analytical category. Academics and activists alike have criticized the problematic use of the term to designate "all the good" of feminism, cautioning about paternalistic and reactionary meanings.

Certainly, speaking of care does not necessarily imply a critique of patriarchal relationships and capitalist exploitation. Coming from the feminist Marxist tradition, scholars from Mariarosa Dalla Costa and Selma James (1975)[15] since the 1970s to Lise Vogel ([1983] 2013)[16] in the 1980s, and more recently Nancy Fraser (2013) and Tithi Bhattacharya (2017),[17] have addressed care through the framework of labor within capitalism. They have revisited Marx's concept of "social reproduction" from a gender-based perspective, arguing that in not addressing reproductive labor as work, Marx failed to develop the notion fully. Broadly, this term refers to the daily material and social maintenance of a group of people and their social bonds, and the restoration of that society generationally. The concept encompasses both a material/economic dimension, which refers to bodies and livelihoods, and a social dimension, which comprises the structuring of the social relationships derived from these specific ways of subsistence. Thus, it is particularly useful to see structures recognize the (exploitative) conditions in which care work takes place under capitalism and understand the role that this plays in keeping the system running and reproducing itself. Thus, Marxist feminists advocate a reorganization of social reproduction irrespective of gender, class, sexual orientation, ethnicity, and/or ability (Vega Solís, Martínez Buján, and Paredes Chauca 2018).

Building on Marxist feminist theory on social reproduction, yet drawing largely from the Latin American long tradition of communal experiences and struggles against colonialism and extractivism, scholars like Amaia Pérez Orozco (2014), Silvia Rivera Cusicanqui (2018), and Raquel Gutiérrez Aguilar (2017, 2018) have advanced the concept of "life sustenance," which in recent years has gained popularity in social movements and academic circles. The notion of life sustenance brings to the fore capital's dependence on biological processes. Theoretical debates take "sustenance" as a starting point in the analysis of the social and the economic, which is one way of stating that the maintenance of our own selves and the world we live in is an essential precondition to any form of social, economic and political organization. Importantly, life sustenance theory links care with theory and debates on "the commons." As Vega Solís, Martínez Buján, and Paredes Chauca (2018) explain, life sustenance theory revolves around the question of what would it mean and entail to think of reproduction as *commons*. Thus, it engages ongoing debates about the community—and the intersection of community with other institutions of provision of care and protection—and ways to reconstruct social fabrics by politicizing the home and the neighborhood.

Care practices are carried out in all these settings and beyond. The geographer Victoria Lawson (2007, 6) contends that "embodied caring practices must be analysed as multisited . . . and as multiscalar." Relational in nature, care has certainly an inherent spatial dimension. Geographers like Katharyne Mitchell, Sallie A. Marston, and Cindi Katz (2004), and Cheryl McEwan and Michael K. Goodman (2010) have highlighted the implications of care in the social (re)production of space, and conversely the role of the latter in the reproduction of inequalities associated with the first. Christine Milligan and Janine Wiles (2010, 739) coined the notion "landscapes of care," which they described as the "spatial manifestations of the interplay between the socio-structural processes and structures that shape experiences and practices of care." This *spatiality* of care is in fact fundamental for the understanding of the aforementioned crisis of care. Conversely, as Lawson (2007, 5) notes, "Researching care relations allows us to more deeply understand the operation of power and the production of inequality at a range of sites and scales."

Besides as a socioeconomic and spatial practice, care has been also conceptualized as an ethics that informs specific subjective formations. In the 1980s, a debate emerged around the existence of different ethical approaches depending on gender. The psychologist Carol Gilligan (1982) elaborated a theory of moral reasoning—grounded in a study of children's stages of moral development in the United States—where she depicted two (opposing) "voices," namely two different forms of approaching ethical problems: one that builds from an understanding of justice as a universal and abstract set of rules, "ethics of justice," and one grounded in empathy and compassion, "ethics of care." According to her, women would be more likely to address moral dilemmas as an issue of clashing responsibilities depending on the context, whereas men would see them as a problem of conflicting rights. Gilligan's controversial theory has been critiqued largely in relation to its gendered (essentialist and homogeneous) approach (Bartos 2019; Wilkinson 1997).[18] Nevertheless, it was key for the development of feminist political theory around a "politics of care." Tronto's (1993) seminal work *Moral Boundaries: A Political Argument for an Ethic of Care* puts forward care as a political concept and elaborates on the previously mentioned definition by herself and Fisher (Tronto and Fisher 1990), has inspired extensive scholarship across disciplines. At present, a nongendered and nonnormative ethics of care is being (re)considered as a political tool to imagine and build other possible modes of existence and relationships in and with the world. The work of María Puig de la Bellacasa (2017) within the field of the posthumanities has profoundly contributed to this endeavor, broadening the very concept of the world and care relationships by including "more than human" beings.

This book inherits and aligns with the diverse traditions that have been presented in this Introduction in that it affirms and reclaims care as both a disruptive and generative force, whose meanings and consequences, nonetheless, cannot be taken for granted. Care as a force with the potential to disrupt the status quo and foster transformative politics, modes of social organizing, subjectivities, and thinking.

CITIZENSHIP

Broadly, the notion of citizenship—born to the Western liberal universalist tradition—defines the relationship between an individual and a political body, and implies affiliation with that entity. In modern history, that political community is preeminently the nation-state. However, the very meaning, subjects, domain, and scope of citizenship have changed throughout the centuries, for history and politics are always being reimagined. As an analytical category, citizenship is difficult to isolate, as it concerns a wide range of issues including law, rights, and duties—what and whose rights and duties—political participation, political institutions, democratic forms, social status, control and agency, processes of belonging and exclusion, borders, welfare, morality, notions of freedom, ethnicity, social behavior, subjectivity, and space. Thus, the question of citizenship can be tackled from a wide range of angles. As a political condition, citizenship is indeed constantly changing as each society redefines what it means to be part of it on a permanent basis. Starting in the second half of the twentieth century, movements for civil rights, women's rights, LGTBQ rights, disability rights, migrant rights, ethnic minorities' rights, as well as movements for the right to housing, public healthcare, and social care, public education, and so forth brought about a deep resignification of the notion of citizenship, its very practice, and the role of the citizen as a political subject. Those movements challenged the conventional understanding of citizenship as merely a legal institution defining and regulating membership (Isin 2009, 2012, 2017; Isin and Nielsen 2008).

The continuing reformulations of citizenship render the debates around its definition and political implications permanently unsettled. In an attempt to address these discussions, Holston (1998) proposed distinguishing between *formal* and *substantive* citizenship. The first would denote membership in a political community, while the second would refer to the series of civil, political, and social rights that individuals can hold as well as the duties they must perform. In its formal sense, citizenship designates a rights bearer and a site of validity of those rights. Thus, it operates as a legal/status marker. In its substantive meaning, citizenship refers to the practice of participating in the political community, the public, by exercising citizen rights and committing to citizen obligations. In its substantive sense, namely understood as political praxis, citizenship can become a vehicle of citizen sovereignty. Implicit in this twofold understanding is the fact that citizenship works simultaneously as an apparatus of inclusion and exclusion, which is controlled mainly by the state, and also as a means through which individuals and collectives claim and regain agency. Thus, despite its original exclusionary foundations, many social movements still draw on its language to make their case and this way appropriate it as a tool for resistance and counterpower. It is collective struggles, which derive processes of (re)politicization, that confer the concept of citizenship a transforming potentiality in political, social, and subjective terms. As such, it is from these experiences of struggle that the concept is worth the (re)engagement, both analytically and politically (D'Souza 2018; Holston 1998; Isin 2009, 2012, 2017; Lister 2003 [1997]).

The engagement with citizenship in this book aligns with these approaches that resonate with the spirit of the ICCs, which are theoretically conceived of as particular versions of Holston's (1998) spaces of insurgent citizenship. The specificity of the ICCs as citizenship instances rests on their articulation and political activation through care in its manifold forms and dimensions. As it will be shown, the ICCs challenge many of the processes that displace populations to the margins of society, excluding them from important social spaces. It is in this sense that ICC's struggles can be viewed simultaneously as struggles over both social reproduction and citizenship. This understanding links with a well-consolidated strand of feminist scholarship and activism that since the 1990s has reclaimed care as a condition of citizenship.

Ever since Thomas H. Marshall (1950) advanced his threefold formulation of modern citizenship, including social rights, the question of social citizenship in the welfare-state model has been a contested terrain, especially for women.[19] Certainly, the relationship between women and welfare states has been an unsettled one and continues to be so. For welfare states are gendered institutions, and as such can promote women's agency and at the same time undermine it by reproducing gender-based discriminatory relations (Pérez Orozco 2014). Ruth Lister (2003) relates this contradiction to what she calls the "citizen–the wage-earner vs. citizen–the carer" divide. She explains that irrespective of the type of welfare state, access to social rights and welfare benefits is always conditioned to the type of work and the sphere in which this work is carried out so that work in the labor market is privileged over care work in the private sphere. From this critical standpoint, she advocates the need to recognize the value of care work to citizenship, and in so doing reformulates its very meaning and scope. She adds that this must be done irrespective of gender because, otherwise, it risks reinforcing the role of women as private caregivers, which has prevented them from active participation in the public sphere, hence from power.

Lister's (2003) critique constitutes a valuable contribution toward a more inclusive citizenship framework connecting care to rights. Tronto's work (1993, 2015) would further this analysis on the role and implications of care to democratic states. Tronto stresses the interdependence between care and politics and its significance for the functionality and sustainability of any democratic framework. She advocates taking away the centrality of the market in politics and instead placing care at the core of democratic political life. This shift would necessarily involve a change at the institutional level and the citizenry level based on the recognition of the large barriers that prevent it. Importantly, one of these obstacles precisely lays on the very limitations of the rights framework as a mechanism to ensure coverage of care needs for everyone. The welfare state in fact leaves many care needs uncovered and many populations unassisted. The failure of public policies and services in guaranteeing universal care coverage—let alone when those serve to reinforce inequalities along the lines of gender, race, class, and/or ability—evidences the significant shortcomings of social citizenship within the framework of welfare states. Austerity regimes have contributed to exposing and deepening these weaknesses in many countries. Thus, the coverage of care/welfare needs on universal and equal terms must not be left to rest on any rights framework alone. The legal—and particularly the citizenship framework—can be expanded to further guarantee the coverage of those needs in the form of social rights. As noted, this same framework is being used, challenged, and enlarged by groups demanding equal access to welfare for a dignified life. Yet, scholars and activists alike should have always in mind the significant limitations of any legal framework.

A final dimension of citizenship that accounts for its very limitations is space. Citizenship produces and demarcates spaces and geographies in that it establishes the sites or territories in which both those instituted as citizens and those who are not can validate, perform, and/or challenge (citizenship) rights and obligations. As noted, since the instauration of modernity to date, the nation-state has been the prominent site of citizenship. At present, nation-state institutions still monopolize the governance of citizenship *dispositifs* like passports, birth certificates, residency permits, taxes and rights to vote, healthcare, and education. Nevertheless, its role as the hegemonic type of political community and its legitimacy in demarcating citizenship rights is becoming increasingly questioned. Factors derived from the processes of globalization like the creation of new structures and sites of governance, mass migration, and increasing mobility, and the many social mobilizations and struggles against exclusions of different sorts, have brought to the fore the limitations of a singular national citizenship, as well as the violence performed by state institutions to sustain it (Holston 1998; Isin 2009, 2012, 2014, 2017; Isin and Nielsen 2008; Lister 2003). In face of this growing fluidity of citizenship, Isin (2009) talks of "site scales" of citizenship, which are configured through diverse social and political battles. In speaking of site scales, he places the focus on the "acts" (Isin 2009, 2014; Isin and Nielsen 2008) through which subjects—whether citizens or not—enact citizenship, and in so doing alter its very boundaries.

Interestingly, against this background of global reworking and relocation of citizenship, Holston (1998) and Isin (2009) reclaim the city as the principal site eliciting the emergence—and contraction—of spatialities of citizenship. Since antiquity, the city has favored the development of associational configurations in which processes of belongingness, engagement, inclusion, and exclusion take place and are contested. With modernity, the state displaced the city as the main sovereign entity. Nevertheless, the city has endured as a prominent locus of power where citizenship is de facto enacted and exercised (Isin 2009). Today, the city constitutes a paramount site for the expression and organization of emerging local, regional, national, transnational, *diasporic*, or intranational identities.

In this light, Isin (2009) explains that since the twentieth century, the production of citizens in the urban occurs through the articulation of rights in two different manners—or rights of different characters—which he defines as "rights of the city" and "rights to the city." The first refers to those rights that the citizen holds as a legal member of the city. At present, even though it is just the state that bestows citizenship formal rights and status, municipalities do confer substantive rights through a sort of "local citizenship" and, in many cases, they are already seeking to expand it to reach more populations. The second refers to those that are advanced by claimants—who are not necessarily those holding formal citizenship—of new social rights.

Although struggles over the right to the city have existed since antiquity, the condition of the city as a battleground has intensified during the decades of globalization and neoliberalization of the economy (Harvey 2000, 2008, 2012; Holston 1998; Isin 2009). David Harvey explains that the late processes of urbanization, which have acquired a global scale, have been instrumental in restoring the processes of capitalist accumulation to the rich, hence conversely, in dispossessing major populations of any *right to the city*.[20] Urban development and restructuring driven by financial and corporate capital's interests have usually come about through deprivation, repression, and violence against the poor and the disenfranchised. Austerity regimes have sharpened these processes of citizenship erosion and/or destruction. Holston's (1998) suggestion to look at spaces of insurgent citizenship includes these impoverished urban populations organized in social movements and initiatives claiming the right to the city. These metropolitan forms of citizenship enactment provide the conditions to open up questions about the type of institutions we need to imagine and create to overcome the limitations of current citizenship frameworks concerning guaranteed access to the social rights for all individuals, irrespective of whether they hold a national passport.

INFRASTRUCTURE

Infrastructures constitute key sites in the contemporary crisis regime. Across the Global North, accounts of infrastructural aging, failure, disinvestment, and struggle have become increasingly recurrent, populating daily news and reports on media outlets. Although political leaders keep renewing promises of commitment to infrastructural development as a means to address contemporary crises, state institutions—whether national or international—have been long unable to fully finance the infrastructural development needed to sustain economic growth. Following the 2008 international financial crisis, the private sector has gradually withdrawn investments too. The anthropologist Dimitris Dalakoglou (2016) uses the term "infrastructural gap" (IG) to refer to the present deficit in infrastructure development and maintenance. He contends that the IG has prompted the emergence of new infrastructural configurations, particularly in the urban, where new actors, technologies, modes of operation, and ownerships are yielding a shift in the modern paradigm of infrastructural function, governance, and imagination. Given the intrinsic connection between infrastructures and modernity, he argues that these infrastructural reconfigurations are challenging the established social contract, pushing a change in the altogether wider sociopolitical paradigm.

This juncture has prompted a renewed focus on infrastructures in academic scholarship and debates. Attention has been drawn to the emergence of new collective contexts and political conceptions associated with ongoing infrastructural reconfigurations, and the possibilities (and limitations) that those may open concerning more inclusive and sustainable modes of social provision and citizenship (e.g., Alam and Houston 2020; Angelo and Hentschel 2015; Berlant 2016; Corsín-Jiménez 2014; Dalakoglou 2016; Graham and McFarlane 2015; Power et al. 2022; Venkatesan et al. 2018). New conceptualizations have been posed from different disciplinary fields, moving away from modern understandings—where infrastructures are largely seen as homogeneous, uniform, expert-based, and politically neutral systems—toward new analytical frameworks to examine infrastructural transformations and, through them, contemporary crises. Scholars like Hillarie Angelo and Christine Hentschel (2015), Mary Lawhon et al. (2018), and Fran Tonkiss (2015) propose to use infrastructure as an analytical lens, highlighting its intrinsic relational nature. "Infrastructures make things *relatable*" (Tonkiss 2015, 384). Infrastructures can mediate some frequent (problematic) binaries in critical urban studies, like macro and micro, North and South, object and agent, human and nonhuman, political and everyday experience. Others, including Lauren Berlant (2016), Alberto Corsín-Jiménez (2014), Dimitris Dalakoglou (2016), and AbdouMaliq Simone (2018), have gone further to propose infrastructure not only as a category productive of new modes of inquiry, but also as a concept generative of imaginations that can gesture toward modes of organizing the social and the economy at the service of life amid and through global breakdown.

These theoretical debates are drawing largely from studies of everyday engagements with infrastructures in urban contexts, particularly in the Global South, where infrastructure is commonly experienced as discontinuous, heterogeneous, decentralized, and peopled (Lawhon et al. 2018). This rich scholarship has inspired recent studies focusing on the role of the grassroots in the infrastructural reconfigurations taking place in cities of the Global North in response to conditions of crisis and uncertainty that have expanded since 2008 (e.g., Alam and Houston 2020; Arampatzi 2016, 2017; Corsín-Jiménez 2014; Dalakoglou 2016; Power et al. 2020). A broad definition that could be drawn from this growing literature is that infrastructures are relational and moving sociomaterial configurations that enable everyday sustenance and reproduction, through which people partake and transform their social, political, and built environments and produce or reproduce collective imaginations.

The ethnographic work of Simone (2004, 2015, 2019) has been paramount in these recent conceptual engagements with infrastructure. He has defined infrastructures as relational fields that shape and sustain everyday urban life, showing that relation making through experimental practices of collaboration, reciprocity, and entrepreneurship is a fundamental capacity to endure in contexts marked by scarcity and uncertainty. The notion of "people as infrastructure" (2004), based on ethnographic research about everyday economic activities in the inner city of Johannesburg, provides a framework to understand the myriad ways in which people engage the imbrications of materialities and socialities that infrastructures are, and the role that those play in enabling—or disabling—the conditions for inhabitation. Building on this idea of infrastructure as relation making for everyday urban sustenance, the urban scholars Colin McFarlane and Jonathan Silver (2017, 463) propose to think of it as a verb—*infrastructuring*—namely "a practice of connecting people and things in sociomaterial relations that sustain urban life." They contend that a closer look at infrastructures exposes the vulnerability of the negotiations that sustain the apparent normality of everyday life.

Calling infrastructures *relational achievements*—in Simone's (2004) words—alludes to their function as (provisional) supporting structures of urban everyday life. Yet, Simone explains that the notion of "people as infrastructure" does not designate a mere coping strategy that translates as a particular economy of shared knowledge(s) and collaboration among deprived inhabitants. Rather, active engagement and composition of infrastructures constitute modes of intervening in the existing reality, ways of expanding opportunities and opening up the present toward the unknown, and, as such—albeit precariously—ways of performing agency and yielding change. That is, when people operate as infrastructure, they increase their potentiality of transforming the city. The infrastructure in this sense provides both a supporting structure for livelihoods and a site for the exertion of (some) agency.

More recently, Simone (in Venkatesan et al. 2018) has emphasized that a look at infrastructures raises questions about who makes the city, for infrastructures generate different ways of *doing reality*. "The focus on infrastructure allows us to see the kinds of relational knowledges that are at work, that are under threat, that are vulnerable today" (Simone 2018, 49). Thus, attention to infrastructure can reconfigure anthropological approaches to the political.[21] Angelo and Hentschel (2015), Corsín-Jiménez (2014), Dalakoglou (2016), and Graham and McFarlane (2015, xiii) have elaborated on the political dimension of infrastructures from this perspective, referring to infrastructures as sites of continuous political negotiations among different actors. From large finance actors, including international and supranational agencies, corporations, and public institutions, to nation-states, social and environmental justice movements, journalists, lawyers, academics, and artists, all participate in the configuration of infrastructure, its geographies, politics, and imaginations. Importantly, these scholars argue that the capacity of citizens to engage with infrastructures and the ways those are imagined determines citizenship conditions. They explain that infrastructure imaginaries are reflections of how people understand and give meaning to their positions and roles in the social field. Thus, since the emergence of the first infrastructural systems, social imaginaries of infrastructure have been linked to notions of political participation and citizenship. In times of crisis, changes in power relationships affect established perceptions and modes of engagement with infrastructures. In turn, infrastructural reconfigurations induce change in social patterns, practices, and perceptions, and prompt the articulation of new social imaginations.

In light of these insights, infrastructures can be seen as key elements in the material and symbolic sustenance and reproduction of modern societies. Nevertheless, many of these scholars invite us to (re)think infrastructures as alternative modes of social organizing for a world in chronic crisis. Behind this invitation lies the intuition of a potentiality associated with the concept of infrastructure capable of generating fairer systems. In this speculative discussion, the conceptual comparison of infrastructures with institutions has provided further nuance. Arguably, the three dimensions of infrastructure discussed so far, namely sustenance, power, and imagination, are likewise constitutive of institutions. Nevertheless, Berlant (2016) points out a key difference, which lies in movement. This aspect translates into politics and ethics of a different kind. Whereas institutions operate through established norms, roles, and normative reciprocity, infrastructures work through movement, dynamic relationality, and connectivity. Institutions seek to organize transformation based on predictability. They want to "protect" us from change, alterity, plurality, and conflict. Thus, they fix, settle, classify, separate, and control—ultimately closing off. They tend to prioritize their own interests over society's needs and demands. Thus, they concentrate power and interest. Infrastructures, by contrast, circulate, distribute, bridge, and connect. Their functioning and durability are mostly based on use. Thus, they are more porous to power read-justments and rearrangements.

This book takes on this invitation and builds on this ongoing scholarly de-bate to think through infrastructure as a means to examine sociomaterial transformations and reconfigurations amid crisis, and also to imagine or spec-ulate with modes of organizing societies better able to cope with breakdown in more just and generative manners.

Commons: Relational Subjectivities amid Neoliberalism and Crisis

The gradual liberalization of the economy and retrenchment of the welfare state that has taken place in Europe since the 1980s has been grounded in the promotion of a business-oriented management of life, which ever since has deeply informed practices, discourses, relationships, and desires from the cor-porate and institutional spheres to the most quotidian instances of everyday life.[22] The philosopher Marina Garcés (2013) observes a striking paradox in the unprecedented demand for independence and self-sufficiency in a world char-acterized by planetary interconnection—and (ineluctable) interdependence—to an extent never seen before in history. She explains such a contradiction with the notion of "individualist universalism," which she describes as the cli-max of the ideological configuration of modernity. In her view, the universalist ideal was cast as a progressive paradigm, as the ethical and political horizon of a world of equality. However, grounded as it is in the liberal tradition, univer-salism is bound to an individualist conception of the subject that has rendered private their way of being, their mode of experiencing and relating to others and the world.

Aligned with this perspective, the philosopher Amador Fernández-Savater (2018) has reflected on the type of subjectivity induced by neoliberalism through the metaphorical figure of "the maximizer." The philosopher grounds the elaboration of this figure on the premise that neoliberalism suppresses and disciplines as much as it stimulates a desire for ceaseless self-improvement. In this sense, the maximizer builds their self-image on the myths of independence and self-realization through continuous calculation, competition, consumer-ism, and private ownership. Driven by that self-entrepreneurial spirit, the maximizer feels capable of reinventing themselves continuously. Under the present regime of chronic crisis, the overwhelming state of permanent activity, the exhaustion and anxiety derived from the overload of tasks, the ceaseless stimulation of the senses, and the blend or confusion of work with life have resulted in an intensification and expansion of mental breakdowns and depression, which Fernández-Savater argues has become the main condition of our present time. Depressed subjects are easily rendered unnecessary for the system. Those who become "unproductive"—that is, unemployed, on benefits, or in need of assistance—are deeply stigmatized under the neoliberal regime. Denial, shame, guilt, and despair become constituents of the subjectivities forming under the ongoing neoliberal regime. In his ethnography about the Argentinian *piqueteros,* the psychologist and ethnographer Francisco Ferrara (2003) talks of "the disposable" as that subject who has ceased to exist for the system.[23] This expulsion is driven by and entails a number of "desubjectivizing operations," which dismantle the political condition of the subject and redefine the relationship between the self, the "we," and the others.

These two subjective figures, namely the disposable and the maximizer, constitute forms of subjectivation—or desubjectivation—which suppress the political condition of the subject to different extents. Expelled from society, cast outside the labor market, the spaces of consumption and sometimes the very public urban spaces, the disposable is denied the right of participation in the public. For their part, the maximizer is neither used to participating in public matters nor interested in them. After decades of neoliberal rationality promoting self-interested, self-responsible, and self-optimizing subjects, many have ended up isolated, utterly lacking a social safety net to turn to for support and solidarity. Neoliberalism in this way has profoundly transformed the possibilities of both subjective and collective action.

Importantly, as a reworked mode of neoliberal governmentality, the present chronic crisis regime is altering some of the ways in which neoliberalism has predominantly shaped subjectivities until recently. Nowadays, with the normalization of crisis, conditions of intensified dispossession, precariousness, uncertainty, and vulnerability have become all the more prominent in the formation of contemporary subjectivities (Athanasiou 2018). Yet, the way individuals assimilate and relate to these factors can vary radically. Ferrara (2003) argues that in the face of the institution of misery, two possible options emerge, namely either to succumb to the loss of the condition of the subject or to build a new subjectivity.[24]

Foucault ([1969] 2002, 2008, 2017) had already theorized crisis as a liminal field through which the established premises that shape subjectivities are challenged. Thus, crises often provide the conditions for the prefiguration of new subjectivities that seek emancipation from the prevailing order and powers. Building on Foucault's thought, Butler (2015) argues that actually subjects are continuously or repeatedly in formation, that subjectivities are never fixed or singular. They are constantly responding to societal norms, discourses, institutions, environments, life processes, spaces, and bodies—both human and nonhuman—they come across and produce in changing circumstances. In these responses there are always generative moments of interruption or discontinuity. Similarly, Guattari (2015) in the series of essays gathered in the book *Psychoanalysis and Transversality: Texts and Interviews, 1955–1971*, emphasizes the idea of "becoming," that is, as they interact and establish new relationships, individuals experience ongoing and multiple processes of transforming into something different, processes of "becoming other." Certainly, the enduring, multifaceted crisis in Europe over the past decade has had a deep impact on the shaping of subjectivities. It has pushed large populations into indebtedness and poverty. At the same time, it has also incited large social mobilizations and struggles. In this context, new forms and mechanisms of subjectivation have been brought forth while others—(apparently) established—have lost traction.

Amid crisis, social mobilizations and insurgent initiatives open up spaces of encounter in which different subjectivities come into contact. Ferrara (2003) defines this particular type of encounter produced through experiences of common struggle as a powerful experience of shared transformation that enables the displacement of previous subjectivities or established identities—social, professional, geographical—and in so doing paves the way for the formation of new shared ones. So, an encounter with the other that dislocates both subjects facilitates the possibility of becoming something other than what each one previously was. In his view, these encounters hold an emancipatory potentiality in that they enable the formation of new collective "we(s)" capable of (re)gaining agency against the "desubjectivating" operations deployed by the dominant powers—especially during crisis—which override collective sovereignty and the political condition of the subject.

In line with this thesis of the encounter through experiences of collective struggle, the independent collective of thinkers Espai en Blanc (2009) proposes the idea of "anonymity"—or more precisely "becoming anonymous"—as a condition of possibility for transformative encounters to happen and for the emergence of new collective forms of expression, thought, and action. "Anonymity as a collective wager, as a force, as a conquered possibility of the experience of something common that opens up in the face of the resurgence of identities that fragment the map of the global world, and in the face of the strict process of identification and privatization that we suffer today as individuals" (Espai en Blanc 2009). Conceptualized in this way, anonymity, rather than deficit or negation, delineates a force, a potentiality for an existence in common.

The instances of collective care and struggle presented in this book, namely the ICCs, are all sites where the self is to some degree displaced by a sense of collectivity. I will argue that these displacements are enabled to a great extent by commoning practices, which, as the scholar and activist Stavros Stavrides (2016, 2) contends, produce new relations between people. "They encourage creative encounters and negotiations through which forms of sharing are organised and take shape." Stavrides talks of the "we(s)" of the commons as "communities in the making" and stresses that their emancipatory potentiality relies on their ability to remain open. His theoretical work endeavors in fact "to connect commoning with processes of opening: opening the community of those who share common worlds, opening the circles of sharing to include newcomers, opening the sharing relations to new possibilities through a re-thinking of sharing rules and opening the boundaries that define the spaces of sharing" (Stavrides 2016, 3). Akin to Stavrides (2016), Gutiérrez Aguilar (2017, 2018) calls the type of groups that form through experiences of commoning and struggle—particularly struggles over reproduction—"communitarian fabrics," and defines them as communities that are generated by "weaving" bonds.

Commoning practices in the ICCs promote processes that resonate with the concepts of anonymity and encounter elaborated by these authors. As they claim, these processes make new sensibilities, meanings, and identifications flourish with what is "we." In this way, they challenge the neoliberal logic and the subjectivities it produces. They facilitate an understanding of the subject no longer as merely an individual, but rather as an intrinsic relational being capable of inventing new ways of relating to the world. However, none of these practices or processes should be taken as emancipatory factors by themselves or as always-necessary preconditions for radical transformation. Rather, they should be viewed as instances of experiences that in some cases produce ruptures with the dominant orderings—social, political, subjective—but that take place and shape embedded in broader and manifold normative processes, which, as Butler (2015) argues, lead the subject to reproduce, many times unconsciously, the status quo. Processes of anonymity and encounters take place in the ICCs alongside, for instance, tensions around gender norms and identities, which foreground difference rather than commonality. This is important to stress and will be shown throughout the chapters of the book. Processes of subjective formation are determined by manifold factors and events to which subjects' responses will always have a degree of unpredictability.

My engagement in this book with these questions, the problem—and problematization—of (what is) "we" and how such a collective subject takes shape and manifests, derives from my fieldwork in the ICCs. The question about transforming subjectivities and emerging we(s) became apparent to me over time, as my relationship with the people involved in the ICCs grew deeper. Yet, what exactly did "we" mean in each site? Which names were associated with those "we(s)"? What were they made of and how? What exactly characterized those collective subjects? Which commoning practices enabled processes of (re)subjectivation and which did not? Were the emerging we(s) taken as potential sites for emancipation? Did those hold any political potentiality embedded as they were in an individualist universalism paradigm—in Garcés's (2013) words? I will dwell in depth on these questions particularly in chapter 4.

Infrastructures of Caring Citizenship: The Field

Taking inspiration from Holston's (1998) concept of "spaces of insurgent citizenship," this book proposes and elaborates the notion of ICCs in reference to urban grassroots initiatives that combine the provision of care on a collaborative and self-managed basis with political actions articulated within broader social struggles. Having Holston's text as a dear reference of mine to which I would often return, I first considered the possibility of using a reinterpreted version of his concept that would place the focus on care after a primary intuitive approximation to some concrete instances in Athens— particularly in *Athens in crisis*. The eventual elaboration of the concept of ICCs would span years of research through a constant back-and-forth journey from the field to theory and vice versa. Importantly, although primarily constructed from and through a situated (urban) reality, the concept aims to serve as both an analytical framework for other geographical contexts sharing similar characteristics and a potential tool for political action amid regimes of chronic crisis.

The ethnographic field of this work is composed of four specific cases of ICCs, namely a social kitchen, a social clinic, an accommodation center, and a community center, all of which I introduce later in this section. The rationale behind my choosing was to provide a representative sample of four major sectors within the realm of social reproduction, namely food provision, healthcare, accommodation, and education, as the basis to elaborate my situated definition of ICCs. Broadly, the four initiatives constitute responses from the grassroots to The Crisis and the way it has been managed by formal institutions, both state and nongovernmental, local, national, and international alike. They all are political in character, although each one has its own specific aims, organizing methods, political affinities, and actors of diverse backgrounds.

Like Holston (1998), I approached them at first with the intuition that they might potentially open up new pathways or imaginable horizons for the city beyond the imposed state and regime of chronic crisis. Starting from this hypothesis, I set off to explore the possibilities—and limitations—of an emerging radical imagination that takes shape through processes of reconfiguration of the notions, practices and spaces of care, citizenship, and infrastructure. In this light, the guiding questions of this work are as follows: How are care and citizenship changing in Athens as a city facing a multifaceted crisis which is deeply reshaping the processes of urban and social reproduction? How are grassroots initiatives contributing to these transformations? How are these people-driven projects challenging The Crisis politics and its effects? What are the alternatives that they are posing? How are they transforming the city space? And conversely, how is urban space contributing to their expansion?

O ALLOS ANTHROPOS SOCIAL KITCHEN

O Allos Anthropos ("The other person" in Greek) is a social kitchen that was initiated in 2012 with the aim of providing free food for any person in need. The group installs a mobile kitchen in public spaces on a daily basis. They cook there and eat the meal together with the people they serve. At the time of my fieldwork, the initiative comprised a "core group" of six people and others who would partake temporarily or occasionally. On the busiest day, those people were up to thirty-six. Over the years, the initiative has counted on several headquarters located in central areas of Athens, where they store the food and provide other services, including school support activities for children and night accommodation for homeless people.

In Greece, food distribution has been the most prominent solidarity activity since the start of The Crisis. Social kitchens constitute the underpinning infrastructure of many other people-driven initiatives. Beyond their primary goal, initiatives like O Allos Anthropos foster a form of sociality that attempts to break social isolation and the despair and embarrassment produced by the individualization of social problems.

ATHENS COMMUNITY POLYCLINIC AND PHARMACY

The Athens Community Polyclinic and Pharmacy (ACP&P) is one of the multiple self-organized medical centers that emerged in the city from the early months of the austerity regime and are popularly known as "social clinics." At the time of my fieldwork there were twenty social clinics in the Athens metropolitan area and another thirty across the country. The institution of social clinics was primarily a response to the breakdown of the Greek national health system (NHS) and the privatization of the healthcare sector. The ACP&P, located in the area of Omonia in central Athens, provides health services free of charge, prescriptions and pharmaceuticals to Greek citizens and migrants excluded from the NHS. Personnel of the clinic also assist migrants and refugees in camps near Athens, as well as inmates in some prisons in the city. The clinic functions on the basis of donations and voluntary work. It counts on gynecologists, endocrinologists, dermatologists, cardiologists, ophthalmologists, and dentists, as well as psychologists, social workers, and admin personnel. In total, there are around forty volunteers. The ACP&P remained without legal status until 2020, when it was registered as a nonprofit organization called Open Solidarity City.

CITY PLAZA REFUGEE ACCOMMODATION CENTER

City Plaza, today inactive, was an accommodation center for migrants and refugees. It was located in a formerly abandoned hotel in the area of Victoria in central Athens, which was squatted from April 2016 to July 2019. During this time, City Plaza provided safe and dignified accommodation for over 2,500 refugees and asylum seekers, as well as for local activists and dozens of so-called international solidarians, while serving as an active center for the coordination of political actions of different sorts and scales. During my fieldwork, around 400 people were living in the building. The "squat" or the "house," as residents used to refer to it, operated as a self-managed housing community, sustained by economic and in-kind donations.

Along with City Plaza, at the time of my fieldwork, there were around a dozen buildings in Athens that had been occupied to shelter displaced people. In their day-to-day practices—and not exempted from multiple tensions and difficult challenges—they sought to construct and maintain spaces of solidarity, mutual help, and common struggles among people from different origins and backgrounds.

KHORA COMMUNITY CENTER

Khora is a community center, which was set up in 2016 by a group of local and international volunteers on a self-organized basis. The initial foundational statement of the initiative was grounded in a rejection of the European Union (EU) border system and its migration policies. Initially located in Exarcheia,

Khora provided a space for people from different backgrounds to socialize, work, and learn. Until 2018, services included the provision of meals, clothing, and other essential products, dentistry, legal aid for asylum seekers, language and music lessons, Internet and computer access, childcare, a women's (safe) space, and a carpentry and metal workshop. At the time of my fieldwork, there were around 150 volunteers. At present, the community center is registered as an association and runs throughout three buildings in Kypseli and Exarcheia. Interestingly, the notion or the typology of "community center," which was chosen to characterize the initiative, was not previously part of the Athenian urban imaginary and vocabularies.

METHODOLOGY

The research inquiry that drives this book is above all an anthropological one. Thus, the research that grounds it is based primarily on a qualitative, field-based methodology that combined ethnographic fieldwork in the four ICCs previously presented, an online interactive map that registered ICCs set up in Athens from 2010 to 2018, a series of recorded conversations with people about The Crisis and its impact on their personal lives, and three collaborative creative projects inside the initiatives that sought to coproduce ethnographic material with some of the people involved in them. The creative projects, however, turned out rather unsuccessful as methods for ethnographic data production and collection. Although this does not mean that they were unproductive in terms of furthering my reflections, I will not provide a detailed account of them here.

The ethnographic fieldwork in the ICCs was carried out in two main phases, each one lasting six months during 2016 and 2017. Later, in 2018 and 2021, I conducted follow-up interviews with some of my previous interlocutors. The ethnographic fieldwork during the first two phases entailed my participation in three of the four chosen ICCs, namely O Allos Anthropos social kitchen, City Plaza refugee accommodation center, and Khora community center. The main data collecting methods comprised participant observation, field notes, and drawings, semistructured interviews, and gathering and sorting textual, graphic, and audiovisual material produced by these ICCs. At the ACP&P, fieldwork involved semistructured interviews with volunteers at the clinic, as well as primary-source data collection from published documents, records, audiovisual materials, and the social media of the clinic.

More in detail, participant observation in the first three mentioned ICCs translated into an engagement in these collectives' assemblies and meetings, everyday activities—ranging from cooking and cleaning to cultural, educational, and sports activities, training workshops, games, and long conversations over coffee or beer—parties, public events, political actions, and protests. The principal settings were O Allos Anthropos headquarters in Metaxourgio, the squares of Monastiraki and Agios Georgios in central Athens, and Heroes Square in Haidari—where the group used to set up the kitchen—the occupied former City Plaza, and the building that housed Khora at the time of my fieldwork. However, some activities took place elsewhere, outside these main settings. I planned my participant observation sessions in advance and structured them in "spatiotemporal scenarios" of around four hours each, corresponding to different activities carried out in different spaces or by varying actors. I wrote my field notes in a private space right after each session. To guarantee the anonymity of children, people seeking asylum, and activists, I did not take photographs. Instead, I made field drawings in a sketchbook, representing everyday moments that I considered of special relevance. During the sessions, I engaged in conversations with some of the people present. As requested by some of my interlocutors during those conversations and personal communications, I have used pseudonyms when quoting them so as to respect their privacy. As regards my observations, I have processed all of them anonymously.

Alongside these participant observation sessions, I conducted semi-structured interviews with twenty people directly involved in the four ICCs, members of other political and solidarity initiatives in Athens, and researchers. I tried to choose people from different origins and social and political backgrounds to be able to include as many voices and perspectives as possible. The interviews included sets of open questions, which sought to get the interlocutor engaged in personal reflections largely about forms of organizing and management in the ICCs, forms of resistance and building power, opinions about The Crisis, austerity and institutions, observations about the spaces—uses and misuses, personal tastes, views on ownership—personal experiences, and visions for the future.

This series of fieldwork methods afforded me in-depth knowledge of each ICC's respective everyday practices and politics, as well as some processes of subjective formation in the cases of O Allos Anthropos, City Plaza, and Khora. From the analysis of the data collected, I derived three main analytical strands, namely organization, politics, and subjectivities, all of which would be informed by spatial considerations. This analysis, which grounds the definition of the concept of ICCs, is presented in chapters 2, 3, and 4, respectively. Each chapter provides cross-case accounts of what occurs in these four ICCs, which in turn are informed by an engagement with recent scholarly debates on the questions at stake. These chapters conclude with a theoretical-speculative elaboration on the imaginations and political possibilities that I derive from each strand of the analysis.

The online map of ICCs aim was to record and visualize the geography of these initiatives that emerged in Athens during the austerity regime.[25] Due to the informal character of the ICCs, this geography had no official register. On the map, the initiatives were classified according to three main categories: field of activity, distinguishing among them healthcare, social care, food, clothing, accommodation, and education; social infrastructure, referring to the organizational framework in terms of the type of social agent and scale; and material infrastructure, referring to the type of physical space. Importantly, rendering the initiatives visible to the wider public on an open website was not appropriate for some of them, either for political reasons or because of questions related to the migration status of some of the people involved in them. Therefore, a number of initiatives were not marked on the map. This aspect may serve to draw attention to the ethics and politics that are always embedded in maps—and their media—in ways seen and unseen.

Lastly, the series of recorded conversations with Athens dwellers—twenty-three in total during 2018—allowed me to expand on my anthropological inquiry into crisis, and more specifically into Athens-in-crisis: practices of resistance, individual and collective alike, and social and urban imaginaries. These conversations took place across the city, in different locations intentionally chosen by my interlocutors for their significance to their personal lived experiences of The Crisis. Each of these sites served in this way as a catalyst of memories and affections through which the conversations unfolded. Drawing on secondary sources, I had examined, on the one hand, different crisis discourses and representations with a particular focus on the articulation of those crisis narratives through the case of Athens, and, on the other hand, processes of exclusion, dispossession, and transformation of the urban life and urban environment, as well as of resistance. Yet, these conversations grounded my analysis with first-person stories and interpretations about The Crisis—some quite straightforward, others more ambiguous—bringing in the voices of some Athenian dwellers. They informed my examination of Athens in crisis and my ultimate articulation of it, which is presented in chapter 1.

ETHICAL, POLITICAL, AND DISCIPLINARY CONSIDERATIONS

The research process underpinning this book has been a constant back-and-forth journey from practice to theory, from the field to my desk, from individuality to collectivity, from the evidential to the imaginary, from empirically based analysis to playful yet committed speculation and vice versa. My approach has drawn on my mixed background in anthropology, urban studies, and architecture, as well as on my political interests and practice, which are largely informed by strands of feminist theory on care. This disciplinary and political background has colored the ways in which I have navigated my research field, how I have linked different thoughts, voices, and experiences, and ultimately how I have reflected and written about them. It permeates this book in ways visible and less visible, leaving nonetheless an imprint that reflects my attempts—and limitations—at producing a critical work with care. Building on a rich tradition of feminist thought on knowledge politics, in her book *Matters of Care: Speculative Ethics in More Than Human Worlds*, Puig de la Bellacasa (2017) elaborates thoroughly on the affirmation that care can be generative of new modes of thinking.[26] Importantly, in this statement, knowledge is understood as a set of practices and sociomaterial configurations that contribute to (re)making and mattering the world. As she argues, thinking through and with care involves a number of practices and dispositions with inherent politics and ethics that ultimately seek to "generate more caring relationalities" (Puig de la Bellacasa 2017, 66). Care(ful) critical thinking entails first of all drawing attention to neglected things and devalued doings, and unearthing the power relations that underlie them. Besides, it implies engaging with these *matters of care* acknowledging not only a socially situated but also an ethical and political standpoint. Lastly, it entails committing to the possible *becomings* of these matters of care through a speculative, affective practice of imagining and suggesting (nonnormative) openings toward more caring worlds. This approach resonates with that of the feminist geographers J. K. Gibson-Graham (2006) when they both talk of a "politics of becoming" fostered by a theorizing endeavor seeking to channel "fugitive energies of caring" toward something new. That is, asking theory "to do something else—to help us see openings, to help us to find happiness, to provide a space of freedom and possibility" (Gibson-Graham 2006, 7). Similarly, it aligns as well with social-movement researchers engaging with radical imaginations, for whom any form of social research that seeks to challenge the status quo should go beyond description and find ways to convoke, expand, and prolong the openings or the radical imaginations at play in the movements.[27] In the following lines, I would like to reflect on the research work and thinking practice that grounds this book from this overarching framework.

All this being said, I arrived in Athens in 2016 without conscious awareness of the impact that such events could have on my research endeavors. Now, that

I am about to conclude an important phase of this journey, I think that it is with and from them that I intuitively started to develop my personal practice of *careful situated thinking*. Yet, my initial approach to the research field was actually very much influenced by classical science approaches to sociology and anthropology, which I was taught at university and from which I learned I should maintain a rigorous, "objective" distance from my "object of study." This approach, however, would not stick with me for long. Quite early into my fieldwork, I was faced with my first ethical dilemma. There I was—a white, foreign, doctoral student—in initiatives and spaces like the ICCs, which exist in response to pressing vital needs for many and are based on solidarity and commoning practices, having my "own agenda." Of course, this was not hidden, as from the very first day I introduced myself and my research purposes and asked for approval. Particularly in City Plaza and Khora, I would restate this repeatedly as newcomers would arrive almost continuously. Yet, this seemed to me not enough to justify my presence in these initiatives. Eventually, I took the decision to engage fully as a volunteer and separate this time from my fieldwork. I decided not to use that experience as research material, and to a certain extent I stuck to this, as I have not included any personal communication nor any particular event that occurred during those times of "no research."

However, another ethical dilemma arose quickly after. The more I involved myself, worked, spent time, and engaged in long conversations with others, the more I got to know people, eventually forging close friendships with some of them. It is through these friends that I began to acquire a deeper understanding of some of the dynamics and details that I had not seen or realized before. Furthermore, at a certain point, I started to become part of some of the same processes I was examining and trying to make sense of. There were times in which handling the feelings derived from specific situations I happened to find myself in was for me deeply challenging. In fact, I myself experienced what in this book I characterize as an *encounter*—or a series of encounters—through which I found myself transformed on a personal level. The reflection on my own processes of transformation has particularly influenced my analysis of what concerns relationships and subjectivities.

As my sensitivity and attentiveness to subtle transformations and latent possibilities expanded, my hypothesis about the potentiality of the ICCs gained depth and solidity. Yet, at the same time, my affective engagement with the field reinforced my worries about the risk of romanticizing my analysis. Although I believe that my awareness in this regard has always kept me on alert, the fact of feeling aligned—politically and also affectively—with the views and hopes about fostering social change that many of my interlocutors shared keeps making me question to what extent, despite my efforts to account for complexities, contradictions, and limitations, I have been truly able to reflect that wide complexity in my ethnographic account.

It is known that managing distance is a troubled commonplace for anthropologists. I am certainly not an exception in this regard as, besides my concerns about biased interpretations, I still find myself struggling with the thought of having taken from my interlocutors and friends a part of their own lived realities for my own individual endeavor. Considerations about possible forms to collectivize my research process and its outcomes in ways meaningful and inspiring for the people directly involved—or at least for some—emerged early in my engagement with the field, and are still present as I complete this book. The institutional framework of my doctoral thesis, which—as in most cases still—remains rooted in an individual approach, made my efforts toward collaborative research quite a challenging experience. As I have noted before, during my fieldwork time in the ICCs, I tried out some exercises that were aimed at coproducing ethnographic material with the people composing the field. My attempts in these regards were rather tentative and ultimately unsuccessful, as the projects that I proposed did not manage to engage people on a sustained basis for long enough. They failed to provide the conditions for people to make them theirs.

Yet, my challenges *to do collectively* or *in common* transcend the doctoral framework that demarcates this research. Coming from environments heavily marked by individualistic worldviews, where the mantra that goes "I can go it alone" seems to be desired, pursued, and actually enacted by many, there were indeed several times when I myself felt trapped by that paradigm, that way of doing and relating to others. That is, there were times when I found myself caught in a situation where I could not—or was not willing enough—to act other than individualistically. It is in this sense that the practices of producing, weaving, and sustaining everyday life and collective desires that I witnessed and experienced myself in the ICCs interpellated me on a very personal level. I have already mentioned that my experience as part of the ICCs was in many ways a transformative one. I believe that the essence of this transformation has to do with the fact of having allowed myself to be part of a number of *communitarian fabrics* or *communities in the making*—using Gutiérrez Aguilar's (2017) and Stavrides's (2016) words, respectively—as those were made and also unmade, with all the complexities that that entailed.

All these concerns and considerations stemming from an affected and affective engagement with the field have left an imprint on this book, molding my reflections, my arguments, and the tonality of my writing. The experience certainly afforded me important learnings. The shift in approach from one of a "critical observer from a distance" to that of an "active participant who embeds themselves in the field"—with the awareness and the commitment of finding a fair and respectful proximity—has for me no way back. Putting that (supposedly) objective distance in suspension, immersing myself in the field, and letting myself be touched by it afforded me the opportunity to delve into those less visible labors of care that hold things together, and to explore them from an affected and ethically committed position attentive to the possible openings latent in each situation.

Thus, I think that it is through this way of engaging with the field that I started to embrace and make sense of the practice of careful-situated-thinking, which in a way I had begun to practice quite inadvertently in the occupation of Puerta del Sol. To think *carefully* and *situatedly* in this sense implies letting oneself be affected by the situation, participating in it, conjecturing about its possibilities of a break with the status quo, and inhabiting its challenges. Thus, as feminist epistemologists and social movement researchers contend, this thinking practice goes beyond the acknowledgment of one's sociomaterial position. After all, any knowledge is inextricably bound to the social, cultural, and material context in and from which it is produced. Careful-situated-thinking implies a disposition of conscious acknowledgment of this fact and a continuous reflection on one's own specific positionality within the (always relational) research field. Yet, it also involves an ethical commitment to take part in possible transformations and openings toward more caring configurations that the engaged reality holds. Unsuccessful in my attempts at producing anthropological knowledge reflective of the transformative potentiality of the ICCs together with my field, this book, however, has provided me with the opportunity to show my commitment in this regard to a wider readership. At the end of the analytical chapters, I have included a speculative reflection about aspects of the radical imaginations concerning modes of sociomaterial organizing, politics, and subjectivities that I grasped in the examined ICCs, and in which I sense possible lines of flight toward more caring worlds. Let me stress, however, that radical imaginations are a controversial topic within social research. They are difficult to define—more so from an individual position—for they emerge embedded in normally long-established imaginaries that turn these processes of departure into arenas marked by ambiguity, contradiction, and resistance to replacement. Aware of this fact, I nonetheless believe that signaling them, trying to articulate them through words, contributes in some way to their very configuration and mattering. Hence my attempt in this respect.

I would like to close this section with some remarks concerning the cross-disciplinary nature of the research behind this book. I have noted that, at the core, the inquiries driving it are anthropological. Yet, for the elaboration of this work I have felt the need to resort to a number of different disciplinary fields, among them geography, urban studies, history, political philosophy, citizenship studies, and feminist theor(ies) on care. After all, the practice of careful-situated-thinking necessarily overflows established disciplinary boundaries, for it seeks holistic understandings of the engaged reality. The ideas that I have found in these compartments of knowledge have hugely helped me in the endeavor of elaborating my experience and analysis of the ICCs, connecting them with other realities through theory. Weaving (meaningful) connections among theories and between those and the experience in the field has been a challenging yet fulfilling task.

In this process of weaving, I want to highlight the role that my training as a spatial thinker has played. Looking into the ways in which space was produced and transformed in the ICCs and the type of spatiality(ies) that were brought about has notably informed my examination of the type of organizing structures and mechanisms in place in the initiatives and the kind of politics that unfolded in the everyday. It has also provided me with a perspective from which to understand social and personal relationships within these heterogeneous groups of people, as well as the emergence of new subjective formations, and conversely, to explore the effects of those relationships in the spaces inhabited in common. Besides, it is through spatial thinking that I have been able to understand and connect different levels and scales of action, impact, and potentiality of the ICCs. Massey (2005) talks of space as the dimension of the social. She contends that our respective conceptions of the world, relationships, and politics are shaped by the way we think about space. To me, especially after this research work, it is quite evident that the interrogation of space enhances anthropological inquiry and analysis.

I will close the introduction here by restating my belief in and commitment to a research practice that embraces affection, self-reflexivity, cross-disciplinarity, committed theorization, and personal transformation as key elements for the production of critical knowledge from the standpoint of care. Now I leave it for the reader to navigate through this endeavor in this book and judge it.

CHAPTER 1

The Emergence of Infrastructures of Caring Citizenship in Athens-in-Crisis

Urban Development of Athens toward Crisis

During the two decades preceding the global financial crisis, Greece underwent large social and economic transformations. The rapid economic growth boosted the spirit of "modernization"—expanding since the early postwar years—and the social consensus around development through infrastructure construction and urbanization (Dalakoglou 2013; Dalakoglou and Kallianos 2018). During these years, the improvement trend in the living standards of Greek citizens continued, coupled with increasing consumerist practices. The long-established mode of social reproduction of the Greek society, strongly anchored in the (traditional) family, shifted (Papadopoulos and Roumpakis 2012, 2013). New processes and mechanisms for redefining citizenship emerged. The Olympic Games, held in Athens in 2004, would constitute the zenith of these processes of socioeconomic transformation (Dalakoglou 2013; Dalakoglou and Kallianos 2018). However, the alluring future that the games were supposed to bring about was truncated. On the contrary, they would come to signal the end of the so-called golden decade. From the year in which they were awarded (1997) until their implementation, Greece's public and private debt raised dramatically. The Greek growth economic model that started in the 1990s, which was reliant on European Union (EU) funds, the construction and service sectors, the privatization of public services, and increasing credit-driven consumption, would prove highly fragile in the face of the advent of the international banking crash. By 2008, Greece's fiscal situation was one of extreme vulnerability (Dalakoglou 2013; Dalakoglou and Kallianos 2018; Papadopoulos and Roumpakis 2012, 2013; Petropoulou 2008).

The series of socioeconomic transformations that Greece has undergone since the end of the Greek Civil War has a marked urban character. Athens, which experienced exorbitant growth, constitutes an emblematic setting in which all these societal changes can be traced. In the following, I present a historical overview of the development of Athens from the 1950s until the outbreak of the Greek sovereign debt crisis in 2010, focusing on those processes that reflect the entwining of Greek forms of social reproduction and production of citizenship with major urban processes and imaginaries of the capital.

1950S–1974: THE METHOD OF ANTIPAROCHI AND THE POLYKATOIKIA AS URBAN CONSTITUENTS OF THE GREEK MODEL OF FAMILISTIC WELFARE CAPITALISM

After the Greek Civil War (1946–1949) until the end of the military junta (1967–1974), Athens underwent a process of extensive urban development marked by the lack of large capital investments and official urban plans. During these decades, the Greek capital received a large inflow of people who moved from the rural areas seeking employment in the industrial and construction sectors. This internal migration added to the large numbers of refugees from Asia Minor who had settled in Athens after the population exchange that followed the war with Turkey (1919–1922).[1] The resulting immense demand for housing surpassed by far the capabilities of the state to provide a response. Instead, small private initiatives became the main driving forces of urbanization. The urban development led by small builders resulted in the city sprawling in all directions without following any institutional planning (Petropoulou 2008).

In this context, the *polykatoikia*—a multistory apartment building constructed by self-taught contractors through the method of *antiparochi*—would become the most extended housing typology.[2] Antiparochi was a policy framework set by the state as an alternative to a social housing program, which it was not able to finance. This regulatory system allowed landowners to transfer their plots to constructors to build a multistory housing block in exchange for an agreed number of flats. Antiparochi permitted a high degree of irregularities in building regulations and real-estate transactions, and proved to be a rather profitable mechanism for small investors operating within clientelistic networks (Petropoulou 2008). This way, the loosely regulated construction fever from the 1950s to the 1970s, based on "the apparatus of the polykatoikia" (Aureli, Giudici, and Issaias 2012), brought about a high increase in urban density in central areas as well as uncontrolled urban sprawl. Interestingly, the resulting cityscape was one of homogeneity and repetition when looked at on the large scale, and of fragmentation and discontinuity when looked at from the level of individual buildings.

The polykatoikia became one of the most emblematic representations of the social imaginary of the growing middle class of the time, associated with the family and its traditional values. In Greece—as in southern Europe—in the absence of a fully developed welfare state, the family has traditionally played a paramount role in the economy and society. The scholars Theodoros Papadopoulos and Antonios Roumpakis (2013) called this model of political economy "familistic welfare capitalism." The Greek model of familistic welfare capitalism has been remarkably characterized by networks of clientelism and patronage. The "polykatoikia apparatus" performed a constitutive role in this system of favors among family networks. The architectural historian Ioanna Theocharopoulou (2017) argues that the massive expansion of these apartment buildings contributed to the emergence of a middle-class subjectivity grounded in private home ownership. Her examination of marketing campaigns of the interiors of the polykatoikias of the time, which targeted housewives as the principal managers of "domestic affairs," provides very interesting insights into the connection of these apartments with an emerging social imaginary of modernization and development.

Theocharopoulou is among the authors who broadly hold a positive view of the polykatoikia system in social and urban terms. Among the beneficial aspects, authors (e.g., Siatitsa 2016; Boano and Gyftopoulou 2016) have highlighted that the system permitted a rather widespread social control of access to housing, thus protecting its social reproduction function, that the sociospatial conditions of the polykatoikia facilitated the coexistence of people of diverse incomes and origins, thereby favoring processes of social integration and cohesion, and that its flexibility promoted a mixed program of uses while the porosity and versatility of its architectural boundaries—through balconies and arcades—allowed moments of blend between the public and the private. But there are critical views, too. Scholars like Aureli, Giudici, and Issaias (2012) have stressed that this housing model based on private ownership and the subjectivity it produced, marked by "radical individualism" and excessive consumerism, led to an increasing trend toward economic speculation through housing. In their view, this process contributed to the housing crisis that broke out during the austerity regime.

1974 TO MID-1990S: MIDDLE-CLASS SUBURBANIZATION AND "OTHERING" MECHANISMS IN CENTRAL ATHENS

The establishment of the democratic regime in 1974 and the later incorporation of Greece into the EU in 1981 opened an era of important sociopolitical changes in the country, particularly in the urban areas.[3] New urban planning regulations and initiatives were launched, the Urban Restructuring Project in 1982 and the Housing Law of 1983 being the most significant ones. Both enabled the incorporation of several neighborhoods into the city's urban plans. In 1985, the Athens Metropolitan Plan included among its main aims the restriction of the city's urban growth, the reduction of sociospatial differences between eastern and western areas, the enhancement of the city's historical heritage, and the promotion of citizen participation. These urban measures attested to a will to regularize the city's urban development, although they would eventually prove rather weak (Petropoulou 2008).

Due to the political stability and a favorable economic situation, Greeks experienced a significant rise in living standards. The state and the banks started to encourage families to enroll themselves in financial credits and high-risk market practices—like investment in the stock exchange and the housing market—as a way to promote consumption and increase economic growth. A new form of reproduction of the socioeconomic system took form, leaving behind a period of over four decades characterized by cautious economic operations within households (Papadopoulos and Roumpakis 2012, 2013). In these years, Athens witnessed a steady relocation of the upper and middle classes to the outskirts. Many apartments in central Athens were left empty and entire buildings were abandoned. Retail moved to the suburbs as well. Public space in the city center was neglected and the price of houses dropped. Central Athens became a rather derelict area. Nevertheless, and in part for these reasons, from the 1990s onward, the city center attracted growing numbers of migrants.[4] Deprived of protective networks, these people mostly settled in the area, where they could meet acquaintances, and legal and everyday life resources as well as job opportunities and affordable housing were more available. Interestingly, the distinctive polykatoikia model and its associated vertical segregation prevented a high horizontal sociospatial segregation along ethnic lines.[5] Yet, the extreme precariousness of the living conditions of the majority of them would not improve much in the years to come (Dalakoglou 2013; Maloutas 2007; Petropoulou 2008).

Despite the newly settled migrant networks, which set up thriving small businesses, some neighborhoods in central Athens—for years already subject to neglect and underinvestment—became representative of the inner city's decay in the Athenians' urban imaginary. In this negatively connoted imaginary, Omonia Square—and its surrounding areas—stands out. The large square has historically performed the role of the main transportation hub and includes an extensive variety of commercial services, small businesses, and hotels. From the

1990s, the square gradually started to be identified with irregular activities—drug trafficking and prostitution, for example—and marginalized populations, very often stigmatized. Policing in the area increased. This, coupled with corporate media's negative publicity on migration, boosted an image of Omonia as a "no go area." Similarly, Exarcheia—a neighborhood in central Athens with a deeply rooted historical tradition of political mobilization and activism within the spectrum of the Left and of development of social movements—also witnessed increasing policing alongside official stigmatizing discourses by the state, the local governments, and the corporate media during the 1990s and 2000s (Dalakoglou 2013; Koutrolikou 2016).

Athens's case is paradigmatic in the sense that through processes of displacement, policing mechanisms, and stigmatizing discourses, specific urban areas became symbolic of decay and were identified with those "others"—the noncitizens or the "bad citizens"—who in turn became representative of a potential public threat. The series of "othering" mechanisms implemented throughout those years—mostly along ethnic, national, and class lines but also political—were strongly embedded in the urban fabric. The resulting urban imaginary was directly attached to a newly emerged geography of exclusion and fear in the very heart of the city.

MID-1990S TO MID-2000S: INFRASTRUCTURAL DEVELOPMENT AND IMAGINATION

Parallel to the degradation of central Athens, the city continued its frenzied sprawl outside the urban plan's limits. Due to the introduction of new regulations pertaining to public work, a growing role of the banks in real-estate development, and the emergence of big construction contractors, Athens experienced a new construction boom marked by large-scale projects and infrastructures, like the new Athens international airport, the metro, the suburban railway, the tram and the new Athens ring road. Following the new consumerist lifestyles, new leisure areas and shopping centers were established along the motorways, providing new "public spaces" for the middle and upper classes. New suburbs emerged as Athens consolidated its automobilization trend. The magnitude of the urban (re)development of this so-called golden decade was so big that the Greek construction sector was called the "steam engine." In fact, between the mid-1990s and the mid-2000s, Greece positioned itself among the countries in the EU with the highest economic growth rate (Dalakoglou 2013; Dalakoglou and Kallianos 2018; Petropoulou 2008).

The infrastructural imagination that emerged in Greece during the golden decade was one in which infrastructure construction was directly associated with the idea of progress. Such an optimistic assemblage of discourses and images was largely promoted from the top down. In 1997, the capital won the bid to host the 2004 Olympic Games. From then on, Athens's cityscape would experience dramatic changes. The games were promoted on the one hand as an opportunity for the internationalization of Greece and, on the other, as a domestic project for the reinvigoration of the Greek identity as part of the European culture and history—to the detriment of its historical connection with the East. Large amounts of funds and resources were allocated to promote the games by enhancing a collective sense of enthusiasm and national pride (Dalakoglou 2013; Dalakoglou and Kallianos 2018).

Nevertheless, while the games were welcomed with great social optimism, the urban transformations that ensued triggered the emergence of the first urban movements against some of these projects. Alongside new infrastructures—mostly hard infrastructures—a large number of urban regeneration projects were undertaken across the Attica region. Landmark architectural designs were promoted to the detriment of many public spaces, which would be privatized or neglected later on. Within a decade, public opinion about these operations and their effects, this dramatic transformation of the Greek capital, had changed. As per Kallianos and Dalakoglou's account (2018), the "stage of consent" in regard to public works turned quite quickly into a "stage of contestation." The infrastructural imagination that prefigured a brilliant future did not last long. Shortly after the end of the games, the recently built infrastructures and projects became associated with economic collapse, political breakdown, and social rupture. In fact, the games brought disastrous consequences for Athens. Their legacy is that of a *privatized*, *devalued*, and *militarized* city, as was portrayed in the documentary *Future Suspended* (2014).[6] The number of privatized assets, the degree of public indebtedness, and the new policing mechanisms were unprecedented in the history of the city. So nefarious was their legacy that they have been accused of paving the way for The Crisis (Arampatzi and Nicholls 2012; Boano and Gyftopoulou 2016; Dalakoglou 2013; Dalakoglou and Kallianos 2018; Petropoulou 2008; Stavrides 2014).

The Production and Management of the Greek Crisis through the Urban: Narratives, Governmentality, and Space

THE RHETORICAL CONSTRUCTION OF THE CRISIS IN GREECE

The social imaginary of crisis gives meaning to a social reality, but also produces and/or reproduces this same reality and its established social order. Thus, it works as a mechanism that exerts power and control, which as such has been intensely mobilized by the dominant powers (Agamben 2003; Athanasiou 2018; Butler and Athanasiou 2013; Roitman 2013; Tsilimpounidi 2017). From January 2009, when the International Monetary Fund (IMF) formally announced a global economic recession after the global banking crash, the production and mainstreaming of official discourses and images to explain the nature and causes of the global financial and economic crisis was extraordinary. In Greece, from the early months of the economic recession, discourses of what came to be commonly referred to as The Crisis were spread widely, aimed principally at the middle classes. Greek crisis narratives have been framed to a large extent in (macro)economic, security, and humanitarian terms. The three crisis "types" intertwine with and build from each other, yet each one draws from specific events and has had particular impacts.

Initially, the most salient crisis narrative was that of the sudden collapse of the national economy due to the high levels of the national debt. When in 2009 the global financial crisis hit Greece, the Greek economy was already in jeopardy due to the continuous expansion of public debt that had been going on since the 1970s. The steady economic growth that started in the 1990s vanished all of a sudden. In the face of a possible default, in 2010, the PASOK government sought financial assistance from the Troika.[7] That event signaled the "official" entry of Greece into The Crisis. Citizens were bombarded with explanations about its causes, coming from politicians, different media, and experts alike. At first, the narrative explained The Crisis in terms of a domestic failure ascribed to a society that "had consumed beyond its means," corrupt governments, and an inefficient public sector, and this explanation dominated over those that pointed out systemic factors within the Eurozone or the broader global economic system. This point actually came up in a few of the conversations that I had about The Crisis with my interlocutors. Stelios, a young student of economics, expressed it in this way:

> They've been trying to make us believe that it was all our fault because we like the *kafeneios* too much. Because we, Greeks, are lazy. For them [at the time, the Néa Dimokratía (New Democracy; ND) government], it was just us, not Europe, not Germany, not the banks. Now the golden years are gone and we have to pay up. We, our parents, and grandparents who have been working all their lives trying to make some savings for the future. They are cutting everything—the pensions, the salaries, the healthcare—and worst, they want that we feel guilty. (Stelios, July 3, 2016)

Nevertheless, in one way or another, what was made clear was that the country had fallen into a situation of emergency and the conjunction required an immediate response. Therefore, any measure to meet the debt and "save the country" would be deemed reasonable. In May of that year, the PASOK government would sign the first Memorandum of Understanding (MoU) with the Troika of lenders, which would signal a turning point for the national economic sovereignties not just in Greece but also in the rest of Europe. A new financial crisis framework was instituted with the subsequent implementation of legal amendments and new regulations to accommodate the approved austerity package (Domoney, Dalakoglou, and Filippidis 2013; Papadopoulos and Roumpakis 2012).

A second way of constructing The Crisis revolved around the idea of the increase of insecurity in people's everyday lives—particularly of Greek citizens. Accounts of public revolts and riots coupled with criminalizing narratives often targeting those most socially vulnerable populated much of the mainstream media.[8] Existing social problems were emphasized and new ones were invented in order to introduce new political and judiciary changes (Domoney, Dalakoglou, and Filippidis 2013). A number of "othering" strategies and practices were put in place to redefine and signal "new" public enemies. Migrants, sex workers, drug consumers, and far-left and anarchist groups became principal targets of the police as well as far-right groups (Boano and Gyftopoulou 2016; Koutrolikou 2016). The state repression system was in fact reconfigured as new structures and concepts to address criminality were introduced, for instance, the concept of "anomie," which underpinned a media and police campaign—"Zero Tolerance to Anomie"[9]—targeting demonstrators, anarchists, and migrants (Boano and Gyftopoulou 2016; Domoney, Dalakoglou, and Filippidis 2013). The creation of this climate of fear was used in some instances for electoral purposes. The electoral campaign run by Antonis Samaras (ND)—the future prime minister—in 2012, in which, among other things, he promised to open thirty new detention centers for undocumented migrants, is telling in this regard.[10]

A third big representation of The Crisis was characterized as "humanitarian." It was largely built on a press release by Médecins du Monde in November 2010, which read "Athens, a City in Humanitarian Crisis" (Médecins du Monde 2010; see also Koutrolikou 2016). For the first time since the creation of the EU, a member state was facing a humanitarian emergency—normally the case after wars, civil conflicts, epidemics, or natural catastrophes. This crisis declaration would be followed by many others, coming largely from international but also local NGOs,[11] which addressed national governments and international institutions and condemned the harmful effects of the austerity measures on Greek society. This narrative would partially ameliorate the negative image constructed about many of those most affected by The Crisis, namely migrants and socially excluded people. Interestingly, the large-scale arrival in 2015 of people from the Middle East and North Africa seeking asylum in Europe did not initially result in further criminalization of the immigrant. On the contrary, the previous threatening image changed quite significantly. As Lafazani (2018) accounts, the striking scenario of thousands of asylum seekers packing parks and squares such as Omonia Square and Victoria Square in central Athens triggered the launch of an extraordinary solidarity movement integrated by great segments of civil society that served to prevent discourses of an "invasion" and the like. A new image of the immigrant was configured, that of the "refugee family" fleeing war.

> My grandmother told me that this [the sudden arrival of thousands of refugees in the city] reminded her of what her parents had told her about the *exchange*, when they had to leave Turkey overnight and arrived in Piraeaus together with many other people.[12] Victoria Square was packed. There were also many children. For days, people created chains to supply food, clothes, and also toys. It was very moving. I think that the image of that little boy Alan Kurdi, drowned at the seashore, hit people deeply.[13] We [Greeks] are suffering, but we can't close our eyes to this reality. They are fleeing from a reality of death. Everybody deserves a good life. (Eleni, June 27, 2016)

When we met in 2016, Eleni was a middle-age woman who was working as a cleaner at some offices. Her account illustrates the aforementioned image of the deserving refugee family. However, that first wave of arrivals between 2015 and 2016 was taken by and large as "temporary," which underscored that attitude toward refugees as deserving of help and compassion, though not of citizens' rights. The media would feature a wide range of individual stories about the perils of their journeys coupled with others showing the generosity of many Greek citizens who welcomed and hosted them in their houses. The so-called refugee crisis—which added a new facet to the already-declared humanitarian crisis in the country—would bring hundreds of NGOs and charity organizations to Greece. As the refugee crisis extended in time, and against a backdrop of "NGOization"[14]—facing increasing rejection by growing sectors of the civil society—the image of the "good refugee" started to decline while the rhetoric of the threat gained ground once again.

THE PRODUCTION AND MANAGEMENT OF ATHENS-IN-CRISIS
AS PART OF THE CRISIS

Throughout the unfolding of the Greek crisis, Athens played a central role in the production and management of The Crisis itself, proving the common link between financial and economic crises and urban space. The city underwent major transformations, becoming a territory of governance experimentation and thus the setting of harsh clashes between competing interests and powers. Quite quickly, Athens went from being considered the spearhead of the modernization of the country to a space in decay and turmoil—a city in crisis—where, on the one hand, increasing processes of dispossession and exclusion yielded the emergence of new social and urban enclosures while, on the other, the formation of insurgent forms of resistance created new social bonds and solidarity practices challenging those very enclosures. Athens, as a crisis-ridden city, was the focus of a set of discourses and images that drew on different yet interlinked (declared) urban crises—some of them already underway before 2008—to eventually feed The Crisis grand narrative. Local and international press and television outlets, human rights agencies, NGOs, and politicians,[15] all contributed to constructing "Athens in crisis," albeit in different terms. This rhetoric and imaginary were used by the political and economic powers to legitimize the implementation of a plethora of new measures and mechanisms of social control at the local level, ultimately contributing to the institution of that new phase of neoliberal governance through the city (Boano and Gyftopoulou 2016; Koutrolikou 2016).

Athens-in-crisis narratives shaped the ways in which a series of crises in the city, which unfolded or became more acute during the next ten years, were managed and governed during the austerity regime. The "crisis governmentality" in the case of Athens comprised a number of different strategies and mechanisms, among them the enforcement of exceptional policies, disproportionally violent or discriminatory police operations, and privatizations and sell-offs of public land and properties—some of them followed by the announcement of new urban regeneration projects. The following examples illustrate these points.

Premised on emergency, Athens saw a striking increase in police presence in the streets, to the point where, for many, the city's experience became one of a militarized zone (Domoney, Dalakoglou, and Filippidis 2013; Filippidis et al. 2014). To enforce the acceptance of the new (repressive) order, the authorities launched a series of police operations in response to the so-called public safety crisis in the city. An exemplary case was the evictions in 2013 of long-standing political squats such as Villa Amalias, Patission 61, and Skaramagas, all of them bearing great symbolism in the Athenian urban imaginary of resistance. Prior to the raids and dismantling of these self-organized spaces, a campaign accusing them of degrading the urban fabric was widely mobilized. The evictions took place with the use of disproportionate violence, and images and footage were spread to the public. As the lawyers Kutrovik and Ladis in *Landscapes of Emergency* (Domoney, Dalakoglou, and Filippidis 2013) note, "The symbols of resistance had been brought down and the message sent was clear: those resisting the new state of affairs were to be disciplined."

Following the same rhetoric, some of the most socially vulnerable groups were subject to discriminatory criminalizing campaigns with the eventual violation of individual rights in some cases. The following two events epitomize this issue. The first took place in 2012. Sex workers in Athens were detained and forced to take HIV tests. They were publicly named—their names and photos were posted online by the police—criminally charged, and pinpointed as a threat to public health. Rather than looking at the cuts in social budgets and programs as the cause of the emerging health crisis, the government blamed sex workers for it.[16] The second occurred between 2012 and 2013. The police carried out the operation Xenios Zeus, which comprised police raids, abusive searches, and arbitrary detentions targeting undocumented immigrants on race or ethnicity grounds.[17] Over 84,000 migrants were arrested and forced to prove their immigration status (Amnesty International 2014; Boano and Gyftopoulou 2016; Human Rights Watch 2013; Koutrolikou 2016).

As already argued, the strategies of naming and configuring specific groups of people as threats translate materially in the city space and its geographies. The center of Athens has been a particular target of these discourses and operations. Alongside The Crisis grand narrative, a crisis of central Athens was constructed as well, drawing on years of gradual deterioration due to infrastructural disinvestment and urban neglect. As analyzed by Koutrolikou (2016) and Boano and Gyftopoulou (2016), since the early years of the national economic downturn, a representation of some areas of the city center as "hotbeds of crime" or ghettos—like Omonia Square and its surroundings, (Gerani), Vathis Square, Victoria Square, Acharnon Street, and Amerikis Square, or (to a lesser extent) the neighborhoods of Metaxourgio and Kypseli—gained attention in some media, eventually becoming a matter for urgent action. Those narratives and images depicted the center of Athens as an enclave of those "others," namely the immigrants, drug users, sex workers, and refugees. Dwellers of the margins—these groups who represented a threat to the economy, security, and health—were portrayed as responsible for having transformed the area into a site of decay and criminality. This sociospatial stigmatization intensified the climate of fear and insecurity with different repercussions. On the one hand, it was used by groups of the political far right to push their claims into the political discussions as well as to make their presence—and violence—felt in particular public spaces. On the other hand, it served to legitimize the exceptional measures taken.

What came to be known as the "crisis of the center of Athens" was used by local authorities and real-estate developers to present new programs for the redevelopment of some areas, aiming to attract "decent" residents and tourists. Between 2012 and 2013, several urban design competitions for public spaces, such as Theatrou Square, were launched alongside research-design projects, like *Re-activate Athens: 101 Ideas* and *Re-map Athens*, and new "revitalization" projects, such as *Re-think Athens* (Boano and Gyftopoulou 2016; Kaltsa and Maloutas 2015; Koutrolikou 2016; Tournikiotis 2015). Given the declared critical state of the city center, they were all considered urgent. In a way, this series of projects could be viewed as an attempt to develop an urban imaginary beyond crisis. Nevertheless, as various scholars have highlighted (e.g., Boano and Gyftopoulou 2016; Dalakoglou 2013; Koutrolikou 2016), the context in which they emerged was one of rapid urban transformations under a reworked form of urban governance based in part on a redefinition of the concept of the public to accommodate private interests. Thus, they should be read in parallel with the policies and measures for Athens's metropolitan territories that were put in place as remedies for the debt crisis, which included privatizations and sell-offs of public lands and properties, sweeping demolitions of "abandoned" buildings, and an extensive list of planning deregulations.

The examples gathered here are illustrative of how city-in-crisis narratives and the imaginary they promote are part of a specific governance apparatus that uses the city—its specific social dynamics and processes, its lands, buildings, and space—as a medium to implement new policies, judiciary changes, and mechanisms of social control, benefiting the interests of major financial, economic, and political powers behind the national crisis of debt. This governance apparatus, as Athanasiou (2018) argues, is nothing more than a reconfiguration of the neoliberal governmentality through a state of permanent crisis, which builds on loss, dispossession, and fear. Indeed, the management of The Crisis through an austerity regime can be viewed as the intensification of the processes of neoliberalization that gained traction in the country during the 1990s. The debt crisis came to rearticulate certain aspects of the state, which redefined its relationship with the citizenry by actually subjecting them to unprecedented measures involving violence in different forms. Massive mobilizations would contest that newly imposed state of affairs.

Dispossessions and Exclusions

The global financial crisis that broke out in 2008 rapidly spread to the European economies. By the end of the year, Greece was plunged into a profound sovereign debt crisis. In 2010, prime minister George Papandreou (PASOK) announced that the country might fail to meet its debt commitments with the EU. To avoid default, in May of that year, Greece's government agreed to the first MoU with the Troika of lenders, namely the IMF, the European Commission (EC), and the European Central Bank (ECB), by which Greece was required to implement a program of structural economic adjustments through austerity policies and measures. From that point until May 2017, fourteen austerity packages comprising a wide range of economic, social, and political reforms would be approved and adopted in the country. The bailout program formally ended in August 2018. The austerity regime implemented to refinance the debt and reinstate the favorable performance of the economy failed and proved detrimental, not just in economic terms— Greece was mired in a long-term recession until 2017—it also brought about deep political and social crises. Structural adjustment was delivered by means of curtailing salaries and pensions, increasing direct and indirect taxes, making cuts in the public sector, privatizing public infrastructures and assets, and decreasing welfare provision, as well as through the weakening of workers and civil rights and of the social security system, among other reforms. The way the successive Greek governments—PASOK (2009–2012), Néa Dimokratía (2012–2015), SYRIZA-ANEL (2015–2019)—dealt with such a multifaceted crisis was through a marked macroeconomic approach seeking to prioritize the country's financial obligations with its international creditors and the recovery of financial stability and trust within the Eurozone.

Importantly, austerity policies and reforms especially targeted urban populations and areas. Dispossessions and exclusions took place at several levels and within all the spaces of social life, bringing about devastating effects on the processes of urban and social reproduction. In a short span of time, many Greek households found themselves facing unemployment, indebtedness, poverty, and threats of eviction or forced displacement from their homes and neighborhoods. At the same time, the provision of public social protection was drastically cut. Inequality based on people's access to work, housing, and social services increased dramatically after 2010, together with poverty rates. Many family networks were broken, putting in jeopardy the safety nets that they had traditionally provided. This translated into the displacement of many people to the margins of society and the subsequent increase in the number of people at risk of social exclusion. Urban space played an important role in these processes of creating new urban and social enclosures, not only as the setting where they took place and manifested but also as the very means for their implementation and development (Boano and Gyftopoulou 2016; Chalkias, Delladetsimas, and Sapountzaki 2015; Kalandides and Vaiou 2015; Koutrolikou 2016; Stavrides 2014). In what follows, I go through some of the key effects of the Greek crisis with a focus on Athens.

Of the processes of dispossession and exclusion, the first to hit was that of the labor market, which especially targeted women and the youth.[18] In 2011, the youth unemployment rate reached 39 percent. The unemployment benefit was cut from €450 to €360 per month, and the percentage of people receiving the benefit dropped by 44 points from 2008. Additionally, collective bargaining rights were restricted as a condition of the first MoU. The increase in unemployment rates came coupled with a steep decrease in salaries and pensions. Subsequently, households' income and purchasing capacity experienced a sharp decline, while, paradoxically, the cost of living rose.[19] Prices of basic products and social goods increased, the price of electricity being one of the most striking examples.[20] The increasing economic stress left many households unable to meet their financial commitments (bills, loans, etc.), plunging them into indebtedness. From 2010, the burden of private debt increased dramatically.[21]

Public welfare was deeply affected too.[22] Budgets for healthcare, social care, and education were severely curtailed at both the national and the local level. Additionally, many people were excluded from healthcare and social care services and deprived of educational and cultural resources.[23] The public healthcare system was profoundly restructured, both in legal and organizational terms, to rationalize costs. Entire hospitals and clinics were closed and medical staff was reduced. Both the range and quality of healthcare have worsened significantly ever since. Public social services for the elderly, the youth, and people with special needs and chronic illnesses were also curtailed, placing the burden back onto the families, particularly on women. The cuts in and restriction of access to welfare, as well as the downsizing of the welfare state institutions, at a moment when support was needed more than ever, significantly worsened the conditions of the most vulnerable groups, namely women, children, the elderly, and migrants. For many women it meant losing those services and benefits for themselves and other members of their families, losing their jobs as workers in those services or—for migrant women—in home care.

The rise of insecurity and despair directly translated into an increase in illness and mental health problems. Unemployment and indebtedness directly curtail people's capacity to earn a living, yet they also entail the loss of a space of integration and position in society, with serious psychoemotional implications. By the end of 2011, Greece had the highest suicide rates in Europe. The story of Dimitris Christoulas, a seventy-seven-year-old pensioner who in April 2012 committed suicide in Syntagma Square in front of the Greek Parliament, tragically made apparent this new reality to society. I learned about Christoulas's immolation through my friend Electre.

> He chose a tree in Syntagma Square to take his life in the middle of the day. He left a note saying that it was not him but the government that killed him by cutting the pension he had saved working as a pharmacist during all his life. He said he chose to die that way instead of losing his dignity by having to look for food inside garbage containers. . . . He also addressed young people, saying that he hoped we rebelled against the government. (Electre, August 18, 2016)

Christoulas's suicide sparked far-reaching reactions beyond the national reality. In Athens, his funeral was followed by a massive demonstration against austerity measures. He became a symbol of the deep suffering but also of refusal to subjugation that would distinguish Greece during the austerity regime.

At the city level, in Athens, many small businesses closed down, which contributed to the gradual deterioration of urban spaces and neighborhood social life. Continued cuts to municipal expenditures for urban services and infrastructures, which sustain the city's reproduction, affected services like garbage collection, the maintenance of streets, parks, and city infrastructures, and the functioning of transport systems and public cultural and sports facilities. The decaying Olympic infrastructures stand among the most striking examples of urban abandonment and neglect. The adverse impacts of the austerity regime can still be traced in the city's streets and squares, many of which are in degraded conditions.[24] Parallel to public disinvestment, privatization and deregulation policies were put in place to facilitate the sell-off of urban land, public infrastructures, buildings, parks, and commercial spaces.[25] These dispossession strategies yielded the emergence of new urban enclosures. At the neighborhood level, many of these operations prompted processes of displacement of long-established residents in neighborhoods like Exarcheia and Metaxourgio, which are ongoing in the present.

The series of enforced measures in the form of privatizations and cuts in public budgets as well as in social and civil rights transformed the very notion of public space and the way it was experienced. Increasing racist violence, including forced evictions from many public spaces, became a quotidian experience for many groups who faced the violence of either far-right groups or the police. On the other hand, political activism in public spaces was repressed and the right to protest was curtailed. As denounced by the International Federation for Human Rights (FIDH), the implementation of austerity measures in Greece paved the ground for the violation of political and civil rights.[26] Exceptional operations to evict some self-organized spaces as well as migrant- or refugee-occupied buildings were carried out in the name of public safety.[27] Paradoxically, parallel with an increase in policing, drug trafficking and organized crime grew in presence in the public space, which contributed to the expulsion of many residents from the public squares, specifically in areas in central Athens.

Last but not least, austerity is also a key cause behind the emergence of a Greek housing crisis in the form of a pronounced recession in the housing market and the construction sector, on the one hand, and the increase in household indebtedness, in overdue mortgages, and homelessness rates, on the other. As Siatitsa (2016) explains, as opposed to other countries, such as the United States or Spain, in Greece, the housing market was not directly linked to the initial financial crash. Three austerity policy frameworks, involving both legal and institutional changes, contributed to turning housing and real-estate assets from a family resource into an unsustainable burden for many low- and medium-income households. This series of strategic reforms brought the long-established Greek housing and land regime—comprising construction, ownership, and access—to a turning point, jeopardizing a system that for long had facilitated the social control of housing and land as well as the wide distribution of assets.

The first of these policy frameworks concerned the introduction of new taxation. A controversial property tax to was passed by the PASOK government in September 2011, affecting more than five million properties. The new tax was set to be collected through electricity bills. Failure to pay would translate into electricity supply cut-offs. The second was related to the management of private debt toward international and public debt repayment, for which real-estate assets were marked as ideal sources of revenue. The legal framework that had been set to protect citizens' primary residences and prevent mass foreclosures was revoked at the end of 2014 by the mandate of the Troika. In 2017, the SYRYZA-ANEL government—which had promised that no house would be seized and sold by the banks—gave the green light to online auctions of foreclosed properties as a facilitating mechanism for creditors targeting nonperforming debtors. Finally, the third policy framework had to do with the recreation of the real-estate sector in favor of speculative practices, for which the role of the state in the housing question had to change dramatically. No longer a facilitator for the social mobility of the working classes and migrant newcomers, the Greek state would actually shift its facilitating mechanisms to serve large real-estate investors, foreigners mostly. Noteworthy, the Workers Housing Organization (Orgánosi Ergatikís Katoikíes, OEK)—the only and rather minimal public institution for housing programs—was dismantled in 2012 following the second MoU. At present, processes of property conversion, reallocation, and sell-off toward the concentration of land and property, as well as processes of deregulation of urban development, are underway under a tailored "safe environment" set up for real-estate investors.[28] On the other hand, increasing numbers of privately owned flats are being placed on the rental market, many of them for touristic and temporary lets.

This all translated into rising numbers of households that could no longer afford to buy a property, and still can't. This has particularly affected young people, who cannot afford to buy their own homes, but also existing home-owners, who started to sell or rent their houses and rent more affordable ones to live in. Ever since, many loan holders have seen how the banks have taken away their houses, which they no longer could afford to pay. In Athens, the number of rough sleepers in the streets increased throughout the years of The Crisis.[29] The situation especially worsened in 2015 and 2016 with the large-scale arrival of migrants and asylum seekers—Syrians and Afghans comprising the largest numbers[30]—and the EU-Turkey agreement.[31] A reception system was set up by the state under the Ministry of Migration Policy and managed by National Center for Social Solidarity (Ethnikó Kéntro Koivonikís Allileggís, EKKA), alongside the UNHCR accommodation scheme—in place since 2015—and a series of other agents. The accommodation facilities included large-scale (temporary/emergency) camps—mostly located outside urban areas and lacking access to public transportation and services—hotels, flats, and other facilities run by NGOs. However, the number of asylum seekers, particularly young single men, facing homelessness has not stopped growing since 2015. The official multiagent reception system has proved insufficient and inadequate in both quantitative and qualitative terms.[32]

In summary, the myriad multiscale processes of dispossession and exclusion—in economic, material, spatial, and rights terms—triggered by the austerity regime in Greece, and particularly in Athens, seriously undermined people's forms and means of social reproduction, as well as citizen sovereignty. In losing their access to the labor market, healthcare and social services, housing, and public spaces, as well as some of their labor and civil rights, many people were deprived of the means to sustain their livelihoods, at the same time as their political agency or citizenship. The structural reforms implemented as mandatory conditions for the bailout programs proved devastating and enormously dangerous for a large majority of the Greek society, with serious implications in all areas of economic, political, and social life, as well as in the very urban space and experience.

Critical Responses: The Movement of the Squares and Its Legacy

The economic downturn and the austerity regime started in 2010 did not take long to hit the population. Nevertheless, the reaction of the citizenry was prompt as well. Since the early months of the economic recession, people took massively to the streets to protest and express their rejection. The Crisis would bring about a cycle of mobilizations without precedent since 1973—when the Junta was contested and eventually overthrown. In December 2008, the killing of the fifteen-year-old Alexandros Grigoropoulos by a policeman in Exarcheia prompted a spontaneous revolt, which spread beyond Athens and lasted several days. The riots were a direct reaction to the increasing police repression over the past years. Yet, they were also reflective of a growing discontent—mainly among the youth, but not only—with the economic situation, as well as a deep dissatisfaction with institutional politics and parliamentary parties.

In May 2010, upon the signing of the MoU, an antiausterity movement broke out. Massive demonstrations were held in Athens and Thessaloniki, with slogans against the government—and the Greek political class in general—the European institutions, and the IMF. They were violently repressed by riot police. These demonstrations were followed by numerous workers' strikes and blockades—among them a number of migrant workers who carried out specific actions as well—a countrywide prisoners' hunger strike, a series of occupations of institutional buildings, recurrent episodes of riots in urban areas, and also violent attacks. In 2011 alone, 445 strikes were called, including eight general strikes.

Unlike countries of the Global South, for which enforced structural adjustment programs in response to debt crises were already familiar, in Europe the new austerity regimes were unknown. As was the case in the Global South, the austerity measures would prove not only inefficient in economic terms but extremely devastating for many. Additionally, the state of emergency added further restrictions and sometimes violations of fundamental democratic and civil rights like the right to pacific protest or freedom of speech. This way, austerity in Europe—and particularly in its southern countries—came to aggravate the long-underway global crisis of social reproduction, as well as the crisis of representative democracy systems. It is against this backdrop that thousands of people coming from different social sectors would mobilize, protest, and eventually self-organize to cope with and fight back against the devastating impacts of the austerity regime on everyday lives, welfare, and liberties.

In Greece, the antiausterity movement would reach its most emblematic moment in mid-2011. In May of that year, in the wake of the so-called Arab Spring and the 15M Movement in Spain, large demonstrations took place in most major cities in Greece, including Athens, Thessaloniki, Larissa, Patras, and Volos.[33] On May 25, in the capital, thousands gathered in Syntagma Square, eventually setting up an encampment that would last for more than a month. A temporary city equipped with self-organized kindergartens, infirmaries, information points, kitchens, and concerts emerged in the heart of Athens. It provided the supporting infrastructure for a growing movement demanding a radical political and economic overturn, becoming a truly social experiment of self-organization based on direct democracy and mutual support.

The documentary *Utopia on the Horizon: Documentary on the Greek Debt Crisis* (Oikonomakis and Roos 2012) gathers accounts from participants in the occupation against the backdrop of The Crisis. Dimitris, a mathematics tutor, and Maria, a freelancer, talk about their personal experiences in this way.

> They're refusing to see the reality. . . . They're afraid of the new, the other thing. So they're kind of closing to their selves and saying: it's not happening. Everything is gonna be alright. Nothing is gonna be alright. . . . It wasn't a call from a specific party, let's say, political party. I thought: here maybe there's something happening. From the people. That's why I participated. I had used to participate in demonstrations, strikes. . . . Ok, I did all this. But always it was under someone's flag. Now it wasn't. (Dimitris Timpilis, interviewee)
>
> I feel hurt. I feel exploited. I feel that my personal field of action—you know—creative and economic, is closing down on me. . . . There is fear and anxiety. . . . We didn't know why we were happy. I think it was just because simple people, actually met each other in the public sphere again. . . . In a way we lost our political innocence, let's say, that of the voter. . . . This was an important battle, because in a way it was an inner battle between fear and

rage. These two contradicting collective feelings are now inside the Greek society, the Greek people. (Maria Kanellopoulou, interviewee)

Dimitris's and Maria's interventions speak of transformative experiences of
political awakening. Amid a climate of extended distrust and discredit of institutional politics, the occupation of Syntagma Square—which, as Dimitris
notes, took place without the leadership of any political party, group, or
union—introduced an inflection point in the Greek collective consciousness
since the outbreak of The Crisis. The government and the main media had put
a lot of effort into picturing austerity as the only alternative to overcome the
economic recession. However, the slogans in the protests—for example "Δεν
αντέχω στην ανεργία ούτε να πάω στην Αυστραλία" (I cannot stand up to
unemployment or go to Australia), "Χουμε ξυπνήσει—τι ώρα είναι;—ώρα να
φύγουν" (Wake up—What time is it?—Time to leave), "Καλυτερα στο
Συνταγμα να ειμαστε μαζι, παρα σαραντα χρονια σκλαβια και φυλακη" (Better to be in Syntagma together, than forty years of slavery and prison)—boldly
reflected a different view. Citizens had been made responsible for a crisis triggered by the financial sector, and the new market-driven policies to counter it
were severely undermining their life conditions and rights. Under the premise
of austerity, international economic and financial institutions had become the
principal agents dictating national economic programs and public policies.
Thus, the imposed austerity regime entailed a serious undermining of national
sovereignty. This collective understanding brought to the fore a narrative of
"the top versus the bottom" that refused any sort of political leadership coming
from parliamentary parties, thus undermining legitimacies and normalities
that for long had seemed rather solid. The same narrative of rejection and
delegitimization included slogans against corruption and clientelistic practices
so rooted in Greek society.

The occupation of Syntagama Square, which became part of a broader
"Movement of the Squares" that spread out through over thirty-eight central
squares in cities across the country, was innovative in many aspects, distanc-
ing itself from the traditional forms of protest of the political Left. During the
time that the occupation lasted, decisions were made collectively in open assemblies following principles of direct democracy. Yet, it was not only the assemblies but the entire everyday life that was self-organized in common. Thus,
the potential to open new possibilities was not so much in the general assemblies as in the myriad practices of organization and running of infrastructures—
food, caring, learning, rest, and so on—that hold together the temporary autonomous territory. There was a conscious collective effort to care for each

other and make the space habitable for everybody. Self-organization and autonomy in the squares constituted indeed a building-capacity experience for
many. They became elements of a new politicization that emerged in the
square. A new idea of emancipating politics gained ground, a politics stemming from the collective engagement in the reproduction of everyday life.

The encampment was eventually taken down. On June 28–29, during a
vote on a new austerity package in the parliament, the police dismantled the
encampment amid scenes of disproportionate violence. The crackdown was a
hard blow to the new confidence and hopefulness generated by the movement. However, the radical imagination of Syntagma endured, finding diverse
prolongations at both the institutional and the grassroots levels. Regarding the
first, despite the dismissiveness of main political parties and the corporate media, the fact is that the change in sensitivities toward the reading of The Crisis,
the party system, and international institutions like the EU and the IMF that
was fostered in Syntagma contributed to deepening the already deep institutional crisis, which led to the resignation of Prime Minister Papandreou in
November 2011 and the emergence of SYRIZA, which came into government
in 2015. As for the latter, the spirit of self-management that emerged in Syntagma and then expanded to myriad squares across the country left a legacy of
multiple self-organized initiatives, including neighborhood committees, cooperative economy structures, and solidarity initiatives, which would reactivate the grassroots of Greek society in the following years.

In Athens, the experience of Syntagma took root in many neighborhoods.
The Syntagma assembly was dispersed across the city bringing about around
forty local assemblies and residents' committees. The activities and purposes
of the neighborhood assemblies were manifold and site-specific. Informative
meetings concerning local issues, public talks, campaigns against construc-
tions or works affecting the area, solidarity actions, open festivals, and design-
build projects were combined with actions and protests where broader claims
were articulated. Importantly, the common basis of all these different activities
was the reinforcement of social cohesion towards the protection of the most
vulnerable groups. In parallel, initiatives seeking alternative forms of economic
relationships and processes such as time banks, alternative currency markets,
farmer networks "without middlemen" and groceries co-ops were also set up.
In Greece, initiatives of this kind were labeled under the name Solidarity Economy.[34] Moreover, alongside this series of neighborhood and economic projects, another type of initiative in response to growing issues and pressures of
social reproduction—deriving from the collapse of public services around
health and social protection—spread across the metropolitan territories. Social

kitchens, social clinics and pharmacies, networks of care services, training and language lessons, accommodation centers with migrants and refugees, legal aid hubs, and mobile laundries gradually became part of an emerging urban geography of self-organized structures providing practical solutions to meet basic daily needs, as well as local and translocal strategies to fight back and safeguard the means of living and social and political rights.

This book focuses on this last type of initiative, which I propose to call "infrastructures of caring citizenship" (ICCs). Throughout the following pages, I argue that the ICCs—many of them still running[35]—have played an important role in the reconfiguration of political conceptions, practices, structures, and subjectivities during, and despite, The Crisis. Overall, they have rendered social reproduction public, and visible, contributing to its politicization in both collective struggles and everyday life. They have made existing movements and new ones to converge and support each other in the fight against austerity and the EU border regime. They have opened up political spaces where radical imaginations have brewed. Last but not least, they have yielded the emergence of new collective subjectivities based on solidarity and collective care, which break away from individualism and isolation.

"We Cannot Go It Alone. We Need to Fight Back": Setting up Infrastructures of Caring Citizenship

> Either we started organizing collectively or they'd take it all. We began to realize that we cannot go it alone. All of a sudden people were becoming poor, depressed, desperate. We began to realize that our own individual problems were in fact the same problems of many others. They wanted us to believe that we were to blame for our situation, that we were the only ones responsible for having spent so much. They wanted us to surrender, to be alone and do nothing. We realized this was a big problem, so we started to tell people otherwise. We needed people to understand that The Crisis was a common problem, that the government wasn't helping us and that we needed to fight back and organize it ourselves. (Eirini, November 27, 2017)

With these words, Eirini—a young Greek lawyer and activist—answered my question regarding the reasons she thought had driven people to engage in solidarity initiatives. Her statement exemplifies well the collective sentiment of the need to "take matters into our own hands," which grew remarkably among segments of the Greek lower and middle classes, especially in the wake of the Syntagma occupation, and is a common feature across the ICCs examined in this work. Calls to organize collectively from the ground up to cope with the ordeals inflicted by the austerity and the EU border regimes and test out alternatives for social provision and protection were part of the statements that the initiatives posted on their respective social media upon their formation. The question was also brought about by many of my interlocutors, who used it as a key argument to explain the role and purposes of the initiatives. In what follows, I provide an account of when, why, and how each of the four studied ICCs were set up, where this stance shows in diverse ways.

O Allos Anthropos social kitchen was initially set up in 2012 by Konstantinos, a middle-aged Greek man. When asked about the origins of the initiative, he tells the story of how after two years of unemployment—during which he had to return to his mother's place and faced several periods of depression—he had a "wake-up call" when he saw children fighting for an apple they had found in the trash bins of a street market. "Seeing those kids, I just knew that it had been enough. Enough of those bastards squeezing our lives. Enough of me doing nothing" (Konstantinos, July 13, 2016). He then found a way to set up a stall in the street market where he began distributing food. As he recounts, he soon realized that some people were reluctant to approach the stall as they considered the act of seeking free food somehow shameful. Others would come more for a chat than for the food itself. He changed the approach. Instead of just offering food, he started inviting people to cook with him the meal they would then all eat together. Some friends joined him and the initiative grew, especially after Fotis joined the group after having won a supermarket gift voucher, which the local activist donated to the kitchen. They decided to call it O Allos Anthropos (The other person) in allusion to "that other person we can all potentially become," and started to install the kitchen—announced by a colorful self-made banner—in different locations across Athens on a daily basis.

The Athens Community Polyclinic and Pharmacy (ACP&P) has a statement on its website that explains the reasons behind its foundation—in January 2013—as driven by the urgent need to provide a response to the accelerated disintegration of the Greek National Health System that followed the implementation of the directives by the Troika. In line with this statement, my interlocutors from the clinic repeatedly stressed that such a critical situation left them with "no choice" but to engage personally and collectively. Based on this standpoint, an initial group of people with diverse professional backgrounds followed the initiative of a number of other social clinics that had been established in the Athenian metropolitan region since 2011, and after securing some funds provided by the organization Solidarity for All for the rent of a space, they agreed with volunteer doctors of various specialities to start providing health services and prescriptions free of charge, as well as donating pharmaceuticals to Greek citizens and migrants excluded from the NHS.[36]

For its part, City Plaza—or Plaza alone, as it came to be eventually called by many residents—was initiated in April 2016. Local activists engaged in the project since the beginning explained to me that the idea of a "large-scale housing squat for refugees" was forged over months during which the need for housing for displaced populations in the city skyrocketed. The EU-Turkey agreement and the subsequent closing of the so-called Balkan route in March 2016 had left more than 50,000 migrants blocked in mainland Greece.[37] The state responded with the institution of camps, most of them set up in isolated areas away from the city. By that time, solidarity initiatives had started to face increasing demonization by some mainstream media and repression by state authorities. Many groups were banned from entering the camps and providing any aid. Given this juncture, people organized under the Initiative of Solidarity to Economic and Political Refugees (ISEPR) decided to occupy an eight-floor building in central Athens that had been abandoned for some years.[38] Following some days of preparation for the takeover operation, the building was eventually squatted on April 22, 2016. Several of my interlocutors highlighted how the project was conceived as a response to the camps, to the social and spatial exclusion that those created, as well as to the illegalization of the antiracist movement. The public statement on behalf of ISEPR used to introduce City Plaza on Facebook reflected this view. The statement included the following claims:

> Let's create a world of mutual aid and co-existence.
> Against racism, solidarity. We will all live together.
> Down with the shameful agreement between E.U.-Turkey. Open borders, safe passages for refugees.
> Full legalization of all refugees. No deportation to Turkey or elsewhere.
> Accommodation for all refugees in appropriate buildings, within the city core. Requisition of hotels and empty houses for refugees' accommodation.
> Free access to health and education services for all refugees. Participation of the refugees' children to programs of school insertion.
> Closing of all detention centers, no exclusion of refugees from the cities.
> No criminalization of the solidarity movement.

Khora was the last of the four to be set up. Like City Plaza, the initiative followed the EU-Turkey agreement. It was set up in September 2016 by a group of independent volunteers who had previously met in Lesvos, an island in the north of the Aegean Sea where thousands of migrants and asylum seekers arrived in 2015 and 2016. After the agreement was signed, all the informal refugee camps on the island were closed down. This group decided then to set up a project in Athens with a more long-term perspective, which—in the words of Becca, one of the founding members of the ICC—"tried to meet not just the basic needs but also the social need that would help to integrate and empower people who were quite obviously now going to settle in Greece for a long time" (August 8, 2017). Becca also highlighted that "there were so many gaps left by the large NGOs and the government, that it just felt that we needed to do something to cover those gaps." Khora's first website made clear this political positioning too. The section that explained the meaning of the name of the project used to read:

> Khora is a multifaceted word with many meanings. The meaning we take from it is "a radical otherness that *gives place* for being." The current EU border system creates the illusion of the "other." It divides humans into categories of those who have freedom of movement and those who do not, those who have valuable lives and those who do not, those who have the right to make choices and those who do not. We stand in opposition to this system and want to create a space in which all people can come together, where everyone is "other" in standing against this mode of oppression and thus equal.

As can be seen, these statements on behalf of the initiatives and by my interlocutors reflect a common will to self-organize, which goes beyond coping alone to actually embrace a deliberate endeavor to resist The Crisis's politics of dispossession and exclusion. Thus, more than a specific ideology, worldview, or identity, what drew people to the ICCs was, first, a context of crisis (politics) and second, the will—or necessity—to act and organize collectively to resist that situation and oppose (some of) the powers that were seen as the very drivers of those processes. It is primarily on this basis that the initiatives have managed to gather people from diverse socioeconomic and political backgrounds, ages and countries—from retired locals to students and professionals (some of them unemployed), homeless people, people with prison experience, foreign volunteers, migrants, and refugees. Importantly, women have had a prominent presence and have usually constituted a majority within each group. Besides, the ICCs have also attracted the interest of researchers and journalists, who in some cases have got involved for some time. In each ICC there have been people with life-long experiences of political organizing— within the left side of the political spectrum—others who have come as volunteers from abroad in groups or individually, others for whom their engagements have constituted their first experience of self-organization and struggle, others who have come in search of support given their situation of pressing need, and others who have returned as volunteers after having being supported in the first instance. Thus, some arrived already "used" to self-organizing—albeit for various reasons that may range from previous experiences in activist groups to life experiences in deprived contexts where collective organizing and mutual aid come practically as a given for people to get by—while others found themselves in the ICCs as part of a personal search for forms of relating to others, of living and/or working together, different from the ones that dominate in their home environments—largely in countries of the Global North.

CHAPTER 2

Care Commons Infrastructures

To Infrastructure Care by Commoning

The current infrastructural gap in the global North derived from the cycle of crisis that started in 2008 has brought about new infrastructural configurations, especially in urban areas (Dalakoglou 2016). Novel forms of operation and ownership, and new technologies and actors, are prompting a shift in long-standing models of infrastructural governance and the very imagination of infrastructure. These reconfigurations are in turn related to the emergence of new collective contexts and political conceptions and practices. A rich body of scholarship addressing this juncture (e.g., Alam and Houston 2020; Angelo and Hentschel 2015; Corsín-Jiménez 2014; Dalakoglou 2016; Graham and McFarlane 2015; McFarlane and Silver 2017; Morado Castresana 2021; Power et al. 2022) has raised inquiry about the possibilities and challenges that these infrastructural transformations may bring about regarding social provision— and social reproduction more broadly—and citizenship in contexts marked by deepening crises and the retreat of the welfare state.

Yet, questions regarding more just and sustainable modes of social provision and organization of social reproduction associated with the concept of infrastructure are not new. In 1994, the scholars Liisa Horelli and Kirsti Vepsä coined the terms "Infrastructures for Everyday Life" and "New Everyday Life." They were proposed as conceptual tools for urban planning and policy from a gender-based perspective. In particular, they were conceived to serve to develop a new type of social and cultural infrastructure for the support of everyday practices in the Scandinavian context. To this end, Horelli and Vepsä (1994) included in their theoretical proposal an archetypal model of urban social organization based on independent entities that would self-manage neighborhood resources. The urban scholar Inés Sánchez de Madariaga (2004) argued that Horelli and Vepsä's concepts contributed to questioning long-standing notions in the urban disciplines like that of infrastructure, with important implications for sustainability and wellbeing. According to her, contrary to the notion of "facility"—associated with social expenditure for specific populations in need—the concept of "infrastructure" was intentionally chosen to highlight the universal character that welfare systems must have and pursue, and to help understand welfare as public investment. Underlying this word choice was the overall intention of claiming social reproduction as a political and societal issue everyone ought to be responsible for and not just women.

Horelli and Vepsä's (1994) proposal had a major influence on a series of urban and architectural projects that were realized in Europe during the 1990s.[1] Yet, their infrastructures for everyday life were to be designed and implemented top-down, namely by experts and the public administrations. This would prove rather limiting regarding the ultimate aim of yielding social change. Feminist approaches to urban planning within the tradition in which Horelli and Vepsä (1994) are inscribed have been subjected to extensive critique on this ground.[2] Their overreliance on public resources and control by the administration would most of the time prevent active citizen engagement in the processes of design and governance of the projects in the long run. And, after all, citizen agency is a necessary condition for any profound transformation. Taking on this critique, I nonetheless argue that the concept of Infrastructures for Everyday Life can be worth revisiting in the present context of crisis and reconfiguration of welfare regimes. What would it be like to think of infrastructures for everyday life as a redistributive mechanism through which people could (re)gain political agency for the transformation of their urban conditions?

This is actually one of the main questions at stake in this work. The myriad grassroots initiatives and networks that have emerged in cities since 2008 in response to conditions of crisis and dispossession have opened up possibilities in this direction. Their infrastructural qualities differ substantially from Horelli and Vepsä's (1994) proposed entities. Recent ethnographic studies (e.g. Alam and Houston 2020; Aramptazi, Kouki, and Pettas 2022; Corsín Jímenez 2014; Kapsali 2020; Morado Castresana 2021; Power et al. 2022) have shown that by engaging in collective practices of *infrastructuring* participatory modalities of social and cultural provision, these people-driven initiatives and movements are bringing about new ecologies of urban relations that foster socio-technological innovation and open up new pathways for political action and governance. Dalakoglou (2016) has further argued that they are driving a shift in the (European) infrastructural paradigm with broader implications for the socio-political order and its institutions.

The analysis of these grassroots initiatives as infrastructure draws largely from a rich body of urban scholarship about everyday citizens' engagements with infrastructures, particularly in the Global South. In 2004, Simone coined the term "people as infrastructure," which has provided a productive framework to examine the myriad sociomaterial practices through which people engage with ever-shifting and multiscale networks of transaction of goods, services, resources, information, and knowledge(s), and the role that this plays in the sustenance of everyday life in urban contexts marked by scarcity and uncertainty. Simone's (2004, 2015, 2018) extensive work has shown that people's embodied engagement in these exchange webs increases their capacity to intervene and transform their respective environments. Namely, acting as infrastructure—or becoming infrastructure—affords people in deprived contexts a way to both secure livelihoods and acquire (some) agency. In this sense, this form of embodied infrastructural engagement and composition can be viewed as a way of exerting the right to the city, according to Harvey's (2008) and Isin's (2008, 2009, 2017) affined articulations of the concept. Despite lacking an insurgent purpose, acting as infrastructure nonetheless holds a transformative potentiality that turns its protagonists into urban agents, hence into citizens in substantive terms. Arguably, it could be spoken of as a form of or way to citizenship through infrastructure—or through infrastructuring.

Noteworthy, however, in what concerns the main focus of this book, that is, social reproduction, is that Simone's (2004) notion was defined on the basis of economic or productive activities alone. Could the notion still serve for the examination of reproductive activities? I think so. "People as (reproductive) infrastructure" certainly exist and the role that they play in the maintenance of life and livelihoods is paramount. The so-called global care chains are examples on a planetary scale.[3] So are many extended safety nets of relatives, friends, and/or neighbors who provide different sorts of support to members in need by coordinating and distributing tasks and sharing resources and responsibilities. However, as "nonproducers" in the realm of the private, caregivers and care receivers have historically faced invisibility and have been deprived of rights. All the more because they positioned themselves at the bottom of society. The double "vulnerability" that marks these types of peopled reproductive infrastructures undermines the capacity to transform the public and urban realms that Simone attributes to his concept.

Among the grassroots infrastructural entities that have emerged during the last decade, many address care needs and a wide range of social reproduction issues—related to food, healthcare, housing, and education, to name arguably the major ones. They are different from the cases just mentioned—as well as from Simone's (2004) instances—in that they frame their (care) practice as a social struggle, which they connect to broader movements in the quest for social and ecological transformation from the local to the systemic. Building on the tradition of autonomist Marxism, scholars like Federici (2019), Gutiérrez Aguilar (2017, 2018), De Angelis (2017), Stavrides (2016), and Zechner (2021) have attributed their transformative capacity to a mode of functioning based to a large extent on "commoning" practices, which broadly designate modes of producing, organizing, governing, and maintaining any collective resource on a collaborative basis.[4] The framework of "the commons" is being recurrently used to examine this type of collective struggles and initiatives as prefigurative instances that gesture toward postcapital modalities of social organization. In the view of commons advocates, contemporary commoning practices challenge both ongoing capitalist *extractivism* and state co-optation. Thus, they defend commoning as a force toward social transformation, stressing that commoning practices bring about new social relations that foster democracy, agency, and creativity. "Commoning practices, thus, do not simply produce or distribute goods but essentially create new forms of social life, forms of life-in-common" (Stavrides 2016, 2).

The connection between the epistemological traditions on the commons and care has brought—or brought back—"the community" into feminist debates and scholarship, especially in contexts of the Global North where decades of neoliberalization have destroyed most forms of communal life. Importantly, these current debates and studies draw largely from the Latin American tradition of thought on the question of the community. Unlike in Europe and the United States, the community in Latin America has been a major constitutive part of feminist political analyses and debates since the beginning of the expansion of global neoliberalization processes in the 1980s. Experiences and initiatives of solidarity economy, popular kitchens, communitarian mothers, and neighborhood self-help, among others, were already set up across countries in the continent to cope with and challenge those early neoliberal processes of dispossession and exclusion, many of which came hand in hand with structural adjustment policies. Gutiérrez Aguilar (2017, 2018) uses the term "communitarian fabrics" and defines it as structures that emerge, develop, and are sustained by practices of weaving.[5] In resonance with Simone's (2004) notion of people as infrastructure, communitarian fabrics allude to people-driven life sustenance networks, comprising both material and immaterial elements, which are marked by permanent flux and continuous (re)construction.

In a similar fashion, Stavrides (2016) has referred to them as "communities in the making." He has studied and theorized about these commons-based communities placing the focus on the space—or *spatiality*—that their doing brings about. He explains that the constant negotiation of the boundaries of these communities informs the very form in which they produce space. He uses the metaphor of the "threshold"—defined as a "spatiality of passages which connect while separating and separate while connecting" (Stavrides 2016, 5)—to characterize both the type of spatiality brought about by (some)commoning experiences and the spatiotemporal condition of these communities marked by permanent transition.[6] The threshold provides not only an insightful prism to understand the praxis of these communities-in-formation, but also a figure for new political imaginations in that it favors (porous) openness over closure.

The commons can certainly provide a productive framework to examine many of the present people-driven social reproduction initiatives, and arguably also a political compass for them. Nevertheless, all the authors mentioned here warn about the risks of idealizing the grassroots as well as any practice of communitarian appearance. Addressing the question of social reproduction from a commons-based approach indeed poses important challenges, especially in contexts of pervasive crisis and/or a hegemonic culture of individualism. What does it exactly entail to organize social reproduction as commons in different contexts? What conflicts may arise? How do experiences of commoning care relate to other forms and institutions of care provision like the family, the state, or the third sector? How can this truly contribute toward ecosocial justice?

All these are indeed high-stakes questions and the truth is that the ability of the commons to yield radical, systemic transformation remains yet to be seen. Thus, authors like Berlant (2016) have manifested a critical stance toward the commons, questioning their value as a truly transformative force. She has actually dismissed current commons claims and rhetoric, arguing that by casting the commons as an uncontested aspirational achievement, its claimants often overlook the complexity of social relations. Yet, she still sees value in the commons as a conceptual framework to problematize what lies behind the normative structures that organize contemporary collective life, and incite imaginations of necessarily provisional yet livable modes of life that can integrate contradiction, vulnerability, brokenness, and loss. It is in this sense that she suggests the commons as a "vehicle for troubling troubled times" (Berlant 2016, 395), and at the same time, invites us to common affective infrastructures that can alter the status quo while admitting their aspirational ambivalence and uncertainty.

In this chapter, I draw on this elaboration that brings in dialogue recent debates on infrastructure, care, and the commons to ground the analysis of the four examined ICCs concerning noninstitutional—or alter-institutional—modes of organization and provision of care, forms of (re)composing solidarity networks and struggles across the Athenian metropolitan territories and beyond, and the type of spatiality that these infrastructural practices bring forth. The chapter concludes with a reflection on the imaginations that infrastructural systems of care commons open up and their political potentiality.

Striving to Care Otherwise

ICCs have been set up at different stages as The Crisis unfolded. Most of them were conceived of as urgent but provisional responses to the ongoing multifaceted crisis and its management through austerity politics and the new European migration regime. However, as The Crisis evolved, turning into a long-lasting condition, many of them chose to remain active, speeding up the reconfiguration of the welfare regime in Greece already underway for decades. The accelerated deterioration of welfare state institutions and decomposition of family structures during The Crisis have prompted in turn the emergence of alternative actors like the ICCs or "shadow care infrastructures"—a term coined by Power et al. (2022) to refer to emerging—if not always visible in terms of policy—hybrid care structures in postwelfare cities, as well as NGOs and charity organizations. As contended by Dalakoglou (2016), these transformations in the welfare regime toward more heterogeneous modalities of welfare provision can be understood as part of broader infrastructural reconfigurations taking place in the country, especially concerning soft infrastructures in urban areas.

In Athens, the emergence of ICCs across the city involved the takeover of many buildings, premises, and open spaces, which were transformed to make room for increasing reproductive needs. The boundaries of the domestic were expanded. Like many of the emerging initiatives, the four ICCs examined in this book had their main action settings in buildings that were abandoned or in disuse. Either via occupation or formal rental of premises, the ICCs made them theirs by repurposing the spaces and transforming them physically. The ACP&P was set up in the premises of a housing block—a polykatoikia—most of whose floors were in disuse. The rented flat was converted into a small healthcare clinic with a pharmacy. A reception and a waiting area were accommodated at the entrance, some rooms were furnished with medical equipment, and one more was arranged with a fridge, shelves, and tables to stock and dispense donated pharmaceuticals. City Plaza was originally an eight-story hotel in central Athens, which had been abandoned for years when the business went bankrupt in the early years of The Crisis. In the span of just a few days, the building was adapted to house around four hundred people—mostly asylum seekers newly arrived in Athens. The new residents arranged private and shared bedrooms, a reception, a kitchen, and a large dining room, a café, a stock room, a doctor's practice and dispensary, and common spaces. Khora, for its part, was initiated in a six-story building that had previously functioned as a printing house. Likewise, it was fully refurbished to integrate a reception area and a playground, a free-shop, a kitchen and pantry, a café, a library and classrooms, office spaces, a dentistry practice, a maker space, a women's space, and a rooftop with planters. Last, O Allos Anthropos set up the initial headquarters of the social kitchen in an industrial building that was similarly rented and refurbished to accommodate a kitchen and a pantry, clothing storage, a computer area, a space for educational activities, a space for meetings and gatherings, and restroom facilities open to homeless people.

In this way, the ICCs turned these buildings and spaces into operative platforms of services supporting everyday needs and practices. Conversely, these spaces would shape how the ICCs operated. The way in which the self-organized groups of people that made up these ICCs at the time of my fieldwork ran these reproductive platforms notably epitomized what Simone called people as infrastructure. The processes by which, for instance, clothing was distributed at Khora, food was served at the outdoor kitchen of O Allos Anthropos, a specific drug was provided to a patient at the ACP&P, or supplies were arranged at City Plaza, entailed extensively coordinated operations where people involved themselves in a direct, embodied manner.

For instance, for donated clothing to be handed at Khora free-shop, it used to take arranging and coordinating four weekly working groups, namely the "admin-media team," the "van team," the "sorting team," and the "shop assistants team," in different shifts. The admin-media team would launch calls for clothing donations via social media and arrange collection with the corresponding donors—locals and internationals alike. When transportation was required, the van team would use a (rented) van. Many times this would entail going to Helliniko city warehouse and coming back with the stock.[7] At the basement of the building, the sorting team would classify, fix—in some cases—and organize the clothes on the arranged shelves, tables, and cabinets. The shop assistants would allocate different turns for people to come and get some clothes.

In the case of O Allos Anthropos, calls for food and monetary donations were made likewise via website, newsletter, and social media. During my fieldwork time, the core team would pick up the food or buy it in wholesale stores and bring it to the headquarters to store it. Each day, a group would take the responsibility for bringing the food together with the kitchen equipment—the mobile stove, the gas cylinder, the casserole, the wooden ladle, the deployable table, the cloth, the banner, the plastic cutlery, and the garbage containers—to a square in the city, previously announced on the kitchen's social media. Normally, they would use their private cars. At the end of the day, after cleaning and tidying up, someone would return the equipment to the headquarters.

The ACP&P, for its part, counted on a bank account for monetary donations, which at that time were administered by the admin team. Occasionally, this team would launch calls asking for specific needs—some of them via social media and some through the network of social clinics in Greece. The admin team, or alternatively the pharmacist team, would organize the delivery of items to the clinic or the collection from other volunteering associations. The pharmacist team would sort pharmaceuticals, classify valid ones and place those in their corresponding place in the pharmacy room. The admin team would do the same for the rest of the items. Drugs would be dispensed primarily at the clinic's pharmacy, which opened twice a week. Yet, volunteers themselves would also bring some medicines and first-aid-related items to other clinics, refugee camps, and prisons.

Finally, at City Plaza—which was the largest of the four examined ICCs—everyday supply logistics would generally require a great deal of work. Thus, everyone in the house would contribute somehow, from children to grownups. Several times I was able to take part in the human chains that were made up when a new delivery arrived at the door of the building. Such an event would be loudly announced by the children, who would run from floor to floor with the news. They were usually the first and definitely the keenest to contribute in the chains, smiling and sometimes singing while passing from hand to hand watermelons, juice, or milk jars, boxes of clothing, and even new furniture or equipment like baby pushchairs, which would be added to the common fleet arranged on the first floor for use by parents and child carers.

People acting as infrastructure, namely as active constituents of the sociomaterial networks they themselves create and shape, is what allows ICCs to work. In this way, they create social, material, and affective systems through which care is provided in dynamic, flexible, distributed, plural, and rather open ways. Importantly, unlike the traders in inner Johannesburg described by Simone (2004), ICCs infrastructure care not only about making the most of what is available in a context of scarcity of resources, but also about deliberately putting into practice democratic and collaborative forms of work based on principles of solidarity and mutual aid. Commoning of knowledge(s), skills, and resources is fundamental to ICCs' mode of infrastructuring. I argue that in this way, namely by infrastructuring care through commoning, ICCs produce and deliver care different from institutions. As shown in the previous chapter, these ICCs strived to do so as a way to consciously oppose the operating mechanisms of established welfare institutions like the state and certain NGOs, which they largely saw as responsible for having created the very conditions for impoverishment and inequality to thrive. Their respective efforts, however, were not exempted from tensions and contradictions. In practice, their declared intentions did not always show coherently. Nevertheless, in the following section, I provide some initial insights into a few ways in which the four initiatives did distance themselves from the institutions they critiqued. The remaining chapters of the book further elaborate on all of them, dwelling on ambivalences and limitations as well.

O Allos Anthropos's attempts to distance from "NGOs soup kitchens," as Fotis—a charismatic local volunteer very committed with the kitchen—noted, showed in the following ways. From the start, the social kitchen placed special emphasis on the act of "cooking and eating together." During my fieldwork time, the group explicitly endeavored to break away from the logic of "the helper" and "the helped" by inviting everyone to partake in the cooking and serving, and then in the meal. They particularly tried to prevent the formation of queues. The whole process was usually accompanied by chats and other socializing activities. In this way, the group reclaimed public spaces in the city for encounters, conversations, and exchanges between neighbors, fellow citizens, and strangers. The daily installation of the kitchen on the street or the square was seen by the core group as an act of resistance, and in fact, there were several occasions on which they confronted the police claiming both their right to the city space and their right to solidarity. To this day, the social kitchen keeps refusing to acquire legal status. When asked about this stance, Fotis explicitly stressed: "We are not an organization." To coordinate themselves, set the weekly program, and distribute chores, the main group used to hold collective meetings. Yet, those had no regular schedule and were usually done on the spot. Certainly, face-to-face interactions and nonbinding commitments have been the basis of the kitchen's day-to-day running since its early days. Quite often, people would approach the makeshift kitchen with homemade food or sweets. This is how they would show reciprocity and support for the initiative. The acknowledgment of interdependence, trust, and the will to reciprocate are indeed key factors behind the social kitchen's functioning and endurance.

For its part, the ACP&P distinguished itself in the delivery of healthcare from state clinics and NGOs in the following ways. Generally, the services provided at the clinic did not follow a prescriptive rule. Rather, they were established, stopped, and/or resumed as new needs or demands came up, accommodating contingencies, which sometimes transcended the boundaries of official healthcare. Volunteers' schedules and shifts were flexible and adaptable to each one's personal circumstances. Aside from doctors, the rest of the volunteers took on roles and tasks not bound to formally established professional demarcations. Most of them would assume manifold duties depending on the day. Some used to assist refugees in camps and inmates in prisons near Athens. Others also provided guidance to patients who needed assistance with registration procedures to claim state allowances and to access public hospitals. The admin team held in practice the principal organizing role, as most doctors did not take part in the assemblies, they just "fitted in," as Maria, a middle-aged Greek woman who worked as one of the administrators, noted in one of our conversations. When asked about this aspect, Panagiotis stated that:

> In reality, social clinics are more about creating the conditions for doctors, that "elite," to be accommodated into a rearticulated system from the ground up.... Social clinics' approach to healthcare, which actually includes social care, aims beyond the hegemonic framework.... You know, that which is based on medical specialities, where everything is disconnected as if the body was not one entity... nonsense. And also very individualistic. (Panagiotis, July 23, 2026)

In Panagiotis's view, healthcare had been individualized, privatized, and detached from structural social, economic, and political factors, and thus it needed to be reconfigured to include a social and community-building perspective. He later acknowledged, however, that for the time being these efforts by the social clinics had been limited, for there were no mechanisms in place to actively integrate patients into this "community." In spite of this, support for the ACP&P has grown over the years. The clinic has become progressively known and accepted in the area, despite initial reservations from some locals. At the time of writing, it is supported socially and also economically by many neighbors—many of them migrants who run small businesses in the area and have benefited from the services and social aid the clinic provides.

City Plaza's founders described the project as an alternative radically different from the refugee camps jointly run and serviced by the state and transnational NGOs. And it was different indeed. By occupying the abandoned hotel, this initial group was making a political statement that touched on several issues, namely the right for refugees to decent accommodation and access to social and urban services, the right to use buildings and premises out of the market and in disuse, and the right to self-organize (their social reproduction). The "introduction team" used to present the ICC to newcomers by saying: "City Plaza looks like a hotel but it is not." Generally, residents defined it as a home where they "lived and struggled together."

Everyday organizing of the squat was premised on collective participation, assumption of responsibilities on a voluntary basis, collaboration, and sharing. Chores and rules were defined by practice according to need, thus they kept changing over time following a logic of trial and error. As in the other ICCs, informal, reciprocal relations and sharing of resources, skills, and spaces was the foundation that made the initiative work. Everyday life was produced and sustained in common as opposed to what happens in the camps, where strict rules and strong divides between aid workers and refugees prevent any sort of communal experience.

Khora was based on a similar view to City Plaza concerning state-led camps and transnational NGOs. Members strived to put in place organizing tools and mechanisms based on principles of horizontality and collective engagement. During my fieldwork time, weekly "building meetings" were held to organize work based on decisions taken by consensus. However, following the meetings, each working group would attend to their respective duties on a rather informal basis, meaning they operated based more on improvisation, face-to-face interactions, invisible affects, and flexible socializing times than on specific rules or preestablished agreements. Actually, much of the efforts devoted to the establishment of written codes via assembly would be eventually deactivated in practice. In the end, this mode of working—decentralized, flexible, and informal—allowed them to accommodate contingent material needs and affects as well as individual or spontaneous initiatives, fostering resiliency to assume unforeseen events. Common among my interlocutors—as Raed notes—was an interpretation of the capacity of the community center to operate in this way as stemming from trust and a willingness to learn from each other.

I think it is trust, mostly, that makes possible what happens at Khora. There are moments of tensions and disagreements, of course. But in the end, people really want to share and learn from each other. For example, I know how to build some furniture and I'm teaching some volunteers to use the machines and tools. I proposed to make some benches for the kitchen and also to be used outside and we are now working on them. On the other side, I'm learning delicious recipes from the people working mostly in the kitchen! (Raed, September 1, 2017)

These varied aspects of each ICC provide some insights into how the four initiatives strived to put into practice alternative forms of organizing a range of areas of social reproduction, making manifest a vocation to care otherwise. Reservation and distrust toward formalized and bureaucratic procedures are generally prevailing dispositions across ICCs, though this varies among the different initiatives and has evolved over time. Although quite tentatively and with significant limitations—which will be accounted for as this analysis unfolds throughout the coming pages—the mode of producing and delivering care of the ICCs through the creation of rather decentralized, peopled infrastructures that operate by commoning knowledge(s), skills, and resources and seek to build trust and distributed reciprocity, proved that other forms of caring are possible. This care modality derives relevant implications regarding modes of relating and types of bonds, forms of building communities, everyday politics, and subjectivities, all of which will be elaborated on in chapters 3 and 4. In the following section, I expand on how ICCs infrastructure care beyond the workings of each initiative, operating as networked infrastructures within wider systems of collaborative actors.

Weaving Geographies of Political Possibility

ICCs in Athens have created a decentralized infrastructural system of integrated self-organized social reproduction and struggle against the politics and processes of dispossession, exclusion, and urban enclosure prompted and/or intensified during The Crisis. Over the years, the work of weaving alliances with other groups—including other grassroots initiatives, political associations, neighborhood committees, local struggle groups and broader struggle platforms, long-established social and migrant centers, solidarity-economy structures, and independent NGOs—has resulted in a dynamic geography of multiple intersecting networks across the metropolitan territories and beyond. The city's central areas concentrate the majority of nodes. Scholars have referred to this complex of self-managed networks of provision of everyday reproductive needs and the articulation of resistance in terms such as a "hidden welfare system" (Rakopoulos 2015) and "urban solidarity space" (Arampatzi 2016, 2017). In turn, this solidarity networked space is embedded in wider ongoing infrastructural (re)compositions made up of ever-shifting interactions and overlaps and also clashes with other welfare actors, including public institutions, third-sector organizations, and families.

For the most part, the nodes of these grassroots networks are autonomous in terms of governance. However, they hold a relation of interdependence and exchange among them that, as Arampatzi (2016, 2017) explains, mobilizes human and material resources, information, services, and social relationships. The four ICCs examined in this book, namely the ACP&P, O Allos Anthropos, City Plaza, and Khora, operated within this networked infrastructural system—and, apart from City Plaza, they continue to do so in the present. The effort to generate connections locally and internationally was indeed a key element of their respective daily management.

As noted, at the time of my fieldwork, the ACP&P was part of the platform Solidarity for All and connected with other social clinics and pharmacies in Athens and Greece, and with local and international NGOs.[8] O Allos Anthropos exchanged resources at the local level with other self-organized kitchens, as well as some social clinics and migrant self-organized centers.[9] They were also connected to several without-middleman networks of food distribution and an urban orchard initiative in the neighborhood of Haidari in western Athens, which provided them with vegetables. Some of its members engaged with various political groups that organized protests, campaigns, and solidarity actions with political activists, migrants, and refugees, and their "core" members had built connections with migrant and refugee initiatives based in other European countries like Spain and Germany. At a national and international level, O Allos Anthropos was part of a network of social kitchens. From time to time, some of them would schedule Skype video calls at a fixed time so as to have a sort of translocal shared meal among several social kitchens far apart. For its part, Khora worked in collaboration with different legal aid organizations providing asylum support, translators, independent education groups, and artist collectives, without-middleman food networks and food supply organizations, local free-shops, a mobile laundry, independent NGOs and charities both local and international, and other migrant and refugee initiatives in Greek islands and abroad.[10] It was in contact with other migrant spaces in the city and activist groups in the neighborhood. The community center used to run a project called the Info Point & Infomap, which collected and registered information about support groups and organizations for refugees across Athens on an online database and distributed this information through leaflets. Last, City Plaza, which was the one that attracted more political activists, bore a close relationship with different political groups and spaces, as well as with other housing squats with migrants and refugees, social clinics, self-run mobile laundries, food, clothing and hygiene products distribution groups, independent education collectives, an independent solidarity

IT collective, and a mobile library.[11] It was very well connected with international groups and platforms in defense of migrants and refugee rights as well.

Apart from their spatial infrastructures, the four ICCs counted on digital infrastructures, which were fundamental for both their internal organizing and building relationships of collaboration with other groups operating within the same neighborhood or across Athens, Greece and beyond. Each ICC had group chats and email groups that allowed them to organize and address internal issues, as well as social media accounts, newsletters, websites and blogs, which they used as platforms to post news, announcements, statements and calls for solidarity actions. For instance, Khora regularly issued reports on the administrative, material and political situation of asylum seekers and refugees through a self-run media outlet.[12] They also set up a radio station, an initiative that was undertaken at City Plaza as well. The ACP&P also used to make active use of social media to provide information about accessible healthcare and social care services in Athens, as well as ongoing campaigns in defense of the NHS.

Besides the use of social digital media, and perhaps of greater significance, is the engagement of ICCs in common events and actions with other groups in Athens, in other Greek cities, and across Europe. Events such as the Anti-Racist Festival, which is held annually in Athens, the No Borders Camp, which took place in Thessaloniki in July 2016, or the Anti-Racist Parade in Hamburg in September 2018, brought together people from various ICCs, as well as from other activist and/or political groups. Parties are also resourceful and popular events to bring people in touch. O Allos Anthropos used to celebrate with a big barbecue and live music and dance at least once a year in the street adjacent to the social kitchen's headquarters. They would always succeed in bringing in hundreds of people—among them neighbors, families, and children. They also organized smaller parties inside the headquarters on occasions such as the celebration of Ramadan or Christmas. For its part, City Plaza used to organize an anniversary party at the squat every April, which they announced openly to invite anyone interested. Religious festivities, the arrival of newborns and birthdays were also occasions for collective celebration. Likewise, Khora used to throw parties inviting neighbors and locals. Other common activities in which the community center used to participate included demonstrations, protests, open assemblies, specific-case solidarity campaigns, open talks with guests—normally scholars, volunteers, and activists—solidarity caravans, and "pot-luck" picnics.

The composition of temporary (trans)urban safety nets by weaving alliances with other groups, apart from affording modes and sites of self-protection and care, serves ICCs as a foundation to organize and spread resistance, and in so doing, amplifies the pressure on authorities and gains strength to claim rights. Kostas, a middle-aged local volunteer from O Allos Anthropos, articulated this point as follows:

> We believe in solidarity.... It also helps us to become stronger. We need to connect with each other [solidarity initiatives] to be able to resist, and to protect ourselves better. Taking to the streets is very important. There we meet with others who are in struggle like us. It's reassuring. It helps us keep active and keep the fight on for our rights, for the rights of everyone.... And also doing other things together like parties and festivals is important. Because we feel active and less powerless. Despite most of the time we don't achieve our goals at the institutional level, I believe this is also about politics. (Kostas, September 8, 2017)

Certainly, ICCs' politics operate at different levels and in different spheres of social life. Arampatzi (2017) uses the term "expansive politics" to refer to the capacity of these grassroots networks to raise and spread awareness about growing structural inequalities affecting people's everyday lives, but also to (re)activate an always in-the-making political life in the here and now. Politics in this light exceeds not only discourse and representation but also public protest and power struggle to encompass a wide array of practices of different natures, all of which nonetheless contribute to expanding collective agencies and possibilities concerning the organization and sustenance of common life.

Continuous relation making affords ICCs endurance and agency. This resonates with Simone (2004) when he says that by acting as infrastructure people in conditions of deprivation expand their power to transform their (urban) context. Importantly, ICCs do so through care. Yet, connections are most of the time temporary, precarious, and vulnerable to economic constraints, ideological differences, external threats, and/or particular individual circumstances. Clashes among actors of these networks are not exceptional. A common cause of disputes, internally and externally, comes from different ideological positions concerning the engagement with state institutions or third-sector organizations. In the ACP&P this relationship has always been rather open, as the clinic has agreements with certain hospitals as well as with nonprofit organizations from which they openly receive pharmaceuticals. Nevertheless, its connection with Solidarity for All has been critiqued by certain political groups, which have accused it of co-opting solidarity initiatives in the interest of SYRIZA. The truth is that while reservation and distrust toward the state and NGOs prevail across ICCs, they vary among them, and they have actually evolved over time partly for practical reasons concerning the very reproduction of the initiatives. When Khora started to provide "qualified services" like workshops for volunteers or psychological support delivered by NGO "professionals" who did not take part in the assemblies, a big debate broke out in the community center. Some expressed worries about potential divides that this could create. Others saw it as a positive move, noting that despite stances against state institutions and NGOs, ICCs and other solidarity initiatives did not mean to replace them.

Conflicts reflective of more broad structural issues, particularly gender-based discrimination and/or sexual abuse, would also affect the cohesion of the networks. During my engagement at City Plaza and Khora, I witnessed several instances in which cases of sexual harassment were collectively reported, followed by a number of attempts to address them and prevent these behaviors at least inside the respective buildings. At Khora, once, the issue transcended the community center, eventually prompting confrontations with a feminist collective that accused Khora of turning a blind eye to gender-based violence. I dwell on this aspect in chapter 4. Overall, these events and disputes show that conflict is pretty much embedded in the geography of solidarity networks, at times canceling political possibilities that had been growing slowly, yet also providing the opportunity to learn new ways of communicating and negotiating different stakes.

All these varied aspects inform and become apparent in the decentralized, diffuse, and ever-shifting geography that ICCs compose. Following Isin's (2009, 2012, 2017) conception, it can be viewed as a geography of site-scales of citizenship (through care). Each site is rooted in its specific, situated setting and immediate urban context. However, their actions purposely expand way beyond the limits of their specific physical sites. Each site in fact operates at various scales simultaneously, local and translocal. At times, this geography is "hidden," as some of the ICCs do not mark or visibly name the buildings or spaces they inhabit for political and/or safety reasons. For the most part, this geography is not registered in the (public) databases of the municipalities. Additionally, it is unsettled and precarious, for some of the nodes are just provisional, or short-lived, or they appear and disappear intermittently—whether for economic strains, external political pressures and repression, or internal issues. Last, it is also contentious and insurgent as this "transurban grassroots safety net," far from a nonconflictual area, is indeed an arena of struggle.

Holston (1998) arguably considers ICCs as "spaces of insurgent citizenship," for ICCs certainly materialize metropolitan formations of citizenship assertion and enactment. Their praxis feeds on and activates the continuous societal and political processes of expansion and erosion of citizenship, which materialize in the urban territories and spaces forming new geographies. Nevertheless, I argue that more than their insurgent character, it is their relational vocation and infrastructural modus operandi that constitutes them as a significant force of action and transformation of the city. Like Simone (2004), I contend that by acting as networked infrastructure, ICCs increase their agency and potential to transform Athens, particularly Athens-in-crisis. Against the logic of separation, segregation, enclosure, and fixation of the city-in-crisis—increasing exclusions from social welfare and public services, growing privatizations and sell-offs of public urban assets, and rising policing and repression—ICCs and their networks enact a logic of connecting and weaving, as Gutiérrez Aguilar (2017, 2018) would call it. That is, a logic of perpetual movement and interchange to enable integration, reciprocity, accommodation, and life sustenance. Thus, it follows that the more ICCs engage in networking with others who resist and the more they strive to strengthen solidarity webs, the more capacity they will gain to effect change in Athens and beyond. This is a fact that participants in ICCs know. More than in the insurgent capacity of each initiative alone, the power to oppose and overcome the politics and devastating effects of Athens-in-crisis rests on their operation as infrastructure both internally and externally.

Challenging Urban Processes of Crisis through Liminal, Elastic Spatialities

The institution of ICCs has been linked to the creation of what Stavrides (2016) has theorized as "common spaces," which have been established through spatial reappropriations, rearrangements, and repurposing of urban spaces in Athens-in-crisis. Following the Movement of the Squares, which linked the protest against austerity with the claim to public space—through the installation of temporary encampments and open-air assemblies—many of the emerging grassroots groups took over spaces and premises in the city to set up their projects. The Movement of the Squares certainly served as the impetus for numerous acts and initiatives that, in a context of increasing dispossessions and exclusions in and through the city, understood access to urban space as fundamental to their struggles. Public acts of claiming rights, open-air assemblies, the installation of self-constructions or temporary settings, the creation of gardens and playgrounds, and the refurbishment of unused buildings and premises for publicly accessible uses, became common practices carried out by the multiple collectives of organized people that emerged in the wake of the 2011 mobilizations. Since their inception, ICCs and other solidarity initiatives have been proof of the fact that cities constitute grounds of relentless struggle, which in times of crisis become even amplified by emerging forms of resistance through which urban space is reclaimed and transformed. Certainly, urban space has acted as a fundamental constituent of these initiatives, not merely as the setting for their practices, but also as their very means for their conformation and development.

ICCs have reactivated and transformed buildings and urban spaces into operative platforms of services supporting everyday needs and practices. They have introduced new uses in the city through the collectivization of many social reproduction activities, many of which have traditionally been considered domestic, and thus private. In so doing, they have contributed to making social reproduction a public—and visible—concern, therefore politicizing it in the everyday. The reorganization and rearrangement of social reproduction functions in the urban space parallel to official institutions have brought about new spatialities and dynamics in the city's everyday life. Starting in the aftermath of the Syntagma occupation, kitchens, dining rooms, laundries, and barbers (re)emerged on the streets and squares, while the latter moved to the living rooms and common spaces in the newly squatted accommodation spaces and community centers across the city. With these subversions, ICCs created spatio-temporal scenarios where encounters, exchanges, and collective deliberations would flourish, reinstating a space of conviviality in many public areas where collective life had actually been lost either to big commercial and real-estate speculative interests or to the neglect and disinvestment by the authorities.

The ICCs examined in this work provide good examples of these spatial reappropriations and reconfigurations. Starting, for instance, with O Allos Anthropos, it was pretty remarkable to see how by informally setting a simple deployable table and a big pot on the square for some hours, the social kitchen blurred the established demarcations between the public and the private, creating what Stavrides (2016) has called a threshold. In such a temporary setting, a kitchen migrated from its traditional interior domestic space to the street, while in turn the street—its life, varying rhythms, and materiality—became part of the action of cooking and eating together. Spontaneous activities like improvised ball games, life-music concerts, puppet shows, and dances would emerge around the kitchen—sometimes to the suspicion or discomfort of police officers—accompanying and amusing the chefs on duty and attracting more people to the provisionally created common space, thereby temporarily upsetting circulation and consumption patterns.

The cases of Khora and City Plaza were also telling in this regard. On the days when the laundry-van served the community center, people would gather and linger for hours on the passage that faced the workshop of the building located on the ground floor. Self-designed chairs and tables, which were built at the wood and metal workshop, would be taken out to this transitional space for people to have a chat and a coffee, a smoke, or a backgammon game, while waiting for the laundry to finish. Sometimes clothes were hung on ropes to dry, adding new layers to this temporary urban threshold where the domestic spilled over onto the street creating a sort of open living room. For their part, residents of City Plaza engaged quite frequently in collective outdoor activities that ranged from communal meals at the entrance of the building—for which they would set a long table, which would take over the whole length of the small street, filling it with conversations between residents, friends, and neighbors around a culinary display prepared by migrant groups like the United African Women Organization Greece—to regular rallies and demonstrations, for which they displayed a full range of self-made placards, flags, and banners.[13]

These kinds of temporary, liminal spaces foster social interactions and face-to-face communications, intensifying and expanding them in time. Urban space is enlivened and rendered more dynamic, porous, and resilient. They might not seem very subversive, but these practices of reappropriation and temporary transformation of urban spaces help nevertheless to bring back collective life to streets and neighborhoods in a crisis-ridden city like Athens, where years of neglect by the local authorities coupled with the closedown of many retail businesses have contributed to the gradual degradation and emptying of many areas. Some of my interlocutors, like Danai, from Khora, highlighted how some of these activities have actually served to challenge processes of urban enclosure and geographies of fear, which largely resulted from crisis politics and discourses instrumentalized by diverse ruling powers to impose (their) order, eliminate conflict, and repress those deemed a threat or a hindrance to capital interests.

> Dinners like the one last night on Strefi make some days special, so days are not just gray as in the camps.[14] We do this so there are days with different colors. Besides, it's a good way to show that spaces like Strefi belong to us, to the neighbors. That there is not just drugs, as they say. . . . It was a big effort but in the end it was worth it. Together with some people of a neighborhood association, we did some posters announcing the event and placed them on the

streets around the area. We also posted it on Facebook and Indymedia. We worried no neighbor would come, but in the end a group showed up. We talked about doing more things like that. (Danai, August 16, 2017)

Certainly, the spatial contours of the ICCs were always in permanent fluctuation, creating a form of fluid and ever-changing spatiality. Their boundaries did not finish at the physical borders imposed by the materiality of the buildings. On the contrary, they challenged those, expanding and contracting according to the constant negotiations and the plethora of varying activities. Through all these activities, people in the ICCs collectively went and opened up to the public, stretching the space of their main respective action settings. However, there were moments when this stretching and opening-up operation reversed; for instance, in City Plaza residents closed the doors and guarded the building against potential attacks by organized far-right groups, and assemblies were closed off to nonresidents—or even to specific residents—to deal with certain issues. Khora closed off the building for a few days to carry out maintenance, both of the building and of "the community," which meant internal issues of concern.

Arguably, this mode of inhabiting urban space, which challenges enclosures imposed from above as well as long-fixed demarcations and reinstates forms of collective life in neighborhoods, brings forth new meanings, dimensions, and temporalities in and of the urban public space. Ultimately, this (re)activation of the social function of public space can be seen as an expansion of the very space of politics in and through the urban. ICCs (re)open the urban territory to a wider public. The type of liminal, diffuse, ambivalent, and elastic spatiality that the ICCs generate reconfigure—albeit temporarily—the urban public as it has been defined and constrained under austerity, challenging the politics and imaginary of Athens-in-crisis.

Infrastructural Imaginations of Care for Life Sustenance

Novel modes of social organizing for social provision from the grassroots, like the four ICCs examined in this work, are creating new care spaces and forms of political engagement and possibility. In this chapter, I have characterized these bottom-up organizational experiments in response to entrenched crisis and state mismanagement as modes of infrastructuring care through commoning. This conceptualization affords an analytical lens that enables connections across scales while drawing attention to questions of sustenance, relationality, affects, ethics, and agency. The comparison with institutions further helps dig into questions concerning alternative modes, structures, actors, governing mechanisms, and spaces for (re)organizing social reproduction and providing care that in turn can open up avenues toward ecosocial transformation in the face of systemic breakdown. Yet, beyond this analytical affordance, I would like to conclude this chapter by taking on the invitation to think of infrastructure as a concept generative also of imaginations of living alternatives amid crisis yet against crisis regimes.

Through the ethnographic accounts presented throughout the previous pages, I have shown ways in which ICCs in Athens infrastructure care through commoning across sites and scales. Infrastructural care through commoning creates systems where resources, capacities, agencies, and affects are in constant circulation and reconfiguration, accommodating themselves to emerging needs and desires. Underlying this mode of sociomaterial organization and provision there is an ethics of care, in which personal relationships and affects prevail over established rules. This aspect will be further elaborated on in chapters 3 and 4. Infrastructural care through commoning affords ICCs political agency, especially at the local level, where as part of different intersecting networks they (re)compose common struggles. Importantly, ICCs never meant to replace other forms of state support. Yet, in the absence of state support, by networking with others, they build political power, creating a foundation from which to articulate collective demands about a wide range of issues concerning the very sustenance of dignified lives. This way they contribute to the (re)activation of social and political life, composing relevant forces of delegitimization and contestation of crisis politics and opening up the realm of the political possible as active (reproductive) actors in the city. In other words, they put in motion processes of assertion of their right to care—and of social reproduction more broadly—in so doing expanding the boundaries of citizenship. Their forms of reappropriating and repurposing urban space enhance these processes that dispute the politics, imaginary, and geographies of Athens-in-crisis.

In Greece, the state and (large) NGOs have failed to ensure people's life sustenance needs during the ongoing crisis. The state has not only withdrawn responsibilities for social provision but has also increased its violence. For their part, third-sector organizations, which ultimately depend on private interests, largely dismiss individuals' political condition, preventing the possibility of nonnormative reciprocity and the formation of durable bonds among people. They impede the possibility of care becoming a practice with the political capacity to challenge existing regimes of inequalities. In contrast to prevailing institutional modes of social provision, which seek to prevent or control change, reciprocity, engagement, alterity and conflict, ICCs contribute to an infrastructural imagination that moves away from ideals of progress, centralized control, and homogeneity, toward values of relationality, conductivity, care, maintenance, and repair. That is, systems in motion, continuously in the making, based on the persistent dot-to-dot (re)creation of connections through the distribution of a plurality of knowledge(s), resources, and responsibilities; systems that allow people to take collective responsibility for sustaining life in a world in crisis.

Through this infrastructural mode of organizing (some aspects of) social reproduction and claiming it as a matter of public concern and social rights, ICCs turn social reproduction into both a site of commoning and a site of struggle. In this way, care in the ICCs becomes a political practice through which people perform citizenship in substantial terms. In so doing, ICCs gesture toward an alternative conception of care as a political practice directly linked to people's democratic participation in society. That is, an imagination of care linked to the assertion and enactment of citizenship. As pointed out by Tronto (1993, 2015) and Lister (2003), such a conception could serve as a foundation to rethink the very political paradigm that structures Western societies and their institutions. For placing care at the core of democratic political life would entail a radical reconfiguration of the modern political order.

Nevertheless, nothing guarantees that infrastructural systems of care commons will necessarily bring about more democratic or sustainable modes of social provision and life sustenance in the long run, let alone the sweeping transformations needed to catch up with the speed of capitalist destruction. As the ethnographic accounts have shown, the challenges facing ICCs are in no way small. Not only hardships and external threats, but important internal conflicts—whether predominantly structural, ideological, organizational, or personal—undermine their transformative potentiality. In fact, ICCs in Athens have gradually become less distributive and less open. The reduction of moments for collective decision making, the establishment of certain fixed roles and the setting up of more (rigid) rules concerning the incorporation of newcomers are elements reflective of a closing tendency over time. These changes attest to the challenges facing bottom-up groups striving to put in practice forms of organizing life sustenance with a commons-based framework under the hegemony of capitalism. Turning care into a truly collective practice at the center of social life, and keeping commoning on an expansive basis, namely as an open practice of insistent relation-making, are both endeavors subject to constraint and ambivalence. Nevertheless, instances like the

ACP&P, O Allos Anthropos, City Plaza, and Khora create the conditions for people to learn to engage in common life and sustain it in ways that expand solidarities and build collective power—even just temporarily. Thus, modes of organizing life sustenance as commons-based infrastructure intensify the possibilities of a transformative politics for a world in crisis, yet against crisis regimes of further extraction and dispossession.

CHAPTER 3

Dwelling as Politics

The Paradigm of Dwelling

Over the past decade, a (nongendered) ethics of care is being (re)considered in scholarly debates and activist settings alike, building largely on Gilligan's (1982) and Tronto's (1993) works, as well as recent experiences of reorganization of social reproduction from the ground up. An ethics of care is being posed as a political tool to imagine and build other possible modes of existence and relationship in and with the world. Recent theorizations of politics through the lens of care (e.g., Chatzidakis et al. 2020; Manrique 2020; Puig de la Bellacasa 2017) emphasize relationality, interdependence, situatedness, embodiment, and transversality across levels. In their manifesto for a "caring politics," Chatzidakis et al. (2020) outline a series of "caring alternatives" premised on the recognition of interdependence and vulnerabilities. They articulate them through five scales: kinships, communities, states, economies, and the world. Although they stress the need for active care "across every distinct scale of life" (6), strikingly, a description of the actual role and implications of space in the formation of these caring systems is missing from their account. Similarly, Puig de la Bellacasa (2017), who extends care webs to more than human worlds, fails to address the spatial dimension in a substantial manner. Noteworthy, despite the extensive scholarship by geographers on the matter, the absence of an analytical gaze from and through the spatial is actually common among recent attempts by political theorists and philosophers to define a politics based on care as an alternative out of the contemporary state of crisis and its politics. Relational in nature, care has an inherent spatial dimension. Space has a key role in constituting and transforming practices of care, emerging subjectivities, and political positionalities.

In a more nuanced take on this endeavor, through a claim "to politicize the domestic and *domesticize* the political," the philosopher Patricia Manrique (2020, 167) describes everyday life and the domestic in particular as the primary realm of biological and symbolic reproduction, where human and material relationships fundamental for social life are first developed, and therefore a "sphere of life with the sufficient entity to vindicate its *politicity*." From this standpoint, she advocates a politics informed by the type of practices, values, and relationships that form within the domestic realm—care, nurture, parenting, attention to life's materiality, to the concrete and the sensible—as opposed to a politics just based on legislation. Although she points to this sphere as the articulating place of the political vision that she delineates, her proposal is based for the most part on a revision of the historical roots of the term *domestic*, but it does not delve into the characteristics and ambivalences of this realm in the present, its different and diverse forms and spatialities, or its enmeshed technologies.

Broadly aligned with this approach in search of a new political conception, the philosopher Amador Fernández-Savater (2020) proposes a theoretical framework that, in contrast to the previous examples, does touch on the question of the constitutive role of space in a more elaborated and critical manner. Based on his experience in the 15M Movement in Spain, he elaborates a theory of two opposing political paradigms, which he uses to reflect on the potentiality of a new political imagination that he intuits as being latent in this movement. In his view, the unprecedented experience of square occupations prefigured a new political culture grounded in the autonomous and cooperative organization of the daily tasks needed to sustain the encampments as sites of protest but also of formation of new collective sensitivities and imaginations. He proposes to reflect on this hypothesis through what he calls the "Paradigm of Dwelling"—as the possible (ideal) model of an emerging form of transformative politics—and the "Paradigm of Governing"—which represents the model dominant in Western societies. Through this exercise of deliberate theoretical abstraction, he invites us to reflect on the stakes, potentiality, and challenges of a political conception grounded in everyday life, commons-based relationships, and practices. He outlines this theory as follows.

Politics under the Paradigm of Dwelling would emerge from any situated reality and space and would develop based on the capacity of sensing, accompanying, and enhancing the potentialities embedded in the embodied experiences of daily encounters with others. Thus, the realm of everyday life would be a key ground for the formation of this kind of politics. This paradigm would be representative of a political form that does not follow fixed rules or proto-cols, but rather unfolds through negotiations emerging in situation. Responsi-bility toward one another would prevail over preset codes of fairness. In this form of practicing politics from/around a radical experience of inhabitation, power is expressed and exercised more through embodied practices of pro-duction, use and operation of spaces and material resources than through par-liamentarian or bureaucratic procedures. In contrast, politics under the Para-digm of Governing follows abstract, universal models of what *ought to be*. Preestablished ideals of how the social must be ruled and organized constitute the frameworks of which political plans and programs are conceived and im-plemented. Its space is that of representation.

Fernández-Savater's (2020) paradigms resonate with Gilligan's (1982) ethics of justice and ethics of care. Like the first, the Paradigm of Governing depicts a form of politics driven by principles of fairness and impartiality grounded in ideal rules for "everybody." In contrast, the Paradigm of Dwelling reflects the rationale of the second in starting from the particular and emphasizing rela-tionships. Connections can be drawn too with Manrique's (2020) proposal to let life "contaminate" politics and her vindication of care and the domestic in the conception of the political. Concerning the spatial element, Fernández-Savater's (2020) theory echoes Lefebvre's ([1974] 1992) notions of "representa-tion of space," which refers to the production of abstract space, and "represen-tational spaces," those that people produce, inhabit, and imbue with meanings in their everyday lives. Lefebvre's ([1974] 1992) also argues that rhythms and space are constitutive of each other and structure everyday lives. By observing them we can shed light to the veiled powers that configure social life and in so doing gain potential to transform our time-spaces.

I argue that Fernández-Savater's (2020) theory provides an insightful framework to dwell on the conditions and characteristics of a spatial politics that can serve as the basis for social change from the realm of social reproduc-tion and everyday life. Not in vain, it stems from an experience of collective struggle, which brought about significant transformations in the political land-scape of Spain, at both the parliamentary and the grassroots level. This ele-ment, namely collective struggle, is in fact of great relevance here. As feminist intellectuals and activists like Federici (2012, 2019) and Gutiérrez Aguilar (2017, 2018) have noted, it is in what they call struggles over reproduction that new political capacities with the potential of yielding a social transformation beyond capitalist relationships are being produced and practiced. Fernández-Savater's (2020) paradigms very much speak to the kind of spatial politics I observed in the ICCs. By spatial politics, I am referring to the mechanisms used to negotiate and rule, the kind of norms that are set, the different stances that people take toward those established rules, the power dynamics that these processes elicit, and the role that space plays in shaping these interactions. Drawing on the philosopher's theoretical formulation, in this chapter, I will conceptualize the form of daily ruling and organizing of the examined ICCS as a "politics of dwelling," understanding dwelling as a set of practices of creation, transformation, establishment, operation, and maintenance of spaces and times in our everyday lives, as well as of construction of new meanings, relationships, and affections with those space-times and with those who inhabit them.

Structures, Dispositives, Codes, and Pacts

> This is not a hotel. This is not an NGO either. Here we are all working and helping each other freely. Because this is the only way we have to sustain ourselves and fight together for ourselves. Everybody has chores to do, except from the ones who are sick. We cook, we have a café room, we clean, we have assemblies, we take part in demonstrations, we also dance and play and have nice activities. (Ahmed, July 13, 2016)

As I have noted in the previous chapters and as pointed out by Ahmed—a young migrant from Syria who arrived in Greece alone seeking asylum in Europe and was very involved in the activities of City Plaza—at the time of my fieldwork, the four ICCS functioned as self-managed and self-funded projects, namely a kitchen, a clinic and pharmacy, an accommodation center, and a community center respectively. Yet, none was just a mere kitchen, a clinic and pharmacy, an accommodation, or a community center. Not just because all of them expanded the activities or services associated with their respective primary function, but also because they constituted themselves as sites and communities of political struggle, which I elaborate on in chapter 4. This showed in the politics that were put into practice and configured in their daily practice.

The mode of governance in and of their respective projects was intimately attached to the everyday administration of activities and resources. People were all invited to directly take part in the day-to-day management and associated decision making. Their organizing structures were characterized by having a rather stable "core" and a diffuse and changing "periphery." The core group was always integrated by some of the people who initiated each project. They were the main point of reference for newcomers and constituted a key organ for the maintenance of the project. In the case of O Allos Anthropos, for instance, the core group decided the weekly schedule and settings for the kitchen, organized everyday logistics, and administrated donations and resources. In the ACP&P, it was the group of people in charge of the administration of the clinic who played this prime role of overall management, housekeeping, and communication. In City Plaza, the main reference group for newcomers—whether migrants seeking accommodation or people willing to volunteer—as well as for those supporting the project from afar, was the so-called reception team. They were responsible for the financial administration. Similarly, in Khora, some of the founding members played the role of financial administrators and the first point of contact. None of the core groups was closed. However, over time, in part for practical reasons, they became more established and thus less keen to accommodate newcomers.

Outside each core group, there was usually a changing group—or set of groups organized by function—comprising people who partook in each initiative occasionally or temporarily. Of the four, the ACP&P was the one where this outer group was more defined and less changing, for obvious reasons as the healthcare services provided require medical professionals. On the other side of the spectrum in terms of structuring was O Allos Anthropos. The social kitchen attracted all kinds of people, from neighbors to occasional passers-by and people who came to Athens to engage in some sort of volunteering activity for a while. These people would undertake different tasks such as chopping vegetables and bread, serving food, or cleaning up, on an informal basis, meaning without any sort of advanced planning or fixed commitment. Some would do it one day for a few hours and never come back again. City Plaza and Khora, for their part, used to have a team dedicated to introducing newcomers to the respective projects and their overall principles. People in the introduction teams would show them the building, explain the ways of organizing the different tasks and activities and how to get engaged. Specific to both ICCs was the fact that many of the people who integrated them were asylum seekers awaiting the decision on their status and destination in Europe to be confirmed. Thus, those in this situation normally left once they get their papers granted.

In part due to their intrinsically temporary character, in part due to the type of politics that they pursued, and sometimes just as a mechanism for self-defense, the structures of the examined ICCs were in general quite unsettled, flexible, lax, and ambivalent. They were made and unmade contingently in response to the ever-renewing necessities and desires of those integrating them. The four ICCs were rather accessible at first, while the politics of expulsion varied among them. The porosity of their borders created groups—new "We(s)," as we will see in the next chapter—that were constantly renovating and reconfiguring, albeit to different extents.

The daily operation of the ICCs was mainly based on two mechanisms, the assembly and the working groups. Like in other grassroots projects, the assembly—in different versions—was the most common device for decision making, and as such it was vehemently celebrated. Some were open to the public while others were reserved just for the "members." The matters and scope of each one varied accordingly. City Plaza, for example, set three types of assemblies: the general assembly (open, weekly, and devoted to discussing broader issues concerning the situation of asylum seekers and refugees, as well as to proposing new activities or political actions), the coordination assembly (held three times per week among "representatives" of the different working groups to provide updates about the running of each respective one), and the house assembly (held on a weekly basis and just for residents). At Khora, broader political issues as well as questions regarding the community center were treated in the so-called building meeting, which was held weekly and tended to last for many hours. O Allos Anthropos and the ACP&P would hold assemblies too. However, given their smaller size, discussing and taking decisions involved almost no preset procedures. Decisions in the meetings of these two smaller ICCs would be taken neither by majority nor by consensus. Rather, they would likely be resolved in the course of the conversation.

In City Plaza, decisions were taken following open discussions by direct individual vote, while in Khora it was by consensus. Appointed facilitators would introduce the topics to be discussed and set the order of interventions and speaking turns. Others would note down the minutes. English was the primary language used. Different people would volunteer as translators in Greek, Arabic, Farsi, and French. Reaching a decision for some issues would entail the formation of "discussion subgroups" and/or "temperature checks," in the case of Khora. Sometimes heated debates and even arguments would arise among participants. General assemblies in City Plaza and building meetings in Khora would tend to extend for hours and even days until a final decision was eventually agreed. However, at times, important questions would remain inconclusive.

> This is not working and I have to say it won't work. I've never seen such an inefficient, well "highly inefficient" way of organizing things. We always spend long, long hours for what? I always leave so confused and exhausted. Guys, we need to change something. This is what I want to say. (Hashim, June 8, 2017)

I disagree. This is the way to do things different, different to the camps and other organizations that don't care at all about us. We know this. The strong democratic effort we are doing here, yes, it is tiring and sometimes boring, but it is the right thing to do. (Jawad, June 8, 2017)

These examples, from a building meeting in Khora, show that some saw the meetings as "highly inefficient," such as Hashim, a man from Pakistan who had been living in Greece for six years and was now very involved in the community center, while for others like Jawad, a man from Syria recently arrived in Athens, it was a sign of a "strong democratic effort." Nonetheless, decisions and agreements were in fact made and would normally translate into norms of mandatory compliance. Often, the new rules were written down in different languages on signs, which were hung on the walls and circulated via diverse communicating platforms. This way the new decision or regulation was made visible and available for anyone to refer to at any given moment.

The collective management of the reproduction of the everyday in the ICCs was constantly punctuated by large-scale political issues, which were posited and engaged with in different ways depending on the situation. The articulation of these different matters and scales of action did not always flow smoothly. On the contrary, it was a ground of frictions, contradictions, and disputes. Miguel—a volunteer from Spain who stayed in City Plaza for over a year—reflected on this issue, characterizing it as an ever-present difficulty to conciliate daily-life politics and what he hesitantly called "active politics."

Sometimes, in the name of pragmatism, you have to do things that you would do differently if you were strictly following theoretical principles. Of course, there are many contradictions between, let's say, "life" and "politics." The issue, in my view, is that we are people in very different life moments, and sometimes we come from very different backgrounds. Not only speaking of the relationship between volunteers and refugees, but also among the same volunteers and the same refugees. In this sense, for me cooking, of course, or working in the everyday, or cleaning the bathrooms, is to feed the project, to make it work, and thus, to do politics. Everything has a political reading. I think nothing should be dismissed, but the opposite. I think that this type of daily work is what keeps the site open. Then, in politics, let's say, more theoretical . . . for example when sixteen people drowned in a small island close to here, including several children, and we decided to celebrate an act in Syntagma Square with their relatives. It was very moving. Many people came. This is, let's say, the level of pressure and "active politics." I never know well how to refer to this. It's easy to say everyday politics, but I don't know how to name the other. (Miguel, August 15, 2017)

During my fieldwork, this tension surfaced quite often in varied forms. For instance, as a dilemma over whether to prioritize pressing needs or, on the contrary, broader political aims. In O Allos Anthropos, the issue of taking part in collective political actions in the name of the kitchen was brought up a few times by some of the regular members. It gave rise to the same argument, usually among the same people. On one side were those who believed that the kitchen should get more involved in political affairs, at the risk of becoming a "kitchen of an organization" like any other. On the other side were mostly women, who argued that what they were doing was "more important" than going to demonstrations, and in their view, it was actually a form of protest too. In City Plaza, for its part, the issue was brought about several times by volunteers in the house assembly. In their view, the time that was being dedicated to the discussion of "mere logistics" undermined the action on more pressing issues for refugees. However, time after time those complaints were answered back. Hassan, a young resident in the squat from Syria, once responded, "Logistics must be democratized as well."

Another issue reflective of this tension was the provision of wages to some of the people, which particularly in Khora prompted numerous and lengthy discussions. At some point, a decision was made to apply for funding (to international charities) that would be distributed as a sort of "grant" among applicants within the ICC. The funding was eventually provided and a number of assemblies followed. Who should be eligible to apply? How should the duration of those grants be established? Which would be the specific responsibilities of the recipients? How would those differ from those of the rest of the volunteers? Should recipients be assessed or monitored? By whom? These questions sparked hours of debate and tensions, which seemed difficult to conciliate. Eventually, the initiative was discarded on the grounds of potential hierarchies, which could undermine the community center's foundational principles, to the disappointment of those contending that it was actually a good opportunity for "committed" refugees whose present situation was extraordinarily precarious.

Alongside assemblies where questions of the like of the above were treated, working groups held smaller meetings to address practical issues. In City Plaza, working groups ranged from reception, introduction, kitchen, cooking, cleaning, security, translators, warehouse, clinic, bar, finance, media/communication—all of these related to the direct sustenance of the project—to children's activities, language lessons, yoga, art workshops, and other entertainment activities like cinema or dance sessions. Timetables with shifts were pinned up on the walls of the squat for people to sign up freely. Similarly, working groups in Khora comprised reception, induction, kitchen, café, legal aid, translators, dentistry, women's space, children's space, education, workshop, art space, free-shop, cleaning, communication, and finance. During my fieldwork, the emergence of new groups was a constant; for example, there was the "purple commission," set up to tackle gender-based issues in the building; the "health accompanying group," to accompany people to the hospital; and the "neighborhood group," geared toward starting actions to inform neighbors about Khora and invite them to the space.

The working groups operated on an informal basis, that is, social interactions were based on presumably agreed codes of behavior and implicit social commitments.

> Each working group has its own mode of doing things and everyday it's a bit different depending on what we have or what is needed. We don't discuss everything all the time. It's more like action to solve things. We trust each other. (Miguel, August 15, 2017)

The awareness of a web of interconnected relationships fostered a tacit acknowledgment of accountability to others. This consciousness was coupled with a disposition toward sharing and caring, which stemmed largely from the daily practice of dealing with issues of social reproduction as matters of common concern. The operating logic of the working groups differed from the rationale of the assembly, whose ultimate purpose was to set compulsory rules or procedures and which was made operative mainly through discourse. Interestingly, decisions via assemblies were questioned and put on hold time after time. Even the safety protocol and the rules regarding admission or ejection were subjected to continuous debates. In City Plaza, for instance, one of those rules established that anyone skipping a mandatory shift more than twice would be expelled from the house. In practice, the implementation of this rule was rather vague since it was unclear whether any specific group had the power to enforce it. Even the expulsion of someone, which did happen at times, could be revoked depending on the case.

In contrast, the working groups' functioning revolved around the materiality and contingency of everyday needs and resources, with informal meetings that resulted in ad hoc pacts open to permanent reworking. They were in practice the executive bodies of the initiatives. Their organic form of decision making stemmed from daily face-to-face interactions and the affections derived from them. Contact was the main driving force. In this sense, they constituted governance mechanisms aligned with the Paradigm of Dwelling, as opposed to the assembly, which would belong in the Paradigm of Governing. Their decentralized and flexible organizing provided a margin to accommodate newly emerging material needs and affections, as well as individual or spontaneous initiatives. Thus, it fostered resiliency to accommodate unforeseen events. In City Plaza, a woman started a "library working group" on her own, sometime after her proposal was accepted in the assembly but no one joined her effectively. She managed to gather a collection of donated books in different languages. The initiative became quite popular, especially among the children. In Khora, another woman used to replenish the stock of beauty products in the women's space on her own initiative. Individual actions like these indeed contributed to expanding the projects and sustaining them. However, at times, independent initiatives would bring about tensions, as was the case with a man in Khora who used to take goods from the free-shop and distribute them among some refugees or give people of his choosing an additional meal. When he was told off, he would argue that "the bureaucracy" implemented was extremely inefficient.

Discussions and arguments over the implementation of certain procedures were in fact rather common in the ICCs. Some contended that the lack of settled norms was confusing, while others said that it was unfair and even discriminatory. Asymmetric power relations would tend to break out and prompt conflicts whenever people felt their say was not being equally heard or respected. A common cause behind power imbalances was the stagnation of the rota system, meaning specific people remaining in the same working group for a long time. Over time, these individuals' opinions would become more prominent to the detriment of others', giving rise to positions of power and subordination, respectively. At other times, the argument would break out just over a failed personal communication, or the seeming impossibility of an agreement, or simply because people just felt detached from each other for whatever personal reasons. In those moments, the lack—or scarcity—of fixed norms was sometimes used by some individuals to take advantage of others. In fact, used as an opaque resource for individual purposes, informality no longer worked as a mode of interaction that builds on the recognition of interconnection and interdependence among people. It was no longer a form of reciprocity, but rather a form of accumulating power.

The different nature of assemblies and working groups as governance mechanisms translated into different forms of dealing with conflicts, which generated different power dynamics. The assembly produced a form of power that tended to concentrate around those with more salient oral communication skills, following common structural gender and ethnic biases. In City Plaza, for instance, at least at the beginning, it was rare for many refugee women to attend assemblies, and those who did would usually remain silent. In contrast, in the working groups, those who had been involved for longer would retain some power as long as they were able to maintain a good relationship with the rest. Generally, turning to the established norms was not a common resort in the everyday practice of the initiatives. Usually, affections, embodied commitments, and personal relationships prevailed over rules, and conflicts were mostly addressed through face-to-face communications. So, an ethics of care prevailed over an ethics of justice. Normally, the awareness of interdependence fed a sense of mutual responsibility and engagement that was what kept the initiatives running. However, at times, informality did not translate into reciprocal relations of support. Composed as they were by very diverse people, the values underpinning unspoken modes of behavior were not always aligned. At times, informality actually became an internal threat for the initiatives, all of which needed transparency, trust, and openness to keep going.

These contradictions are reflective of a form of daily ruling and organizing that emerges in situ, attending to everyday social reproduction in a direct and embodied manner and as a form of common struggle. Politics is embedded in the web of bonds that are woven in the day-to-day, and thus evolves and transforms according to the contingencies of life and personal relationships—as opposed to the abstract, anonymous, and individualized relationships of capital. In this sense, I argue that this political praxis tends toward the Paradigm of Dwelling in that it is grounded in and takes shape through collective practices and relationships that emerge through a commons-based inhabitation of everyday life. Interpersonal power dynamics and conflicts are part of this hands-on politics concerned with the impure and ambivalent realm of care in everyday life, with the ever-reconfiguring processes of construction of "as well as possible" modes of living and sustaining our world—as per Tronto and Fisher's (1990) definition.

Spatiotemporalities of Their Own

As expounded in the previous chapter, most ICCs in Athens undertook construction or refurbishment works to repurpose buildings or premises across the city as reproductive infrastructures. Lina—a young lawyer from Greece who took part in the works of transforming the former hotel into a commons-based accommodation and hub of struggle—noted the following when talking about the experience: "Although we realized with surprise that most of the equipment still worked perfectly, we had to reimagine the building so we could fit in" (Lina, June 22, 2016).

Metaphorically, this "reimagining of the building to fit in" encapsulates beautifully the meaning of dwelling as a multidimensional praxis that involves in the same operation the creation of space and time—the act(s) of making room, making time for—and of meanings through which to find and claim belongingness.

These initial conversion operations would actually become recurrent practice in the examined ICCs—especially in City Plaza and Khora. The transformation of space would take place organically alongside many of the daily activities. Marta—a Spanish volunteer at Khora with a background in architecture—noted this fact when talking about her experience.

> As an architect, the magnitude of the building, the fact that everything is taken advantage of, impresses me a lot. That every nook has five or six uses a day. We [architects] always predicate that each space should have its own use. However, here [at Khora] people get by with whatever they find at hand; for example, the legal assessment team, which is one of the cores of Khora, just has a little table at *info* [the reception desk at the entrance of the building]. I feel impressed by all this. I feel space is very necessary. That there is always a demand for space—"Ay! Where do we meet? Here. No, here"—You eventually go to the café or wherever. I like that in one way or another everyone collaborates in the space changing so much, and that it changes through Khora itself, that is when everyone asks for it to be changed, and then it's changed through the workshop. It's like a life-being that keeps changing. It's super beautiful. It's a project that I love that it's so ephemeral and so continuous at the same time. (Marta, August 24, 2017)

Each ICC established its own operating rhythms, which was reflected in the type of spatiality that came forth. Most of the emerging spaces were never finished, they remained in-the-making—as happened with the communities created in and through the initiatives. City Plaza, for example, underwent complete transformations in the course of the day. In the mornings, the reception hall of the former hotel was a hairdressing salon. The staircase connecting the different floors of rooms was a playground when children arrived from school in the afternoon. Some evenings the café hosted meetings of the media working group, which turned it into an operational office. At other times, it hosted talks with special guests, becoming a lecture room. The dining room was converted into a meeting room on the days when the house assembly was held. On special occasions, it would become an auditorium and dance hall. At times, the rooftop would be transformed into a "chill-out place," arranged with cushions and mats to accommodate a relaxing and safe space for women. And some summer nights, it would host an open cinema. There were even some days when the entire building was turned into a film studio with different sets arranged across the different areas that resulted in various films.[1] Similarly, space in Khora was subject to a rather intensive transformative speed too, involving also architectural (re)construction works. Quite amazingly, over a year and a half, the building underwent two self-managed large refurbishments. In the last one, the entrance was completely redesigned to move the kids' space down to the ground floor, and the fourth floor was rearranged so that the dentistry and the legal aid office had separate waiting rooms. The rooftop was populated with pots to grow vegetables, and the kitchen was divided to accommodate an office room.

Space and material resources were indeed fundamental common assets to care for and defend on a daily basis. The role of space nonetheless transcended this material function. It was an active constituent of the forms of organizing daily work and activities, and ultimately of the politics that were enacted. "If you want to take power, take over the kitchen, the women's space, the classrooms, the warehouse" (Angeliki, July 3, 2016)—said Angeliki, a Greek woman volunteering and residing in City Plaza.

Such a statement made it explicit that space was a determining factor in the relationships established day to day in the squat. In the ICCs, negotiations, agreements, and conflicts were plainly shaped by the material resources and the spaces. The kitchens of both City Plaza and Khora provide good examples of this spatial and materially embedded power. In City Plaza's kitchen, for example, there were three different daily shifts in which different people with different roles would take part. Every day a different room had to fulfill one. Meals were contingent on the food available. Yet, special meals for residents with specific needs were also provided. There were the chefs, people who chopped vegetables or meat, people who cooked in the stoves, people who served, and people who cleaned and washed. All the roles were interchangeable, even the chef's position, which was normally covered by actual professional cooks—refugees and locals alike. The different tasks were usually distributed according to the preferences of each individual. Yet, it was common for those working on a regular basis to take the role of distributing chores and organizing the process. There was always time for a break, for a chat or a smoke on the balcony. Usually, music was played. Generally, everything would run smoothly in a joyful atmosphere. However, there were moments when arguments over changing tasks, what to cook, the quantity of food to use, the inefficient control of perishables, or not completing the "full shift" would break out. There were times when certain people took food and cooked it for themselves outside the established shifts. This situation prompted a big discussion in the squat about whether to lock the kitchen and appoint key holders or not. The initiative was eventually dismissed on the grounds of the necessity of building collective trust, as it was articulated by Rahmi, a resident in City Plaza from Syria: "A house needs to be reliable and equally accessible for everyone" (Rahmi, July 27, 2016).

Another interesting space in both ICCs, City Plaza and Khora, was the women's space. In City Plaza, it was not until several months after the occupation that this initiative was finally set up by a small group of international female volunteers. Over time, female residents did take the initiative as well and started organizing their own meetings, workshops, and/or classes. Unlike the kitchen, which obviously had a permanent setting, the women's space took over different spaces across the house. In the summer it was set on the rooftop with pads, cushions, and chairs, arranged around rugs on which coffee, tea, and different snacks would be laid out. In wintertime, they used a room that they arranged differently according to the varied set of activities. A working group was in charge of taking good care of it and keeping it served with materials for activities ranging from beauty sessions to fanzine or collage workshops to movie screenings. The space remained open to suggestions of new activities as well as to newcomers, as long as they were female, which was the only strict rule—though it was contentious. As had happened in Khora, the existence of a women-only space was a controversial issue from the onset. Although in both cases they eventually made it, both spaces remained subject to disputes arising most of the time whenever a man did not respect the established rule and entered the space.

Space and material resources in the ICCs were indeed active constituents of social relationships and politics. Shared spaces and equipment channeled the emergence of common codes, commitments, agreements—and disagreements. Everyone's direct participation in the production, operation, and maintenance of the spaces and equipment was fundamental for the running of the initiatives. A funny anecdote that happened to O Allos Anthropos collective illustrates this point. Two representatives of a design collective based in Germany came to Athens to test a "mobile solar kitchen." They offered it to replace the makeshift kitchen the group used to display. The two men started the kitchen, certainly attracting a lot of attention from passers-by and children who showed a curiosity for its quirky design. But just before the water began to boil, the kitchen stopped working. For a long while, the two designers unsuccessfully tried to restart it, to the bewilderment of all those present. None was capable of helping them, as they were not able to figure out the functioning of the machine. Members of O Allos Anthropos eventually decided to bring back their ordinary kitchen. This anecdote speaks to the "experts-users" divide at play in our societies. Those appointed as experts are given the power to apply their knowledge, while those designated as users are considered passive subjects devoid of any significant knowledge. To a certain extent, the ICCs challenged this, for the simple reason that the ability of different group members to understand the functioning of things was crucial for the daily running of the projects. This is why they explicitly endeavored to share tasks, skills, and knowhow.

If dwelling is about creating, establishing, operating, and taking care of spaces and times to accommodate evolving needs and desires, certainly, the multiple spatial practices of the ICCs constituted manifested acts of active dwelling. Nevertheless, dwelling encompasses also a symbolic dimension that comprises the creation of new meanings, relationships, and affections with the space and the rest of the inhabitants. In this sense, dwelling comes often associated with the notion of home. Participants in the ICCs would frequently manifest their will for building "homeplaces," for "homemaking," in multiple ways. Among residents in City Plaza it was common to actively engage in the decoration of the common spaces, whose walls—full of photographs, drawings, and signs—served as an open multilayered archive of the many stories and faces of its dwellers. For many of my interlocutors, this was a way of creating a space in which their stories mattered and the space was fundamental to nourishing a collective capacity to cope with and resist the multiple hardships and threats facing them. Decorating and taking care of the squat fostered a loving sentiment and pride for the space they collectively inhabited.

"City Plaza is a home. We are one big family. Everyone knows each other here" (Moustafa, July 7, 2016). Often, residents would invite nonresidents to show them their "home"—as Moustafa, a resident from Syria in the squat said to me when he invited me to have lunch with his family in their room. The intimate spaces of the bedrooms of the squat would transform into makeshift kitchens where meals and tea were shared with neighbors and visitors. At times, balconies would serve the function of kitchen tables to prepare homemade pasta and bread dough. Keeping the tradition of their home-cities in countries in Africa and the Middle East, some families would leave the door of their rooms open and instead replace them with a makeshift curtain. Shoes would be lined up after the newly created entry, creating a small hall or passage that extended the distance between the outer corridor and the interior of the rooms.

Khora was also referred to as a home by some of my interlocutors. As in City Plaza, the internal walls of the building were covered with multiple and colorful paintings, posters, and signs in different languages, which were added to, removed, and added anew on a constant basis. Efforts to create a "home feeling" were particularly tangible in the women's space, which provided women and girls from different origins and cultural backgrounds with a safe space for recreation, rest, encounter, exchange, and bonding. It was often regarded as a space with a healing or therapeutic character. References to "home" were also common among those participating in O Allos Anthropos. The collective liked to emphasize that their meals were "home-made," implying that they were cooked by them and with care. They would also stress the importance of creating a welcoming atmosphere, a home feeling, so people could overcome feelings of shame and eventually develop some sense of belonging in the collective.

These accounts show that space and material resources were fundamental for the forms in which each collective organized and governed itself, the type of relationships that were forged, and the creation of collective significations—particularly around the notion of home. The practices of putting into use(s), taking care of, and maintaining the different spaces, objects, and equipment reinstated the agreements among the people, though they gave rise to conflicts too. Nevertheless, collective participation in the production and operation of the different spaces and infrastructure was an essential requirement for the initiatives—as the incident with the "new" solar-powered kitchen attests. Thus, it could be argued that governance in the initiatives was embedded in the space, the objects, and the material infrastructure. The production, management, use, design, and maintenance of them were central to a form of politics articulated around experiences of dwelling, which in its ultimate sense is the very agency to (re)create spaces and times of one's own—or our own—and imbue these practices with meanings that help us make sense of ourselves.

Gender: A Factor that Undermines Life in Common and Resists Change

Examined from a gender perspective, the first thing noticeable in the ICCs was the presence of a majority of women. When asked about this fact, several of my interlocutors said that women have been always trained carers. Nonetheless, beyond this, during my fieldwork, I could observe other less apparent aspects where gender featured as a condition behind discriminatory and/or abusive behaviors. It was in City Plaza and Khora that I could observe this more extensively, thanks largely to several initiatives to counteract discrimina-tion, abuse, or violence against women. I present two examples below. I was able to talk with several female participants about personal experiences of un-wanted attention and sexual misconduct that they had unexpectedly faced in the spaces. Complaints about sexual misbehaviors as well as about unequal participation of some women—often refugees—in assemblies and meetings were in fact not unusual and such misbehaviors were denounced straightfor-wardly on numerous occasions.

In Khora, I took part in the attempts to set up a "purple commission," whose function was to report—both orally and in a proposed "harassment record book"—any case of sexual misconduct in the building. The idea was put for-ward after several cases of sexual harassment in the café were reported. The purple commission was short-lived and the idea of the book did not make it in the end. However, soon after, an unnamed working group of female volunteers initiated a series of internal campaigns to secure better conditions for the women coming to the community center. They brought to general attention questions concerning the spatial arrangement of the building—for example, the inconvenience of having the women's space and the children's space on separate floors, the lack of a fitting room in the free-shop, and the intimidating atmo-sphere at the reception for (some) women due to an "excessive" sitting area, which was normally fully taken over by men only—and other issues like the insidious noncompliance of the rule of no men access in the women's space. Some of their proposals were eventually realized, like the creation of a fitting room, the removal of chairs from the entrance, and the hardening of the rules of entry into the women's space. They also managed to organize the delivery of reproductive health workshops and training workshops meant to raise aware-ness about cross-cultural aspects of women's issues.

In City Plaza, I was able to witness and participate in a number of collective efforts to counteract sexist behaviors. One of these initiatives comprised the production of a text about gender-based discrimination and/or violence in the squat, to be distributed to all rooms in the building. The initiative was led by a woman, who took action after denouncing two cases of sexual harassment. They were ignored and met with no response, action, or consequence for the perpetrators, who continued to reside in City Plaza. The text aimed first at raising awareness about the issue of ongoing cases of sexual abuse in the squat, and second at launching a campaign to set "mandatory" rules against sexist behaviors and subsequent procedures in case they were not respected. Several meetings were held in which different women—refugees and solidarians alike—actively participated in the elaboration and edition of the text in question. The text was presented in the general assembly and distributed among the residents. However, it did not achieve its ultimate objectives as, in the end, little collective action was taken to address the issue. In the face of this inaction, the women who fostered the initiative eventually decided to step out from City Plaza.

These two examples show that gender remains a factor of power imbalance and violence that still lacks widespread recognition, let alone action. People involved in the ICCs certainly endeavored to promote equitable forms of organizing (some areas of) their social reproduction. However, forms of discrimination and/or abuse against women were unfortunately present. The efforts by the women presented here yet again prove that women's struggle against oppressive powers remains (at least) twofold. Namely, women who struggle for a more egalitarian society continue to find themselves simultaneously fighting for their own freedom. Gender-based discrimination certainly undermined the potential of the politics expounded in this chapter, and so the possibility for an existence simultaneously in common yet in diversity.

Dwelling as Politics: An Emancipatory Praxis of and through Care and Space in Everyday Life

The ICCs examined in this book constitute examples of grassroots responses to a situation of enduring crisis sternly manifested in the everyday lives of a social majority. The devastating consequences of the austerity measures in Greece proved that the regime was nothing more than an upgrade of the neoliberal system. Despite difficult material and political conditions, the four ICCs were rather successful in enacting forms of organizing social reproduction and modes of care different than those of the state institutions and (large) NGOs, which largely failed to assure people's life sustenance needs. Their daily practices combined the (self-)organization of (some aspects of) social reproduction with political actions of protest and resistance. I have argued that this integrated praxis entailed a reconfiguration of care practices and imagination. Drawing on Fernández-Savater's (2020) theory of the Paradigm of Dwelling and the Paradigm of Governing, in this chapter, I have conceptualized the politics of the ICCs as a "politics of dwelling." I contend that this politics holds an emancipatory potential in the face of the ongoing neoliberal offensive against life, which is based on two main aspects.

First, it is a form of daily ruling and organizing that attends to the sustenance of everyday life in a situated and embodied manner, evolving according to the contingencies of life and personal relationships. It is a politics embedded in the web of bonds that are woven in the day-to-day. It is sustained by the capacity for reaching and performing agreements to take care of one another and for what is shared. Thus, it is marked to a great extent by an ethics of care, so that power dynamics are shaped largely by interpersonal relationships, affections, tacit obligations, and the acknowledgment of interdependency. Mechanisms that seek to establish certain rules are used too. However, in practice, conflicts are largely addressed on a case-by-case basis by those directly affected, and rules are revised constantly. In this sense, it is a politics of proximity, embodiment, and direct engagement with the ambivalent tasks of (collective) caring—as opposed to a politics of abstraction, representation, and delegation.

The second key aspect concerns space and material resources. Through diverse and never-ceasing spatial practices, the ICCs provided themselves with space(s) and time(s) of their own through which to (re)imagine the ways and conditions in which they wanted to (re)organize and sustain their everyday life. This agency is what ultimately defines the act of dwelling. As noted, dwelling comprises practices of both space production and meaning making, which in turn inform feelings and subjectivities. In this light, the space that mediated the form of self-government of the ICCs was a (collectively) inhabited one, namely a space in which objects had a use-value, and which was shaped through practices of housekeeping and homemaking, which are ultimately practices of care. As such, this space was characterized by being permanently in-the-making, unlike the space of representation of institutional politics.

In these two aspects, which characterize the politics of dwelling as a political praxis of and through care and space, lies a transformative capacity. However, limitations are also apparent, as the ethnographic accounts have shown. At times, interpersonal power dynamics and conflicts posed significant threats for the actual sustenance of the ICCs' life-in-common. Most importantly, gender forms of discrimination and/or abuse were present. Common across many grassroots groups, these forms of violence constitute in fact a major challenge that hinders the emancipatory potential of their politics. Still, I contend that a shift toward a politics of dwelling can offer a desirable path to fairer and more meaningful forms of life beyond the present regime of chronic crisis. As Fernández-Savater (2020) highlights, the war on life by the ongoing neoliberal regime(s) is carried out by a power of abstraction. The continuing processes of dispossession and extraction of bodies and natural resources alike are enabled and fostered by the fact that there is no sensitive connection with what is exploited. We are governed by instances of power far removed from our everyday life, and through increasingly diffuse and intangible apparatuses. However, our material and social reproduction are resolved for the most part in places outside the spaces of power. This is why, despite the limitations, I believe that *dwelling* as a political praxis offers valuable insights to those seeking to dehabituate themselves from capitalist forms of living and relating. As a political praxis that attends to the necessities and desires of those who practice it, it actually brings about forms of relating as well as modes of inhabiting space and time capable of yielding significant changes in subjectivities and forms of life.

The politics of dwelling of the ICCs elaborated in this chapter is just an example of what a situated politics leaning toward the Paradigm of Dwelling can look like. The ethnographic accounts attest to the complexity of scales and scopes at play in present struggles over reproduction. I suggest the concept as a framework for empirical research on existing examples of groups coming together to sustain—or socially reproduce—themselves, and the type of everyday spatial politics that develop from those experiences. Federici (2012, 2019) and Gutiérrez Aguilar (2017, 2018) have repeatedly asserted that the stakes of reimagining care and social reproduction are at present higher than ever while pointing to everyday life as a key site where practices of resistance and struggle are being conceived of and performed, and where new social imaginations are actually flourishing. That is why it is necessary to broaden the scope of empirical research on these existing instances as generative of transformative political imaginations.

CHAPTER 4

The More We Come Together, the More We Become Political

Becoming Anonymous Collectively

The proposition by Espai en Blanc (2009) to think of "anonymity" as a collective experience with the potential of eliciting the emergence of new collective forms of expression, thought and action provides an insightful framework to articulate what, throughout my fieldwork in the ICCs, I recognized as a first moment or initial condition for encounters. Encounters of the like Ferrara (2003) refers to in that they have a significant transformative potentiality, and as such would promote the emergence of new subjective formations. However, it is important to note, as I will show below, that not all the experiences of becoming anonymous hold such a transformative capacity.

Anonymity certainly defines a dimension of the experience—both personal and collective—of the people who partook in ICCs. It is an aspect that would come up frequently in conversations with my interlocutors, especially when asked about their arrival and first days in the initiative. Some described the experience of becoming anonymous as empowering or liberating. This was the case of Leonidas (July 14, 2016), who said that joining O Allos Anthropos had been a life-changing experience for it had enabled him to "erase his past" in prison, and Aris (July 14, 2016), who told me that becoming part of the social kitchen had made him no longer feel a homeless person. For others, on the contrary, it felt frustrating or demoralizing. Maria (May 11, 2017) from the ACP&P noted in this regard that many male patients would see her "just as a woman" and for this reason, they would not trust her capacity in providing them with any relevant support.

Another way in which anonymity took form in the ICCs was when it was used as a group strategy for self-defence. As expounded in the previous chapters, at the time of my fieldwork, ICCs shared a rather generalized distrust in formalized procedures and thus, they were unwilling to register the initiatives as official entities. In City Plaza, for instance, the lack of legal status and the ambivalent organizing structure were intentional tools to protect the squat in the face of possible legal actions from third parties or police raids. Playing anonymity in this way, in legal and organizational terms, limited to an extent potential charges against both the entire ICC and individuals. Interestingly, there was a time when the house assembly discussed the convenience of establishing a sort of ID card for residents, volunteers, and visitors. The proposal was eventually dismissed on analogous grounds, namely the rejection of surveillance-driven mechanisms of identification.

These different accounts make reference to forms of experiencing or enacting anonymity. Leonidas's, Aris's, and Maria's testimonials do so from a personal experience. In the case of City Plaza, it was a collective mechanism played for self-defense. However, none of these forms of anonymity holds the genuinely transformative potentiality that Espai en Blanc (2009) refers to. Anonymity became a truly interesting aspect of the ICCs when it constituted a collective exercise and experience of erasing hierarchies, using the kinds of practices that challenged established identities, social statuses, the distribution of roles, and the meaning of ownership. In so doing, it paved the ground for new collective names and common benchmarks to emerge.

These experiences emerged mostly in the mode of organizing and operating the ICCs, when they usually challenged, for example, the establishment of permanent representatives. Yet, this varied depending on the case, as for instance O Allos Anthropos clearly had a visible face, which was Konstantinos. Over time, members of the respective core groups in each ICC would eventually become the "established" reference points and somehow got instituted as representatives of the initiative. However, practices like the alternation of shifts and change of roles in spaces like City Plaza and Khora; the presence of translators in most of the meetings and assemblies; the continuous dissemination of open statements against racism, sexism, and homophobia; the rejection of any flag belonging to any political group, union, or country in the actions of protest each ICC would join or undertake; or the ban on wearing clothing labeled by any particular organization and using any of their branding at an event, were nonetheless reflective of an effort to dismiss any previous category, condition, or status that could undermine everyone's right to have a say and participate.

Another way was their determination to remain officially unnamed. In this way, ICCs challenged the idea of ownership and property linked to a legal and defined name. Who owned O Allos Anthropos, the ACP&P, City Plaza, or

Khora? It was difficult to determine from a legal perspective. ICCs deactivated ownership, whether private or public. On an internal level, as well, individual ownership was challenged by practices of sharing, commoning, and coproducing—material resources, spaces, skills, and knowledge(s)—through which individual names or personalities were diluted, making room for the collective to emerge.

In this way and, further, as a self-defense mechanism, anonymity in the ICCs took on that subversive character which Espai en Blanc (2009) referred to, becoming thereby a "force" that challenged established power devices, settled codes, conventions, categories, and fixed social and political identities—though not fully in the cases of gender roles or gender-based discrimination—all of which separate, privatize, and isolate more than they bring together, foster, and sustain collective processes, knowledge(s), and creations. Anonymity can be truly claimed as a condition that shapes spaces where the existential and the political intermingle, where the social ordering is disrupted and the map of the possible is reconfigured. In the following sections, I elaborate how this collective "becoming anonymous" was an enabling factor for transformative encounters and the emergence of processes of (re)subjectivation and politicization.

Enacting Encounters: Displacing the Self

Generally, ICCs formed heterogeneous groups populated by people from different cultural, social, and political backgrounds. They all inhabited a shared space(s), which was produced through their everyday practices of work, struggle, and life in common. A prevailing collective will of creating inclusive spaces of coexistence and structures of mutual support made ICCs a fertile ground for the growth of new subjectivities. "Either we started organizing collectively or they'd take it all. We began to realize that we cannot go it alone," said Eirini (see quote in chapter 1). This very consciousness, which the examined ICCs contributed to fostering and spreading, provided a foundation for processes of subjective construction—and deconstruction—to unfold. Nevertheless, despite a publicly proclaimed common ethos, there was neither a single nor a clearly hegemonic subjectivity that could be differentiated in the groups. After all, subjectivities, as Butler (2015) reminds us, are manifold, unsettled, and often self-contradictory. Subjects are always in formation in response to multiple interactions, connections, and disconnections.

Furthermore, the fact that people who arrived at the ICCs came from very diverse life trajectories, and thus from experiences and apparatuses of subjectivation of very different sorts, left room for subjective interferences as well as for considerable tensions and clashes. Acknowledging this, however, for the sake of analytical reflection, I distinguish between two "arriving" subjectivities at the ICCs for which I will use the metaphorical figures of the "disposable" and the "maximizer," by Ferrara (2003) and Fernández-Savater (2018), respectively.

Neither the disposable nor the maximizer stands for any particular subject or group of individuals who partook in the ICCs. They depict two different forms of subjectivation rather than two specific identities. The disposable, as subjectivity, develops from the experience of misery—or more precisely, from enforced impoverishment—which alienates the subject from their very human condition, namely their capacity to act politically. Misery turns subjects into bare lives of no value to the socioeconomic system (Ferrara, 2003). Some of my interlocutors recalled such experiences or moments and their difficulty in making sense of them, like Ahmad—a young resident of City Plaza from Syria—when he talked about his time in Turkey.

> Some days I was forced to work twelve, thirteen, fourteen hours. I was nothing. They didn't respect me because I'm handicapped. All my body hurt. I started to just look down. I felt as if I was shrinking. My attitude toward other people changed. (Ahmad, August 27, 2016)

Or Dimitris—a middle-aged Greek man who used to participate in O Allos Anthropos social kitchen from time to time—when he remembered the almost three years he stayed formally unemployed.

> I was fifty-two when I got fired. I lost myself. I fell into depression. For three years I did nothing. I didn't want to see anyone, so I lost many friends. I started to suffer from sicknesses that I had never had before, but I didn't care. For days I wouldn't clean up myself, I wouldn't shave, I even wouldn't eat.... I was going crazy. Nothing interested me any longer. I couldn't take joy from anything. (Dimitris, August 3, 2016)

Indeed, The Crisis in Greece has fostered the increase of practices, mechanisms, and conditions profoundly disempowering and humiliating for many. From sustained unemployment to housing evictions, indebtedness, and homelessness, from denial of access to healthcare to the loss of any social insurance, from physical attacks and expulsion from certain public spaces to the very asylum system, its border policies, and physical facilities like the detention camps where undocumented migrants and asylum seekers are retained indefinitely, labeled with numbers—subsequently losing their own names—and often subjected to violence of different sorts, they all have become powerful desubjectivating devices, many of which seem to be officially endorsed or accepted as The Crisis endured. This climate of increasing coercing and suppressing mechanisms lay the groundwork for the proliferation of "othering practices," which often came up inadvertently in comments and manifest in individual behaviors. From her experience in City Plaza, Elisa—a young volunteer from Spain who arrived in the first months of City Plaza—commented on this aspect as follows.

> No matter how much you think you know about it, you've read about it [referring to the crisis of migration of 2015–2016]. It is seeing it, interacting with the people that makes you understand really what this is all about. It made me realize that in the Western world we look at refugees as a whole, not as a bunch of individuals, and as such we dehumanize them. After I left City Plaza I wrote an article on my blog, which talked about this, how we tend to say things like: "Oh! Poor refugees," and there were actually some volunteers who came to City Plaza—for example with the kids you can see this so clearly—there are these people who come with the kids, they hug them, they kiss them and say: "Oh! Poor little children!" So the kids would be so confused because suddenly they get this huge amount of love from a total stranger who would immediately leave without doing anything about their situation. . . . I think this is a huge mistake that many people do *unawarely*, they cannot understand that there is no way you can ever empower a person by telling them that they are victims, that they are poor things. They already know they are victims. (Elisa, January 3, 2017)

Mohammed—a sixteen-year-old Syrian volunteer at Khora—talked of "the humanity" he had found in the ways relations and things were handled in the community center.

> The humanity with which we serve food to people. They just sit there and feel very comfortable, like in a restaurant. Not to wait in any queue like in the camps. That's what I love about Khora. . . . (There are some things that can be improved in) the café. Sometimes we are so busy, it's so complicated to know who needs food, go take it. . . . About that (organizing problem at the café), every single meeting we talk about it. But, actually, it's so hard to find a solution for it because our goal is to give food in a human way. We could do it

really organized if we ask them to queue and gave them a card. There are guys who say: "Why don't we give cards?"—"Show me your card, I'll give you your food." No, we are not going to do it. . . . Because it's against our goal, helping people in a human way, so they feel like persons. For sure in a restaurant, they don't ask for this, "Give me your card," "Give me your ID so I give you food." (Mohmed, August 18, 2017)

On the opposite side, the subjective traits of the maximizer, like the constant search for new ways of self-improvement, the struggle to reconcile multiple jobs with life, or the need to prove competitive and efficient no matter what the situation, came up as well in quite a lot of my conversations. Coupled with these dispositions was often an expression of some sort of anxiety derived from that very drive of constant self-improvement and competition. The account of Roy—a volunteer at Khora from the United Kingdom—provides an example of this. His narration of the reasons that drove him to join Khora as an international volunteer reflects this tension and personal struggle.

Together with a friend we had the idea of an activist café, and we eventually decided to go for it. . . . It wasn't just for activists, but the idea was to let the space for different collectives of activists have meetings and organize events. . . . We manage to get a loan from the bank, which was actually easier than we had expected. So that was ok, but for over a year and a half, we worked very hard until we finally could open the place. We knew we were madly indebted, but we had calculated that we should be able to repay the debt within two years or two years and a half. By the end of the fourth month, we had to close it down. No way we would be able to make it. We failed. We failed massively! My friend did sort of alright, but to me was really hard. It really hit me. For years already I had changed job after job, all them shit. So I guess I believed I could do my own thing. That's what they tell us, right? After that, I've realized there is something wrong with all this. . . . I guess it's this idea that we can all succeed. And I was sick of it. So this is partly why I decided to come. To be indebted anyway, I prefer to be here until the money runs out. (Roy, June 28, 2017)

These accounts by my interlocutors reveal characteristic traits of the two subjective figures mentioned above, the disposable and the maximizer. In the situated reality of the ICCs, both met, collided, and *contaminated* each other. According to Ferrara (2003), in situations where people become part of a common struggle, embodied encounters among those coming from different contexts and diverse experiences of subjectivation allow the emergence of specific moments when the self is displaced and "the other" fades and reemerges as an ally, a comrade, or a friend. Alma—a teenager volunteer from Israel—provided an account of one of her most meaningful experiences at Khora, which is rather illustrative in this regard.

> So the first time would be when I worked in the cafe and I talked to one of the volunteers there and he said he had a friend from Palestine, and I asked if he is in the building, and he said, "Yes!" and I said, "Would you think that you can ask him if he would like to speak to me?" And . . . when the guy came he told me—in the beginning, I wasn't very . . . I didn't really want to come to talk to you, but he said it was important. And we started talking and it kind of tore me to pieces, because he was a Palestinian refugee from Lebanon and he was a survivor of something called "Sabra and Shatila," which was a horrible, horrible, horrible massacre that the Israel army did in one of the villages there. He was talking to me about his views of the whole situation and it changed my perspective, and it broke my heart a little bit. And now in Khora, we are in the same boat. . . . I think this talk really I will remember it forever. (Alma, August 11, 2017)

Elisa talked about her encounter with Rabie—a young activist from Syria who got very involved in City Plaza—in a similar way, stressing how their mutual support and work in common enabled her to become an insider of City Plaza—no longer a "complete stranger."

> In the beginning I was a complete stranger. . . . We started doing movie nights and Rabie, who was one of the main organizers at City Plaza and the most sensitive person toward kids that I met there and that I've ever met in my life . . . he believed in me for the first moment, he thought I was going to be ok. He helped me to do the signs for the cinema in different languages and we did it and the kids loved it. And it was a very good experience. Little by little I met a few other volunteers and we started creating a program for kids. And by the end of my stay, just two weeks later, the kids had a full program from noon until the night of activities, cinema, and other things. And I couldn't believe it because that first day I just took my ukulele and played it and it was a disaster. From that to how things were at the end there was a whole world. (Elisa, January 3, 2017)

Life expectations, the types of relationships wanted, and the very way in which the subjects spoke of themselves, they all experienced a change. Rosa from City Plaza and Christina from Khora offered examples indicative of these personal self-recalibrations that stemmed from those encounters.

The most changing thing for me [at City Plaza] has been to be able to share some of our lived experiences, which at the beginning I found quite challenging as I was very aware of the fact that many people here have very difficult stories. But I've learnt that when there is no exchange, it doesn't work. I also have my problems, even though when I speak about them may sound ridiculous. But still, if you don't open yourself up to share something, I think you miss the best of this place. (Rosa, August 16, 2016)

Indeed, as these accounts show, many of my interlocutors referred to their experiences in the ICCs as illuminating and transformative. Their accounts resonate with those described by Ferrara (2003) in his ethnography about the Argentinian *piqueteros*, where he calls this metamorphic experience an "encounter," that is, a moment of realization among different others in which otherness gives way to affinity and recognition of belongingness in a same collectivity.

Emerging New We(s)

Experiences of becoming anonymous in collective manners favored transformative encounters that enabled displacements of the self and the emergence of new subjectivities. Yet, what were the constituent elements that shaped these emerging subjectivities in the ICCs? What were new we(s) made of? In the following, I elaborate on some of them based on my ethnographic observations and conversations.

SPACE

Fundamental for the encounters of the type we have been speaking about to take place and be enacted is space and the way it is produced and managed. For space and subjectivities bear a dialectical interrelationship. Guattari (2015) suggests the notion of "smooth space," namely a space that is always in-the-making and open to new potential connections, new possible *becomings*.

Talking about one of her memories in City Plaza, Elisa referred to this co-constitution quite eloquently.

When you are everyday spending twenty-four hours with the same people in the same space your brain makes this connection by which you think they belong to this space. Seeing them taking over the public space in Greece and yelling and asking for . . . demanding, not asking, to open the borders, to "let us in" . . . that was a very powerful moment. (Elisa, January 3, 2017)

Indeed, space shapes our relationships, our fields of desire, and imaginations. Conversely, our practices and interactions produce space (Lefebvre [1974] 1992; Massey 2005; Stavrides 2016). Quite often, when asked about their first impressions and moments in the ICCs, my interlocutors would refer to a feeling of disorientation, of difficulty in finding their place. Elisa underlined this aspect by recalling how lost and "out of place" she felt at the beginning when she arrived with her backpack and ukelele. Similarly, Miguel (August 15, 2017) remarked that it was not until he "found his place" that he started to fully understand the functioning dynamics of City Plaza.

As discussed in chapters 2 and 3, the spatiality produced in the ICCs was one of indeterminacy, contingency, and liminality. It was through spatial negotiations and the management of proximities, that encounters—as transformative subjective experiences—thrived. Some of my interlocutors provided beautiful examples of the sort, like Lina, when recalling one of her most meaningful moments in City Plaza; Mohammed, who talked about the celebration of Ramadan at Khora; and Marta, who defined Khora as a "meeting point."

My personal favourite experience was in a demo, the first demo that we organized along with the other housing squats. There were some other people, not from City Plaza but from other squats—I'm not sure—some Syrian people who—let's say—were saying more patriotic slogans about Syria. And a group of people from City Plaza approached them and told them: [they were also people from Syria] "We should fight together, we should fight united, all of us together." I thought it was a really moving. . . . (Lina, June 29, 2016)

The spaces I like the most [in Khora] are the kitchen and the café. . . . I like the many activities that we have. It's not just the organization of food or clothes. We have different activities and sometimes we have parties there. It's so nice! I'm just remembering how Ramadan was. Ramadan is a holy month for Muslims and we had a celebration with them. We reorganized how we served food just for these people. So all Khora was reorganized just for them. It's so kind! . . . We had a party for three days. We got food, we made food, and we ate it. Also, some sweets coming from our cultural celebrations. It was amazing. I still remember how it was. We were open until night and it was so hard work, but it was amazing. Everyone having fun. And we had some gifts for the children. (Mohammed, August 18, 2017)

I would define Khora as a meeting point, not just on a physical level among people themselves, but also among resources and needs, and that eventually grows and feeds itself because it's something that changes every day, and it changes according to the needs that are demanded. Despite being so many people, it always adjusts. (Marta, August 24, 2017)

In the previous chapters, I have recounted how by installing the deployable table and a big pot on the square, O Allos Antrhopos collective (re)activated a spatiotemporal scenario of encounter, conversation, and exchange, where social and personal connections were enhanced and extended in time. Similarly, rooms in City Plaza provided versatile spaces for gatherings and conversations. Residents would visit their friends and neighbours for coffee, tea, lunch, play cards, listen to music, and converse. The same occurred in Khora's women's space, which was intentionally devoted to enabling encounter and communication among women through a common effort of creating a space of safety and trust for and among them. These all provide examples of what Stavrides (2016) calls "in-between spaces," meaning spaces in which established identities blur and new subjective configurations emerge. For it is through embodied encounters rather than by predefined identitarian demarcations that those are constructed. As such, they configure meeting grounds through which constitutive others recognize themselves as such, or in other words, through which the other is seen as part of one's self. The in-between spaces that were produced in and through the ICCs generated new connections, which challenged established orders fostering transformations holding a political potentiality.

CRISIS AND STRUGGLE

Khora is a community that accepts all members of society. It's an open community.... Things happen due to collaboration, due to exchange among the people and also due to collective struggle in the everyday and in the streets.... I've seen how some refugees are very closed off in their first days due to their own experiences, and then they become more and more confident. This has to do with the friendly environment, because we all try to be supportive.... For me, the experience at Khora has entailed a personal change. It's been tough, but rewarding at the end of the day. The Crisis changed our priorities. In my case for the better, I think. I mean, I had a very tough time. I was jobless for a year. But it helped me value more real relationships with people. I got closer to some friends. Because this is what helps you in difficult periods such as the one we're facing.... Then in Khora, after some refugees told me their personal stories as we collaborated with each other in the day-to-day, I started to ask myself what really matters in life. Sometimes you think your problems are very big, but when you hear those of others you realize many things. And sometimes you relate to the experiences of others, and in some aspects, they are not that different to yours. So I think I've changed in this sense. (Christina, August 24, 2017)

As it has been expounded throughout the chapters and Christina's words reflect—in her case particularly to Khora—ICCs have comprised heterogeneous groups, making it difficult to determine single social and political identities for each one. Socially, as I argue in this work, what may initially define ICCs is "crisis," as an experiential and subjective condition that has marked the people arriving at them—albeit in very different ways. Broadly, to all of these people, crisis implied a form of loss, dispossession or displacement, whether in economic, social, political, or geographical terms. These lived experiences, although different, were the basis that brought them together in the first instance. Politically, no dominant ideology or political tradition could be truly assigned to ICCs, although those who manifested a political position would largely situate themselves somewhere along the political spectrum within the Left. Nevertheless, more than any specific ideology, what has kept people together in these initiatives has been mostly embracing the need to self-organize (some aspects of) their social reproduction in the face of crisis (politics). At the core, it was the act of being together, that is, putting into practice common modes of living, working, and struggling, that gave rise to processes of politicization or repoliticization, more than belongingness to any specific social or political group.

COMMONING AND ETHICS OF CARE

Creating commons-based modes of work, life, and struggle underpinned by a prominent ethics of care—what I have suggested as a situated politics of dwelling (Fernández-Savater 2020) or a politics "contaminated by life" (Manrique 2020)—fed an atmosphere where transformative encounters certainly flourished. ICCs constituted groups that were more than a mere aggregation of individuals. Interdependence—and the acknowledgment of this condition—determined their initial existence and defined a praxis based on affections, solidarity, and accountability that made possible their very sustenance over time. This sense of community became tangible in moments like the one described by Miguel:

I've experienced a sense of community many times but the time I lived it more intensively was when we were on alert due to the issue with Macedonia, when members of Golden Dawn, fascists, and people with far-right ideologies in general came to Athens from all over Greece to demonstrate. We made a safety plan that was craziness, it was dozens and dozens of people working at Plaza, doing shifts of everything you can imagine, watching out for everything everywhere. It was a very beautiful moment because somehow everyone got involved and became aware—well, this was a consciousness already existing— but that it was manifested there at that moment in the form of "this is my house, we live together, we organize and cooperate. Now that we face a real threat from the outside, we defend ourselves." It was very beautiful because the place was boiling with activity during that weekend, and everybody was willing to help. The atmosphere was one of comradeship and friendship. Residents got involved a lot. Shifts of fifty to sixty people actively working, each one carrying out different tasks. (Miguel, August 15, 2017)

A sense of community was manifested as well in the networking endeavors that ICCs undertook. Whether as a form of seeking out means and resources to sustain themselves, as a way of securing protection for their groups, or as a means to gain a political voice, building networks, "building community," was a key feature of the ICCs. The following excerpt of my interview with Lina at City Plaza reflects how this community building through praxis particularly translated into collective demands for public action.

Apart from how we organize internally the life of four hundred people who live here, we try to push as well a greater agenda regarding what is going on in the camps, what is the condition of the access of people to the healthcare system and to the educational system, how we are going to demand better and decent housing conditions for everybody. In this aspect we try to create a center for struggle, that many antiracist and migrant communities, or maybe trade unions or people who are doing solidarity in camps or in other places can come here and coordinate somehow a greater struggle. (Lina, June 29, 2016)

Certainly, ICCs' praxis enabled the emergence of collective formations and meanings. Over time, new collective names emerged in the ICCs, namely new forms of naming the emerging "we(s)." "We are City Plaza. (We live together, we struggle together)," "City Plaza girls," "City Plaza is (still) our home," "The Khora family," all of them were names of the several "we(s)" that appeared in some of the ICCs. A material register of these new names could be found on the walls of the buildings that the ICCs inhabited, on the banners that they created and displayed in demonstrations, or on the building's facades, and on their respective social media.

These new collective names and other significations referred to a "sensing community," namely an embodied collectivity, which was not defined by a common identity but rather by a shared sensibility. Thus, the communities brought about in the ICCs fit within the theoretical approach elaborated by Gutiérrez Aguilar (2017, 2018), who describes communities—or more precisely, "communitarian fabrics"—as the structures that emerge, develop, and are sustained by weaving, namely by a sustained praxis of creating and prioritizing bonds over abstract rules or codes. The ICCs' different and varied communitarian fabrics certainly stemmed from an everyday practice, which was shared and worked out in common. As elaborated above, the "force of anonymity," namely the act of "vacating our usual and recognised places of enunciation" (Espai en Blanc 2009), was a condition that enabled the new collective name(s) to emerge. All these aspects imprinted these communities with an inherently unsettled, undetermined, and unfinished character. Stavrides (2016) calls them "communities in the making." The beautiful term is appropriate, for it evokes both their unsettled nature and their vocation to remain porous to newcomers, new needs, new desires, that is, to transformation.

Nonetheless, here it is important to remember that the communitarian fabrics or communities-in-the-making formed in the ICCs were diverse and not all driven by radical emancipatory desires. At times, practices that foregrounded difference and rupture more than commonality also figured strongly. As Butler (2015) reminds us, subjects—whether unwittingly or not—tend to reproduce the established orders and norms. Processes of subjective (re)formation depend on myriad factors and circumstances.

REWORKING THE FAMILY

Despite conditions of hardship or even evictions, many of the communities-in-the-making brought about by the ICCs have not disappeared. For example, as noted in the statement the ICC made public after the keys of the building of City Plaza were returned to the former employees of the hotel in July 2019, the residents "will actively look for new ways to keep the community it created alive in a different context," so "the community will continue to exist" (Refugee Accommodation and Solidarity Space City Plaza, Facebook, July 11, 2019). This willingness to carry on cut across the four ICCs—even City Plaza—at the time of finishing my doctorate. During my fieldwork I came across multiple moments in which people involved in the different ICCs expressed their desire to sustain not only the relationships they had established, but also their shared experience of engagement in projects they saw as deeply transformative—both on a personal and on a collective level. Interestingly, quite often, this desire to remain, to last, to continue, came articulated in relation to the idea of an "emerging family." Indeed, references to the group as "a family but different"—in Moustafa's words (December 7, 2016)—were rather common, especially in City Plaza, where "a new family" was present not only by being talked about, but also in the form of murals of photographs covering several walls with the faces of many of the residents and memories of emblematic moments.

> Most of all, to me, City Plaza means a new family—a family but different. I have friends from different places; Syria, Pakistan, Afghanistan. Also from different religions. Somehow, we all feel connected. Nothing to do with what we felt in the camp! (Moustafa, City Plaza, December 7, 2016)
>
> I think that the objective that City Plaza has is to create a sort of community. To create strength through unity. Thus, many times I compare it with a big family. Especially for the people who have been here for long, a family emerges. Even in families there are tensions and conflicts, but in the end people tend to take care of each other, people know a lot about each other. Sometimes it works as a small village. You can see this type of questions at the demos. People are very engaged, they are very keen to make their voices heard, and a lot of care is generated. (Miguel, City Plaza, August 15, 2017)
>
> The kitchen is a sort of extended family for me. It is a very important part of my life now and of my day-to-day. I support them and they support me. It's not just about food, you know. (Fotis, O Allos Anthropos, August 3, 2016)
>
> I think I could define Khora as a kind of a family or many families with people from many places who have become friends. So maybe more of a 'friendmily'! (Roy, Khora, June 28, 2017)

Each of these articulations reflects a personal signification of each individual's experience in the ICC through an idea of the family, which in turn is simultaneously shaped by wider cross-cultural conceptualizations and by each one's personal background and culture. Common across the expressions above though, is the framing of the family as a site of care, affection, and belongingness, while aspects of conflict, control, and/or suppression—which are also constitutive of families—were absent. The negative side of the family was clearly left out. This, which is not uncommon, in fact quite commonplace, nonetheless revealed not only the importance of a sense of belongingness but also the search—whether fully wittingly or more unconsciously—for committed and lasting bonds based on mutual support and solidarity. As opposed to families in which affiliation is bounded to kinship and relationships are marked by the normative model prevailing in each society, the type of familial belongingness, form, and practice that ICCs brought about was grounded in the awareness of the need for organizing life—and its sustenance—in common and the desire of creating the conditions for this to be possible and also durable. In other words, the familial formations and meanings that emerged in the ICCs developed through gradual processes of practicing and imagining collectively desirable forms of working and/or dwelling together, all of which enabled trust, affection, and conscious care to thrive.

Obviously, these processes of formation of "familial fabrics"—in reference to Gutiérrez Aguilar's (2017, 2018) notion of "communitarian fabrics"—were far from idyllic and continuous. ICCs' emerging families certainly constituted important assemblages of affection, solidarities, and support, but they were precarious ones, strongly marked by transit—especially in the case of migrants—permanently in-the-making, and always situated and contingent. Nevertheless, I argue that, despite being sometimes contradictory and uncertain in the long run, these processes of community formation and their particular signification in terms of family were valuable in themselves, for they opened the family "from below" to new possible meanings, forms, and practices rooted in solidarity, equality, and freedom.

The Political Capacity of Embodied We(s)

The Movement of the Squares, initially driven by discontent, indignation, and rage against The Crisis and the austerity regime, would become a powerful collective experience where people of diverse life backgrounds and worldviews would enact a new radical imagination, which defied the future of austerity and deprivation that had been imagined for them by the institutional economic and political powers. This new radical imagination was grounded in principles of collective and citizen-led struggle, self-organization, solidarity, and mutual support. At the time of my fieldwork, the radical imagination of the squares still permeated many of the practices in the ICCs and would come up in conversations and discussions, colloquially in the everyday and also in assemblies.

Yet, it was through encounters and the sustained embodied experience of an everyday in common that this imagination took on actualized meaning. Thus, to a certain extent, the ICCs provided a space of prolongation of that primary encounter that took place in the squares and which was reenacted through everyday coexistence. As argued by Ferrara (2003), encounters allow at first a displacement of the self, namely of individuality, which opens up the subject's field of desire to reevaluation and reconfiguration. Life expectations, the types of relationships wanted and the very way in which the subject speaks of themselves, they all experience a change.

ICCs constituted sites where the self was to an extent displaced by a sense of collectivity or community. There emerged a willingness to connect to one another beyond given formulas and to project new forms of attachment and belonging. This relocation of the self challenged hierarchical classifications and given rules. It enabled a rupture with instituted subjectivities and fixed sociocultural categories or identities, and paved the way for the emergence of new common benchmarks. In this sense, the kind of subjective formations that developed in the ICCs had more to do with processes and ways of relating than with transformations of the self on an individual basis. As Fotis stated: "What we want is people to change their feeling about society, to take part and feel integrated" (Fotis, August 3, 2016).

The processes of subjective formation or (re)formation that ICCs enabled speak of Garces's (2013) argument about the relational condition of the subject. ICCs indeed constituted examples through which resistance to the "individualist universalism" paradigm was embodied and enacted. Certainly, ICCs' praxis enabled the emergence of common formations and meanings. Yet, can the emerging collectivities in the ICCs be considered political? As elaborated in the previous chapters, everyday social reproduction, namely the sustenance and maintenance of the groups and the spaces on a daily basis, merged with political action and struggle beyond the very domestic domains of each ICC. The spheres permeated each other, albeit not exempted from frictions and clashes. ICCs indeed fostered processes of politicization—and depoliticization—which transformed or affected the subjectivities of many. Miguel explained this very effectively.

> We have seen people who have arrived as travelers and have left with a different political consciousness and with a perception of reality that—I believe—is different. This also works conversely; people who have arrived knowing where they were entering, with very clear theoretical political ideas, have left with a more humane approach, less theoretical and more practical. (Miguel, August 15, 2017)

Similarly, Lina noted:

> I think the more people get involved [in City Plaza], the more they will get involved on a political level as well. The more we come together, the more we

become political. . . . If you just stay on the level of just helping someone, I think this is a bit selfish. If you don't help to change the system, the larger structure that creates this type of inequality. . . . So I think that if you want to make a change you should work at the same time on many levels, in many layers. (Lina, June 29, 2016)

There were indeed many actions that took place in the ICCs that fit into what Isin and Nielsen (2008) and Isin (2014, 2017) denominate as "acts," particularly acts of citizenship, which as such are inherently political. These are practices that disobey, disrupt, interrupt, and transform established orders. In performing them, people constitute themselves as political subjects. As Lina remarked, "The more we come together, the more we become political." The embodied performance of solidarity fostered the emergence of political subjects in demand of their own rights, as well as allies and coparticipants in their struggle(s) for social justice, who in so doing became political as well.

We had organized a demo in the center of Athens along with other housing occupations, which was very nice actually because of the number of refugees . . . they were the majority. So it is nice to see how they can rise as an autonomous subject. . . . I have to say that refugees here, in this past year, have been very active and they have been doing protests and hunger strikes and demonstrations. They are very active subjects, in contrast to what governments and mainstream media try to sell that they are doing stuff that other people are pushing them to do, or how a more NGO concept of working performs in an active-passive way. We try to do it in another way here, collectively, Greek people, people from all over the world and refugees, and fight for the same struggle, for an open Europe, an open society. (Lina, June 29, 2016)

As we have seen, as time passed, new collective names, that is, new forms of naming the emerging "we(s)," emerged in the ICCs. As Fernández-Savater (2012) remarks, words are material forces, which make and unmake us. In his view, those emerging shared names are constitutive of spaces like the ICCs, and essential to their configuration as spaces of encounter open to subjective displacements and relocations. They have a strong transformative potentiality. They have the capacity to disrupt the existing reality and produce a new one, and there lies their political potentiality. "The political fiction interrupts and creates, creates and interrupts. Simultaneously. It is a power of de-classification and a power of creation. It makes the common by unmaking it, it unmakes the common and remakes it" (Fernández-Savater 2012). In this respect, for instance, the very name of the social kitchen O Allos Anthropos bears this disposition toward transformation and becoming. As explained by Konstantinos, O Allos Anthropos refers to "that other human being one can become (through solidarity)." All these embodied instances hold a transformative capacity, more so if we consider the contemporary context in which ICCs are embedded, on the one hand, marked broadly by the prevalence of the individualist universalism paradigm (Gracés 2013), on the other, by an imposed chronic crisis regime.

Epilogue

Written in the context of the multidimensional crisis in Europe that ensued from the global banking crash in 2008, triggering sweeping processes of dispossession and exclusion via austerity and renewed border enforcement systems in the EU, this book has investigated instances of collective struggle in response to this juncture, where the praxis and imagination of care, citizenship, and (urban) infrastructures are reconfigured through practices of solidarity and commoning.

Crisis, more particularly chronic crisis, is the condition that determines, imperils, and threatens the existence of the subversive sites presented in this work and their possibilities of thriving. Yet, at the same time, it is also the very condition that fostered their birth. Thus, I have engaged crisis as a multidimensional condition crossed and shaped by power struggles between hegemonic forces and contentious instituting instances. For crisis is about dispossession, exclusion, suppression, and control as much as it is about opposition, contestation, and radical imagination. From this perspective, I have distinguished four interrelated dimensions, namely *the empirical-experiential, the imaginary, the governmental,* and *the critical-insurgent,* which in turn have been grounded theoretically and empirically in the urban for, at present, crisis is particularly transforming cities worldwide.

I have elaborated and used the notion of the *city-in-crisis* to analyze some of the major transformations that took place in Athens, Greece, from 2010 to 2018—years in which the Greek capital went from being seen as spearheading the country's modernization to the most economically sunken and socially devastated city in the EU. *Athens-in-crisis* has been presented, on the one hand, as a site ridden by processes of dispossession and exclusion through crisis politics as a reworked mode of neoliberal governmentality and, on the other, as an imaginary (through and of the urban), largely produced and mobilized by the dominant powers to mask ever-renewing processes of capital extraction and growing inequalities. And lastly, and despite the above, as a site in dispute, where both established normalcies and emerging discourses from above are contested laying the ground for the emergence of new movements and struggles of counterpower.

Athens-in-crisis is simultaneously the setting and the means of the emergence and development of what I have called "infrastructures of caring citizenship" (ICCs). The concept designates self-organized initiatives that articulate and integrate the provision of care and social protection at the local level in broader struggles demanding social justice and transformative change. Thus, they can be viewed as instances of contemporary struggles over social reproduction and citizenship at the same time. The appearance of ICCs in Athens took place alongside a wider and long-underway reconfiguration of the welfare regime in Greece, where the retreat of the state has progressively led to the emergence and expansion of other actors including third-sector organizations. These transformations can be seen in turn as part of a broader ongoing infrastructural paradigm shift—particularly affecting soft urban infrastructures—where grassroots groups are playing a key role in advancing novel forms of democratic infrastructural practice.

The four ICCs examined in this book—O Allos Anthropos social kitchen, City Plaza refugee accommodation center, Khora community center, and the Athens Community Polyclinic and Pharmacy—can be viewed as representative of a grassroots movement attesting to these transformations. During the years in which this study takes place, ICCs in Athens succeeded in creating a system of provision of basic needs premised on principles of direct democracy, solidarity, and commoning, which reached thousands of people excluded from state services, while acting also as a platform for the articulation of collective demands and organization of protest actions. In this way, ICCs turned social reproduction into both a site of commoning and a site of struggle. Their praxis unfolded a politics, which I have characterized as a "politics of dwelling," grounded in everyday life and its materiality and largely shaped by an ethics of care. The experience generated new collective subjectivities, new "we(s)," which in some cases channelled emancipatory processes—both individual and collective.

As I have argued throughout the book, not only did ICCs create functional systems of provision and protection, in doing so they prefigured new imaginations of care, citizenship, and infrastructure, opening up possible alternative avenues toward fairer futures. I dwell on these potentialities in the Afterword. ICCs, however, faced significant difficulties since their very inception derived from extremely precarious conditions as well as the rejection from opposing forces, which saw in them a threat to their own agendas. In the time elapsed since the end of the study to the present day, ICCs have actually experienced major setbacks, which have ended up dissolving the so-called Solidarity Movement of the previous years.

I finalized the fieldwork that grounds this work in the summer of 2018, when former president Alexis Tsipras (SYRIZA) officially announced the completion of the bailout programs imposed on Greece by the Troika. Exit from the memoranda, however, did not translate into the end of austerity. The dismantling of the public sector and state welfare, the privatization of public assets and companies, the precarization of wages and work conditions, and the restriction of civil rights have continued into the present. The government headed by the conservative Kyriakos Mitsotakis (Néa Dimokratía), which came to power in July 2019 and was reelected in June 2023, has not only maintained this order but has reinforced it with new neoliberal policies.

During the past five years, big investors have transformed entire buildings in central neighborhoods and the municipality of Pireaus into new hotels or short-term rental tourist accommodations, displacing numerous neighbors from places where they had resided for years or even lifetimes. Khora's initial building is now a housing block for high-income residents, whereas O Allos Anthropos's former headquarters has been turned into fancy co-working spaces. These processes of accelerated gentrification are being experienced too in other southern European cities like Barcelona and Lisbon, where they have contributed to an existing housing crisis, leading some administrations to enforce a ban on new licenses for these types of vacation rentals. In addition, more public spaces have been privatized or enclosed. This is the case of numerous neighborhood squares (*plateia* in Greek), which have been fenced off for years and where trees have been cut down under the pretext of the construction of new metro entrances for the new line. This is having a significant impact on the neighborhoods' everyday life and dynamics.

On a national scale, the present government has implemented a ruthless immigration agenda, which has included deadly pushbacks of migrants and asylum seekers crossing to Greece from Turkey, the closure of refugee camps in urban areas, and the construction of new highly surveilled facilities in isolated areas, the end of housing and economic support schemes for refugees, the eviction of self-organized squats and other structures providing accommodation and support for refugees, and raids against undocumented migrants among others. The shipwreck in Greek waters near the town of Pylos on

June 15, 2023, in which over 500 people—mostly from Afghanistan and Pakistan—died or went missing, has been the deadliest event resulting from this new migration regime that in many cases violates international law.

The harshening of immigration policies and measures has come with a heightened repressive approach toward social movements and political activism that has included eviction operations against many refugee and political squats in central Athens and has involved the detention of many of their residents and supporters, the repeal of the Academic Asylum law—in place since the fall of the military Junta in 1974—which gives back power to the police to enter universities, and the increase of police presence in public spaces. The COVID-19 pandemic served to reinforce this "securitization" agenda with highly restrictive lockdown measures, which further curtailed the right to protest.

The repressive measures and operations by the Néa Dimokratía government have undoubtedly taken a toll on the movements arising from the Syntagma occupation, demobilizing people and dismantling groups. By the end of 2019, a sentiment of disillusion and tiredness was vastly palpable across movements, initiatives, and individuals. Some ICCs like City Plaza ceased to exist due to the increasing pressure from authorities or violent evictions by the police. To this day, the building remains abandoned. Others, like Khora and the ACP&P, seeking ways to ensure the continuation of their activities, formalized their legal statuses as cooperative foundations or nonprofits. These changes, however, have significantly altered the management and politics of these initiatives. There are others, nonetheless, that have remained operating on an independent basis in accordance with the principles of autonomy and direct democracy. This is the case of O Allos Anthropos, which, however, is recently facing legal charges.

The crackdown on grassroots solidarity initiatives and networks attests to the fact that conservative and far-right forces see them as threatening to their interests. Despite the mentioned attacks, various ICCs remain active in the present. Some were repurposed to tackle new challenges in the wake of the COVID-19 pandemic, during which they performed a paramount role in the social reproduction of vulnerable urban populations. O Allos Anthropos social kitchen, for instance, distributed daily portions to families, schools, and other people in need. Khora also provided food and cooked meals while the asylum support team continued providing services remotely. For its part, although services at the ACP&C ceased during the lockdowns, an email account for emergencies was provided and the clinic's social media accounts remained active, providing information about accessible healthcare and social care services in Athens, as well as ongoing campaigns in defense of the NHS. The COVID-19 pandemic actually fostered the (re)composition of many solidarity initiatives and networks that set up, among other things, collection points for food, basic goods, and medicines across neighborhoods, phone lines to provide emotional support for those vulnerable, initiatives to provide financial support for people in need, and digital platforms to coordinate actions, communicate, and provide information regarding services and rights. Existing ICCs and other solidarity collectives were crucial in the initiation of these actions, which were joined by other groups such as residents' committees, workers' unions, social economy organizations, and some political associations (Arampatzi, Kouki, and Pettas 2022). Underlying most of these initiatives was an explicit critique of governmental measures and restrictions. Coordination among them served to organize protest actions—despite mobility restrictions—and campaigns. The case of Athens resonates with others in European cities like Madrid, where similar networks were reactivated in many neighborhoods. A number of low-income barrios like Villaverde, located in the south of the capital, are telling examples in this regard. A recent study (Corsín-Jiménez, Tiburcio Jiménez, and Cisneros 2024) shows that despite their socioeconomic characteristics and high density of population, which according to epidemiological criteria predicted a very high incidence of COVID-19, care networks organized by neighbours managed to avoid that scenario. That is, the grassroots fabric in these areas changed the biosocial geography of the city.

In spite of a context of continuing crises and repressive politics, or perhaps due to it, new struggles and movements did form or recompose during the past five years. The feminist movement has expanded quite significantly in the country in the wake of the feminist movement in Spain[1] and the Non Una Di Meno movement in Italy,[2] which have been of great influence. New groups and spaces have emerged in Athens, combining research, cultural activities, and political action. The big demonstrations that took place across the country on March 8, 2023, which were joined by labour unions as well as many people protesting the rail crash at Tempe on February 28, attest to this growth and the fact that people in Greece keep resisting and protesting.[3] University students have been leading important mobilizations and occupations against the downgrading of their studies—such as performing art studies[4]—and the privatization of higher education.[5] Groups in defense of migrants and asylum seekers continue operating despite increased repression—as in Italy, where initiatives against detention centers and migrant-led movements for housing and citizenship and residency rights keep fighting against the backdrop of a hard-right government. In Greece, a group of lawyers and jurists has been formed to take legal action in defense of the victims and families of the Pylos shipwreck.

This series of events shows that crisis (politics) will keep facing contestation and resistance, that the struggle to determine living conditions in the present is not over, just as the future is not closed. In fact, futures otherwise are already present.

Afterword
Relearning to Live in a World in Crisis

Amid a present marked by relentless crises, this book has nonetheless endeavored to explore spaces of resistance to a logic of enclosure of the future imposed from above, where people dare to imagine alternatives rooted in a collective desire for social justice and emancipation, and to put them into practice. I have argued that, besides providing care and social protection and contributing to recomposing struggles through which rights are demanded and advanced, ICCs prefigure and enact new radical imaginations that help us relearn to live in a world in crisis and yet envision a future—or many futures—beyond the chronic crisis regime.

Still, seen from a quantitative perspective or through a macroscopic lens, one could argue that the impact of initiatives like the ICCs should be deemed insignificant or irrelevant at a structural level. Additionally, those seeking responses that can help outline strategies toward state power as the only feasible means for meaningful social change will most likely be disappointed with this book. From the beginning of the study, on the one hand, my position on these issues has sat within a tradition of theory and scholarship that criticizes the dominance of quantitative-based narratives to explain social phenomena in general, and macroeconomic explanations of the many contemporary crises more particularly, and, on the other hand, my work aligns with the premise held by social movement scholars that mobilization from the ground up is fundamental to any process of social transformation. Bottom-up instances like the ICCs are certainly unsettled and vulnerable. Yet, their impact transcends the here and now. For they challenge the hegemonic narratives of what is happening and what can be. They bring about new subjectivities and imaginations that endure over time, capable of manifesting anew there and when history provides.

In the ICCs, importantly, the processes of imagining are intimately linked to practice. Namely, unlike planned or (pre)fixed top-down visions by experts, new imaginations emerge and unfold as a result of collective processes of organizing and sustaining work and dwelling in common driven by a collective will of radically changing structures, forms of doing politics, forms of relating to one another and forms of living and inhabiting the city. Talking about her overall experience at Khora, Mar—an international volunteer—noted: "My concept of solidarity is now wider. I've seen many ways in which solidarity can develop that I couldn't imagine in the past" (July 6, 2017).

This brief statement encapsulates the ever-present possibility of new radical imaginations capable of widening the conceivable and the realm of the possible. In this line, authors like Max Haiven and Alex Khasnabish (2014), Dimitris Soudias (2023), and Dean Spade (2020) have highlighted the pedagogical capacities of initiatives like the ICCs as spaces that channel and manifest critical stances toward the regimes of inequality and the hostile systems we are forced to depend on through the construction of new capacities, resources, and imaginations toward systems that prioritize life instead of capital accumulation.

Broadly, I have presented ICCs' imaginations as alternatives to the contemporary crisis imaginary, which, whether through coercion, repression, control, or incitement to resistance, in essence remains an imaginary of fear.[1] Conversely, I argue that the imaginations prefigured by the ICCs are imaginations of life, for they gesture toward living alternatives rooted in care as the way to live through crisis and against crisis regimes. Aiming to prolong these learnings, in this book I have outlined three conceptual proposals concerning infrastructures, politics, and subjectivities, which might shed some light on similar initiatives that have likewise emerged—or will emerge—during this ongoing crisis regime in other places. I will briefly summarize them here as a way of closing this work.

First, I have characterized the ICCs as *infrastructural modes of care through commoning*. As such, ICCs open up, on the one hand, a new infrastructural imagination that demarcates from modern ideals of uniformity, continuity, neutrality, expertise, and centralized control, moving toward principles of relationality, conductivity, connectivity, plurality, decentralization, locality, participation, care, maintenance, and repair. On the other hand is a new conception of care linked to the enactment of (an expanded) citizenship. Commons-based infrastructures of care provide a model radically different to the prevailing institutions of welfare, namely the state and the third sector.

The first has been withdrawing responsibilities and cutting social services for decades, at the same time that it has increased its violence and controlling mechanisms. The second, run by private interests through highly hierarchical structures and competitive mechanisms for funding, discriminates among the deserving and the undeserving, often moralizing and even stigmatizing certain populations. Seeking predetermined outcomes fit for evaluation against quantitative criteria, nonprofits disconnect the manifold dimensions of life isolating issues in self-contained categories. Thus, they will never pose a challenge to the status quo. Unlike them, and despite the limitations inherent to their praxis, ICCs' imaginations of infrastructure and care could serve as a foundation to rethink the very political and economic paradigms that structure institutions, particularly welfare, in the Global North.

Second, I have conceptualized the daily ruling and management of the ICCs as a *politics of dwelling*—in lowercase to note its situatedness. This concept points to a political culture that develops in the realm of social reproduction and everyday life that can help us dehabituate ourselves from capitalist forms of living, relating, and organizing common affairs. Whereas the capitalist political imagination grounds itself in abstraction, extraction, ownership, and accumulation, dwelling as politics, on the contrary, represents a political modality of proximity, embodiment, provision, and redistribution. It is a political conception that does not claim an abstract universal model of what ought to be, but rather, depicts a political form necessarily situated that develops as people learn to engage in common life and its sustenance. As such, it has the potential to bring about transformative modes of relating, forms of inhabiting space and time, and subjectivities. It gives ways of inhabiting the world through the sensitive and the embodied, through care and the material time of life's processes, in relation to one another, thus challenging the logic of instrumentality and detachment and its apparent solidity.

Finally, I have foregrounded the notion of *embodied we(s)*, signaling the political potentiality of subjectivities that emerge and develop from encounters between individuals who experience a shift toward a form of subjectivity in which they think and feel as in continuity with others and attached to the world. This shift implies a demarcation from neoliberal subjectivities based on a conception of the subject as an individual, as a consciousness dissociated from the body, the world, their materiality, and their affections. I contend that this process of subjectivation restores the subject's political condition as a relational entity capable of inventing new ways of being in the world, opening up radical possibilities of personal and collective action. Attention to the subjective dimension is in this way crucial, for it is after all where desire takes root and drives us to act.

Let me finish here, with this spirit of hope, which I have sensed and shared with many of the people whose lives have been marked by their experiences in the ICCs. There is no doubt that our present is one in crisis, but it is also a present in dispute. Instances like the ICCs show us that there are always other, and others', futures latent in the here and now. My wish is that this book can contribute to prolonging the radical imaginations of the infrastructures of caring citizenship, promoting new encounters across different contexts amid crisis, yet against crisis regimes.

NOTES

1. Documenta is the name of a contemporary art exhibition that take place every five years. Documenta 14, the fourteenth staging of the event, took place in 2017 in Kassel, Germany, and Athens, Greece. It featured the works of over 160 international artists. Under the title *The Parliament of Bodies*, the public programme of the exhibition gathered artists, intellectuals, and activists in a series of activities that sought to question contemporary democratic institutions and the nature and purposes of contemporary art exhibitions.

In Athens, Documenta 14 was fiercely criticized by many local artists and activists, who accused those who staged the exhibition of conveying yet another stereotypical and romanticized image of the city and its crises.

2. The female vocal group Pleiades was founded in 2006. Their polyphonic singing seeks to preserve an ancient tradition of Greek vocal music emblematic of the Epirus region in northwestern Greece.

3. The Athens Conservatoire was designed by Ioannis Despotopoulos, who studied with Walter Gropius, the founder of the Bauhaus School. The building is remarkable for its distinctive internal raw concrete walls, and especially for the amphitheater, whose design was influenced by ancient Greek theaters.

4. The 15M movement is the common name for the citizen-led series of mobilizations and occupations of squares that took place across Spain in 2011, starting on May 15 after a demonstration in Madrid called by a number of citizen collectives under the slogan "Democracia Real Ya! (Real democracy right now!) It also came to be known as the Indignados movement. The 15M had a strong influence in the Greek Movement of the Squares, and later on in the Occupy Movement (in the United Kingdom and the United States), YoSoy132 (in Mexico), and Nuit Debout (in France).

5. The occupation of Syntagma Square, in front of the Greek parliament, took place in May 2011 without the leadership of any political party, group, or union. The occupation, which followed months of massive mobilizations against austerity policies and measures, ended with an encampment that lasted more than two months. The experience would be key for the later formation of many so-called solidarity initiatives, which are the main focus of this book. A detailed account of the event and its legacy is provided in chapter 1.

6. The term the "Crisis" became increasingly used in Greece by media and citizens for the multifaceted crisis—or multiple intertwined crises (economic, political, social, and so forth)—that followed the official declaration of the national debt crisis in 2010. In this book, I refer to it with capital letters in order to stress its character as a social construct.

7. *Καφενείο* (*kafeneio*) is the Greek word for a neighborhood-based coffee shop.

8. The relation between the processes of signification and definition of reality, namely of production of knowledge and discourses, and the forms of exercising power and control over individuals—whether through top-down state power, mechanisms of self-regulation of one's conduct, or institutional strategies of social control—was called by Foucault ([1969] 2002, 2008, 2017) "governmentality."

Foucault developed the concept between 1977 and 1984, especially throughout his lectures at the Collège de France. The philosopher uses the term "government" in a broad sense, referring to state politics, but also to other control mechanisms, including those of or for one's self-control, as well as those aimed at whole populations and defined as "biopolitical," like forms of institutional social control in hospitals, schools, and prisons. The "mentality" part of the term refers to the forms of producing knowledge (and discourses), which individuals assume and internalize. With the concept of governmentality, Foucault introduced a new way of looking at and analyzing power and power relationships, arguing that the exercise of power is always backed by a political rationality, namely that politics and knowledge bear an intrinsic relationship.

9. The transformative character of crisis is reflected economically, materially, and spatially, but also in terms of perceptions, sensibilities, practices, and relationships, all of which are intimately related to subjective production, namely the formation and transformation of subjectivities. This argument was first posed by Foucault ([1969] 2002, 2008, 2017), who explained that crises bring about the emergence of new subjectivities, for they constitute moments of rupture of established orders, norms, and identities.

10. Castoriadis develops the concepts of "social imaginary" and "radical imagination." They are coconstitutive, that is, one does not exist without the other. The social imaginary comprises the set of images and conceptualizations through which, on the one hand, people within a social group signify and recognize themselves as an entity and, on the other, define "the(ir) real." The radical imagination is the capacity—simultaneously collective and individual—to disrupt established ways of seeing, understanding, and organizing collective life through the creation of new visions and horizons. Where social imaginaries settle, fix, and foreclose, the radical imagination interrupts, breaks down, and opens up. With the radical imagination, the philosopher acknowledges society's creativity and its capacity to break down its very instituted character.

11. The concept of "urban neoliberalism" was developed by critical geographers—among them Neil Brenner, Jamie Peck, and Nick Theodore—based on the work of the Marxist geographer David Harvey. The main theoretical proposition rests on the idea that cities are not just affected by neoliberalism, but rather they constitute fundamental elements for the process of economic neoliberalization—as well as for its contestation. Cities have become crucial components of contemporary processes of capitalist accumulation.

12. Neoliberalization has largely been defined as a political project that rearticulates the relationship between state, market, and citizenship in ways that allow the continua-

tion of the process of capital accumulation in the hands of the economic elites (Harvey 2000, 2007, 2008, 2012). Naming it has helped to analyze its origins, characteristics and effects. In the same vein, naming the "neoliberal city" has created a framework for the investigation of contemporary changes in cities. However, is there such a thing as the neoliberal city? Lately, the overuse of the concept to describe any kind of urban process has been subjected to criticism by a number of scholars. Pinson and Morel Journel (2016) question the proclaimed hegemonic nature of neoliberalization processes in the city by elaborating on the very limitations of the term. They state that for many cities and countries—in southern Europe for example—it cannot be claimed that there has been a complete shift in the national and urban policies toward the liberalization of the market. The widespread tendency of attributing all sorts of urban phenomena to neoliberalization overlooks or misunderstands changes that are not induced or related to it.

13. The notion of "urban enclosures" is used in reference to processes of capitalist seizure of urban resources and privatization of urban properties and spaces, which often entail the expulsion of the populations who used and/or inhabited them. Harvey (2004, 2007) sees urban enclosures as part of a historical process of "accumulation by dispossession" within the history of capitalism. The term "enclosure" was used by Marx in *Das Kapital* to allude to the processes of what he called "primitive accumulation" of capital, which historians date back to the thirteenth century in England, and which would become a far-reaching phenomenon during the sixteenth century. The enclosure was the legal process by which the ruling classes took possession of common lands, which were fenced off (enclosed) and became private property. Subsequently, the direct producers of the land would become wage workers. These events, which involved violence and war, would mark the emergence of the capitalist mode of production.

14. Giorgio Agamben (2003) responds to the concept of "state of exception" as formulated by the jurist and member of the Nazi Party Carl Schmitt. His book focuses on how governments in times of crisis extend their power beyond the established law through the declaration and institution of a state of exception by which constitutional rights are allowed to be restricted or suspended. This process bears a relationship with the production of knowledge. During states of exceptions new "truths" emerge while other voices are suppressed. The philosopher reflects on the negative consequences on citizens' rights when states of exception become an enduring condition.

15. Already in the 1960s women started organizing against the "burden" of care work. They pointed out that reproductive labor, which was performed largely by women, was what kept society alive and running. Under capitalism, this work was mostly unpaid and undervalued, precisely because of the way it was gendered. Earlier in 1952, in the classic newspaper article "A Woman's Place," Selma James had already stated that "when a woman comes home from work at night, there is quite a difference from when a man comes home from work. As soon as she comes home, she starts working all over again." Framing care in this way, namely as labor within the capitalist system, situates it within the epistemological tradition of Marxist feminist thought.

Over time, the concept of reproduction within feminist thought was expanded from its initial focus on work in the home—encompassing childcare and elderly care, cooking/feeding, personal hygiene or daily accompaniment, as well as those tasks related to the maintenance of the domestic space like cleaning, doing the laundry or washing up—to incorporate any form of labor related to the daily restoration of the individual as well as her reproduction from generation to generation.

16. Lise Vogel ([1983] 2013) takes up and elaborates on the Marxist concept of social reproduction, proposing a "unitary" approach, which integrates the two meanings to which Marx alludes in his work, namely the reproduction of both the worker and class society. This perspective is central to the body of work that is being produced at present under the term "social reproduction theory" (SRT).

17. SRT builds on the Marxist feminist tradition, taking on the unitary approach to the notion of social reproduction advanced by Lise Vogel ([1983] 2013). Broadly, SRT is based on the argument that social reproduction is essential for the daily and generational restoration of human life—hence human labor power—and for the very capitalist system.

SRT scholars have shown a critical position with respect to the idea of "crisis of care," contending that such a so-called crisis is just one aspect of a much wider crisis. In their view, speaking of a "crisis of social reproduction" as opposed to a "crisis of care" provides a more comprehensive understanding of our contemporary situation. According to them, the present state of chronic crisis is reflective of the inherent contradiction of the capitalist economy, whereby the system's drive to unlimited accumulation jeopardizes the processes of social reproduction, which in turn are necessary for capital to be produced and reproduced.

18. Care and its associated subjectivities have been—and still are—controversial topics within feminism, in part due to the long-standing associations of care with femininity. Should women defend care? Will they not risk a reinforcement of gender roles in so doing? These are questions still on the table within feminist debates. Pérez Orozco (2014) talks of a "reactionary ethics of care," explaining that the constitution of the self as a woman is linked to an ethics of sacrifice for others, which in her view produces damaged subjects, ultimately at the service of capitalist accumulation. On the contrary, the subjective construction of a man follows a "productivist ethics," which she describes as the construction of the self for the self through paid work. The female-male subjective divide operates as a normative framework by which bodies are read and allocated a specific position and status in the socioeconomic system. Ultimately, it serves to construct—and reconstruct—the socioeconomic institutions, which in turn reproduce this same gender-based binary logic. Today, the "reactionary ethics of care" can certainly be found in many political discourses that defend a framework of normative differentiation between men and women to organize society and the economy. Yet, drawing on the multiple struggles over reproduction and the discussions arising from/around them, the new feminist wave has taken a clear stance against these discourses by (re)claiming care as a driving principle for systemic change. This has prompted new considerations on the potentialities of an "ethics of care" understood in opposition to its reactionary version.

19. T. H. Marshall is regarded as the ideologist of modern citizenship. He advanced a threefold formulation of citizenship, which continues to be taken as a starting point in citizenship studies and debates. This definition encompasses three types of rights, namely civil, political, and social. The distinctive element as regards previous citizenship frameworks is the inclusion of social rights—understood as welfare rights—as part of the rights acquired via citizenship and in turn as part of the states' responsibility. Thus, Marshall's (1950) formulation came to be known as "social citizenship."

20. Note that before Isin (2009), Harvey's seminal essay had already elaborated the concept of "the right to the city" (Harvey 2008).

21. In 2015, the Group for Debates in Anthropological Theory (GDAT)—which, hosted by the University of Manchester and sponsored by the Association of Social Anthropologists, held annual debates on anthropological theoretical developments until 2017—held a meeting to discuss whether attention to infrastructure could reconfigure anthropological approaches to the political. AbdouMaliq Simone was among the scholars who participated in that discussion (see Venkatesan et al. 2018).

22. In speaking of neoliberal governmentality, Foucault ([1969] 2002, 2008, 2017) points out the mechanisms of self-governance that the neoliberal subject would have internalized, which ultimately serve the established political regime. He speaks of the "entrepreneurial self," referring to a prominent neoliberal subjectivity characterized by the administration of the self and one's everyday life as if those were a company.

23. Ferrara talks about the "disposable" in his monograph about the Argentinian *piqueteros* of MTD-Solano (Ferrara 2003), *Más allá del corte de rutas: La lucha por una nueva subjetividad* (Beyond roadblocks: The struggle for a new subjectivity).

24. Ferrara's (2003) conceptualization of the subject is linked to the concept of "bare life," which was coined by Agamben (1998). Agamben contends that the law has historically held the power to define and distinguish individuals as political beings (rights holders) or "bare lives" (deprived of rights, "just" bodies). Following Agamben, the subject, in Ferrara's terms, would refer to a political being as opposed to a bare life.

25. The online map of ICCs in Athens was accessible until the end of my doctoral program on a server provided by University College London. Since then, the geography of ICCs in Athens has changed substantially.

26. Puig de la Bellacasa (2017) builds on the work of influential feminist thinkers like Sandra Harding and Donna J. Haraway to elaborate her thought on care knowledge politics.

27. See Haiven and Khasnabish (2014).

CHAPTER 1. The Emergence of Infrastructures of Caring Citizenship in Athens-in-Crisis

1. After the war between Greece and Turkey (1919–1922), in 1923, Greece and Turkey agreed to carry out an unprecedented large-scale population exchange, which was defined in the Convention Concerning the Exchange of Greek and Turkish Populations and involved more than one and a half million people, most of them Greeks living within Turkey's borders at the time. In the span of several months, nearly a million people arrived as refugees in Greece, which at the time had a total population of slightly over five and a half million.

2. The origins of the *polykatoikia* date back to the 1930s. As Aureli, Giudici, and Issaias (2012) explain, it was devised as an architectural typology catering to the Athenian bourgeoisie.

3. In 1967 a coup d'état led by a group of colonels succeeded in establishing a series of military juntas that ruled over seven years. In Greece, the period is popularly referred to as the Junta or the Dictatorship. It lasted until 1974, when a democratic regime was

established following a series of events, of which the uprising at the Polytechnic in 1973 was key.

4. During the 1990s, the migrant influx into Greece—and Athens in particular—increased significantly. This trend continued during the 2000s. However, as explained by Dalakoglou (2013), whereas during the 1990s it was mostly migrants from Eastern Europe, since the beginning of the new century growing numbers came from the Middle East and Africa, many of them lacking legal documentation.

5. As explained by Maloutas and Spyrellis (2016), vertical segregation refers to the social and/or ethnic stratification by floor within the apartment building. In the polyka-toikia, the poorer households used to reside on the lower floors whereas the wealthier would occupy the higher ones.

6. *Future Suspended* (Filippidis et al. 2014) is a documentary that was produced within the research project The City at a Time of Crisis (completed in 2014).

7. The term Troika is used to refer to the authority group established in the wake of the European debt crisis, starting in 2008, to manage the bailout programmes of Greece, Cyprus, Portugal, and Ireland. It was formed by three transnational institutions, namely the European Commission, the European Central Bank, and the International Monetary Fund.

8. The countrywide mobilizations from 2008 until 2011 were described by some media as "traumatic." Koutrolikou (2016) gathers a number of press news that were featured in some of the Greek newspapers with the highest circulations, like *Kathimerini* (conservative-leaning), *To Vima* (conservative-center), *Eleftherotypia* (traditionally left-leaning), and *Ethnos* (formerly associated with PASOK). An example is Leontaridis (2011).

9. As explained by Kurtovik and Ladis in the documentary *Landscapes of Emergency* (Domoney, Dalakoglou, and Filippidis 2013), the concept of "anomie" was introduced as a new term to redefine new "public enemies." A "Zero Tolerance to Anomie" campaign was spread through some media.

10. Part of Antonis Samaras's speech during the electoral campaign for national government can be viewed at Newsbomb: *Αντώνης Σαμαράς*, March 29, 2012, https://www .youtube.com/watch?time_continue=9&v=v5VhF4UhXdI. An important part of the speech, where the president-to-be promised to implement new measures to facilitate deportations, alludes to immigration as a problem: "Our cities have been taken by illegal immigrants. We will recover them."

11. See for example: UNHCR (2016). See also Human Rights Watch (2016); Politaki (2013.)

12. Piraeus is the second largest municipality within the Athens metropolitan area. In the book *Heirs of the Greek Catastrophe: The Social Life of Asia Minor Refugees in Piraeus* (1989), the anthropologist Renée Hirschon provides a detailed account of a community of refugees from Anatolia who resettled in Yerania, an area close to Pireaus, after the exchange of population and continued to live there fifty years after.

13. Alan Kurdi was a two-year-old boy from Syria who drowned on September 2, 2015, in the Mediterranean Sea, together with his mother and brother, while trying to reach Europe from Turkey. Images of his body went around the globe, prompting responses worldwide. Unfortunately, ever since, many more children have lost their lives in the Mediterranean largely due to the EU border regime.

14. "NGOization" refers to the emergence and expansion of NGOs, normally from a critical perspective. The large-scale arrival of asylum seekers in Greece in 2015 was followed by the establishment of a large number of NGOs in the country, most of them international. This process prompted critiques among some social actors, especially among grassroots initiatives addressing migrant issues and struggling for migrant rights.

15. Koutrolikou (2016) and Boano and Gyftopoulou (2016) gather in their respective papers a number of local press news in relation to the so-called crisis of the center of Athens. A further example is Pouliopoulos (2011).

In addition, I found Lampropoulos (2010) and Katsounaki (2010). Examples from international media and human rights agencies are Kitsantonis (2011) for the *New York Times*, Markaris (2013) for *El País*, Estepa (2015) for *El Confidencial*, Brozak (2015) for *Forbes*, and Human Rights Watch (2012).

16. Paraskevis et al. (2011) show a sharp rise in the number of new HIV infections in Greece.

17. The Xenios Zeus operation was criticized by organizations like Amnesty International (2014) and Human Rights Watch (2013).

18. According to the Organisation for Economic Co-operation and Development (OECD) statistics on Greece, unemployment rates during The Crisis changed as follows: 7.8 percent in 2008, 27.5 percent in 2013, and 19.3 percent in 2018.

According to the Hellenic Statistical Authority data from the European System of Integrated Social Protection Statistics (ESSPROS), unemployment benefit expenditure (in million €) during The Crisis changed as follows: 2,849 in 2008, 2,411 in 2013 and 1,691 in 2016.

19. According to the Household Budget Survey of the Hellenic Statistical Authority, the percentage change in the average household expenditure for goods and services from 2008 to 2017 was as follows: food (−16.9), health (−27.4), education (−29.2), clothing and footwear (−53.4).

The average monthly household expenditure changed as follows: €2120.40 in 2008, €1509.39 in 2013, and €1414.09 in 2017.

20. As noted by Solidarity for All in their report "Building Hope against Fear and Devastation" (2014–215), the total increase in the price of electricity from 2008 to 2013 surpassed 44 percent.

21. According to the Private Debt Project by the OECD (2016), household debt (as percentage of net disposable income) went from 85 in 2008 to 120 in 2013.

22. According to the System of Health Accounts of the Hellenic Statistical Authority, total funding on health expenditures (in million €) during The Crisis changed as follows: 23,193.6 in 2009, 15,201.4 in 2013, and 14,492.2 in 2017.

According to the Hellenic Statistical Authority data from ESSPROS, total funding on social protection (in million €)—including sickness, disability, old age, survivors, family, unemployment, housing, and social exclusion—during the Crisis changed as follows: 57,690 in 2009, 47,049 in 2013, and 45,661 in 2016.

According to the Index Mundi of Education Expenditure in Greece, total funding for education (in US$) changed as follows: 10,002.92 in 2009, 7,426.76 in 2013, and 6,061.12 in 2015.

23. In the Greek National Healthcare System, social insurance coverage is linked to employment. As reflected in the report Economou et al. (2017, 113–124), the fast increase

in unemployment triggered by the economic crisis deprived many people—approximately 2.5 million—of comprehensive healthcare coverage. In 2012, as a response to the Ministry of Health's directive to exclude undocumented immigrants from medical treatment, doctors issued a public refusal statement. However, in 2016, the SYRIZA-led government introduced new legislation, which provided access to healthcare for the uninsured and vulnerable, including people without healthcare coverage, legal migrants, children, pregnant women, and people with chronic conditions, regardless of their insurance status.

24. The City at a Time of Crisis: Transformations of Public Spaces in Athens, Greece (TCATC) was a research project led by Dimitris Dalakoglou at the University of Sussex about the transformations of Athens in the wake of the international financial crisis. It was completed in May 2014 with the conference "Crisis-scapes: Athens and Beyond," which was held at the National Technical University of Athens. The project produced extensive research about how public spaces in Athens changed during the austerity regime. Information about the project is available at https://gtr.ukri.org/projects?ref =ES%2FK001663%2F1#/tabOverview.

25. The article "Seizing Public Land in Attica" (Hadjimichalis 2015) includes a list of sites within the Athens metropolitan area whose sale was underway by 2015. Among them, public land in Glyfada; Faliron Bay; land area in Voula, including Voula Beach B; and land area in Anavyssos.

26. In 2014, the FIDH and its member organization the Hellenic League for Human Rights (HLHR) issued a report called "Downgrading Rights: The Cost of Austerity in Greece," in which they denounced that austerity measures were undermining human rights. The report notes how attacks on certain civil and political rights were enacted and/or reinforced during The Crisis.

27. In March 2017, the police carried out raids in squats in central Athens, which ended with the detention of dozens of undocumented migrants.

28. As explained by Siatitsa (2016), the creation of a "safe environment" for real-estate investors under the policy framework established within the austerity programs comprised new tools and financial products for the management of real-estate property that included dropping taxation for (large) property transactions, the flexibilization of rental leases, and diminishing high rental incomes taxation.

29. Although statistics on homeless people in Greece, and in Athens in particular, vary depending on the source, in 2017, the European Federation of National Organisations Working with the Homeless (FEANTSA), which is supported by the EC, issued a report confirming the rise in homeless people, particularly rough sleepers, during the austerity regime.

30. As per the statistics released by the Asylum Service (Ministry of Migration Policy, Hellenic Republic) from June 7, 2013, to October 31, 2018, a total of 191,825 asylum applications were registered in Greece, 48,263 of them in Attica. Syrians comprise 31.1 percent and Afghans 12.9 percent of the total. Data is available at http://asylo.gov.gr/en/?page_id =110.

31. The EU-Turkey agreement was signed in March 2016 and was in force for two years. It was a statement of cooperation between EU member states and Turkey aimed at controlling and actually reducing the number of people crossing from the latter to Greece. Undocumented migrants reaching the Greek islands would be sent back to Turkey. EU

states would take a Syrian asylum seeker in exchange. Additionally, Turkey would be granted €3 billion of European funds to improve the living conditions of Syrian refugees in the country.

32. As reported by the Asylum Information Database (AIDA) (Konstantinou and Georgopoulou, 2019), which is managed by the European Council on Refugees and Exiles (ECRE), the location of most camps outside urban areas creates a feeling of exclusion. Since 2016, complaints by residents regarding the material conditions of the camps, violent incidents, and lack of security have not decreased.

33. The "Arab Spring" refers to the series of protests, demonstrations, and armed uprisings against autocratic regimes that took place across the Middle East in 2011. The Arab Spring started in Tunisia in December 2010, when the self-immolation of Mohamed Bouazizi—a young Tunisian street vendor—sparked protests nationwide, eventually leading to the expulsion of president Ben Ali. The effects of the so-called Tunisian Revolution reached many other countries, such as Libya, Egypt, Yemen, Syria, Bahrain, Morocco, and Lebanon, among others. In some of them, as in Egypt, the government was eventually overthrown, whereas in others, as in Syria and Yemen, a civil war soon ensued.

34. The so-called Solidarity Economy movement comprises local initiatives of different kinds across all sectors of the economy, namely production, distribution, consumption, and finance. What all of them have in common is their not-for-profit orientation and the effort to transform capitalist economic relations and processes—which are based on the exploitation of the working force and depletion of natural resources—following principles of social justice. Examples include worker co-ops, food-related initiatives, freeshops, and time banks.

35. An update of the situation and geography of ICCs in Athens in 2022 is provided in the Epilogue.

36. Solidarity for All (Αλληλεγγύη για Όλους) is an umbrella organization that provides funding and resources for various solidarity initiatives. It was created in 2012 and is funded by the parliamentary party SYRIZA.

37. The so-called Balkan route was used during 2015 and early 2016 by migrants and refugees to get to Western Europe from Greece and Turkey. Slovenia, Serbia, Croatia, and Macedonia closed their respective borders to new migrants in March 2016 after the signing of the EU-Turkey agreement, leaving thousands stranded in Greece.

38. The Initiative of Solidarity to Economic and Political Refugees was set up in 2015 by Greek activists, anarchists, and international volunteers as a support platform for newly arrived migrants, asylum seekers and refugees in the country.

CHAPTER 2. Care Commons Infrastructures

1. In the 1990s, the EU supported EuroFem, a feminist network that exchanged ideas and experiences of city making and governance with a gender-sensitive approach. The network made an important step toward the introduction of factors of gender equality into urban planning agendas, achieving significant outcomes in some cases in the United Kingdom, the Netherlands, Scandinavia, and Austria.

2. Horelli and Vepsä's (1994) work is part of a tradition of feminist scholarship within the built environment disciplines that started in the late 1970s in the United States and

Europe and has actively contributed to exposing how gender relations shape the configuration of cities and urban life.

3. The term "global care chains" was coined by Arlie Hochschild (2000). Care chains are performed mainly by women across the globe. Women of the Global South are employed by families in the North to cover the daily care tasks in the homes of the latter that the women of those families can no longer perform due to their entry into the (productive) labor market. This way, women of the South migrate to the North for paid care work, finding themselves forced to delegate care responsibilities in their own homes to other family members.

4. "Autonomist Marxism" is the term used to designate a tradition of intellectual work stemming from the convergence of two historic social movements, namely *operaismo* and *autonomia*, which operated in Italy between the late 1960s and early 1980s. Autonomist Marxism's systematic critique of all areas of social life under capitalism has influenced scholars and activists within the political Left over the past five decades, providing a theoretical framework for a wide range of intellectual questions, social movements, and struggles.

5. "Communitarian fabrics" is my own translation of the Spanish terms *tramas comunitarias* or *entramados comunitarios*, used by Gutiérrez Aguilar (2017, 2018) in her intellectual work. Communitarian fabrics speak of processes of community formation through shared practices and activities of different sorts in everyday life, as opposed to identity-bound communities.

6. Stavrides (2016, 2–3) explains that commoning practices are not necessarily open and dynamic in character: "They may either be organised as a closed system which explicitly defines shared space within a definite perimeter and which corresponds to a specific community of commoners." A telling example of this is so-called gated communities, housing estates whose boundaries are fenced off and whose entrance is restricted and controlled.

7. In 2015, thousands of asylum seekers arrived at the port of Piraeus, eventually settling for months in an improvised encampment assisted by volunteers in the absence of an appropriate reception plan by the Greek authorities. After those people were resettled in official camps and other accommodation facilities, the self-run initiative Pamperaki set up a warehouse in the old airport of Helliniko, from which they distributed medical aid and pharmaceuticals, food, clothes, school supplies and toys, hygiene products, and other essential products donated by individuals and NGOs to ICCs and other self-organized structures supporting people in need. The Elliniko warehouse was a key logistics infrastructure for the network of solidarity initiatives across Athens.

8. The ACP&P is part of the network the Social Solidarity Clinics and Pharmacies of Attica, which includes sixteen clinics and/or pharmacies—among them the Metropolitan Community Clinic at Helliniko, Peristeri Social Solidarity Clinic, Solidarity Clinic in Kalamata, and Patissia Social Solidarity Pharmacy.

As reported on its website, the ACP&P has supplied hygiene products, first aid items, baby milk, and/or food in several state-led detention centers like the ones on the islands of Rhodes, Petrou Ralli, and Amygdaleza, in UNHCR-led refugee camps in Diavata, Galatsi, Elaion, Helliniko, Schistos, Skaramagas, and Eleusis, and also in self-run refugee camps like Lavrion. Food was supplied also to refugees settled at Pedion tou Areos Park in central Athens.

Some international NGOs that have collaborated with the ACP&P include Médecins sans Frontières (MSF), Red Cross, and Médecins du Monde. The ACP&P has received funding from solidarity groups from Germany, France, the UK, Belgium and Switzerland.

9. Some other ICCs, solidarity initiatives and political spaces that have borne relationships with O Allos Anthropos include Mano Aperta social kitchen, El Chef social kitchen, Terra Verde free-trade initiative, Notara 26 refugee squat, Spirou Trikoupi 17 refugee squat (no longer active at the present), and Steki Metanaston migrant center.

10. Other ICCs and independent organizations that have borne relationships with Khora include Skouros free-shop, Jafra Foundation, Steps, Melissa, Amurtel, Orange House, Love and Serve without Borders, Hope Café, DoYourPart, and No Border School. Legal aid organizations that have worked with Khora include Solidarity Now and Diotima. Education organizations and artist collectives include Giving for a Better Future, Victoria Square Project, and the Flying Seagull. Among others, Khora has been provided with free food and clothing supplies from the Elliniko city warehouse, which was self-run by the independent initiative Pampiraki. NGOs and charities that have supported Khora include Thighs of Steel, Solidarity with Refugees, HelpRefugees, and Lush. Ithaca Mobile Laundry used to go once a week to Khora. Some refugee/migrant squats connected with Khora at the time of my fieldwork were City Plaza and Spirou Trikoupi 17. Currently, neither of them exists.

11. Political initiatives, education organizations, and artist collectives that worked at City Plaza include Welcome United and Alarm Phone, The Flying Seagull, Manu Chao, Musicorama, and Obrint Pas. City Plaza was supplied with free food, clothing and first-necessity products by Pampiraki, Zaporeak, and SOS Refugiados, as well as by MSF at some point. Ithaca Mobile Laundry used to go once a week. Refugee/migrant squats and centers connected with City Plaza at the time of my fieldwork include Notara 26, and Spirou Trikoupi 17, the 5th School, and Khora. Political associations included Diktio and Nosotros social centers. Migrant spaces included Steki Metanaston. International initiatives that supported City Plaza include Das Beste Hotel in Europe.

12. Are You Syrious? is a volunteer-run media venture initiated in Croatia in 2015 with the initial aim of supporting migrants and refugees through the so-called Balkan route. It was eventually registered as an NGO. It carries out advocacy campaigns and sends shipments of aid to countries like Greece and Turkey. Additionally, it provides daily news digests concerning refugees and asylum seekers' issues and conditions.

13. United African Women Organisation was founded in Athens by Loretta Macauley, originally from Sierra Leone. The group seeks to raise awareness of certain issues concerning African women and their children in Greece, to struggle for citizenship rights of the second generation, and to cultivate solidarities among Africans and Greeks.

14. Strefi Hill is an urban park located in Exarcheia in central Athens.

CHAPTER 3. Dwelling as Politics

1. See, for example, the film made to commemorate the two-year anniversary of the squat (City Plaza 2018), https://www.facebook.com/sol2refugeesen/videos/2053680748257591/. Or "Welcome to the Self-Organized Kitchen of City Plaza Squat" (Aikinis et al. 2016), available at https://www.facebook.com/sol2refugeesen/videos/2026399187652414/.

1. The contemporary feminist movement in Spain gained momentum in 2017 and 2018, when thousands took to the streets across the country on March 8—International Women's Day. The Spanish feminist movement has inspired actions across Europe at the grassroots and institutional and policy levels alike.

2. The movement Non Una Di Meno (Not one less) emerged in Italy in 2016 following the Argentinian movement with the same slogan, which was formed to denounce and protest feminicides and gender-based violence following the murder of Chiara Paez.

3. On February 28, 2023, a crash between two trains took place close to the town of Tempe in the Thessaly region of Greece, killing fifty-seven people, mainly young. In the wake of the accident, massive demonstrations and vigils took place in many cities protesting the government, which was deemed responsible by a large majority of people. The transport minister Kostas Karamanlis resigned following these events.

4. The presidential decree ΠΔ 85/2022 passed by the government of Néa Dimokratía, which equated the three-year higher education degrees of acting, theater directing, and dance to secondary education qualification, officially downgrading performing arts studies, led to the resignation of the entire teaching staff of the Drama School of the National Theater, as well as of the Drama School of the State Theatre of Northern Greece. This was followed by mobilizations and theater occupations by students' associations for over two months.

5. A new bill by the government of Néa Dimokratía—which was meant to be passed in January 2024—that will allow the establishment of private universities threatening the free character of higher education in the country, again sparked large mobilizations led by students and occupations of universities over several weeks.

AFTERWORD. Relearning to Live in a World in Crisis

1. The contemporary crisis imaginary has been broadly presented in this book as a power device of enclosure of the future for the many from above. However, as Ogboh's (2017) artwork reminds us, the crisis imaginary is being produced and reproduced by myriad actors from very different positions and also very different aspirations. See, for example, the crisis discourses promulgated by the scientific community and environmental activists that appeal to the climate emergency to mobilize the citizenry in defense of the planet. Thus, it should not be taken as a homogeneous artifact, but rather as a machine for the production of stories and meanings, so far ambivalent and unsettled. I, however, contend that either way, the contemporary crisis imaginary ultimately seeks to stir up fear, albeit to different ends. Yet, whether to coerce, repress, control, or incite resistance, in essence, it remains an imaginary of fear, which unfortunately many times deters and paralyzes more than it mobilizes.

BIBLIOGRAPHY

Agamben, G. (1998). *Homo Sacer: Sovereign Power and Bare Life.* Translated by D. Heller-Roazen. Stanford, Calif.: Stanford University Press.

Agamben, G. (2003). *State of Exception.* Translated by K. Attell. Chicago: University of Chicago Press.

Alam, A., and D. Houston. (2020). "Rethinking Care as Alternate Infrastructure." *Cities,* 100: 102662.

Angelo, H., and C. Hentschel. (2015). "Interactions with Infrastructure as Windows into Social Worlds: A Method for Critical Urban Studies: Introduction." *City,* 19(2–3): 306–312.

Arampatzi, A. (2016). "The Spatiality of Counter-Austerity Politics in Athens, Greece: Emergent 'Urban Solidarity Spaces.'" *Urban Studies,* 54(9): 2155–2171.

Arampatzi, A. (2017). "Contentious Spatialities in an Era of Austerity: Everyday Politics and Struggle Communities in Athens, Greece." *Political Geography,* 60: 47–56.

Arampatzi, A., H. Kouki, and D. Pettas. (2022). "Re-thinking Solidarity Movements as Infrastructure during the COVID-19 Pandemic Crisis: Insights from Athens." *Social Movement Studies,* 23(6): 777–793.

Arampatzi, A., and W. J. Nicholls (2012). "The Urban Roots of Anti-Neoliberal Social Movements: The Case of Athens, Greece." *Environment and Planning A,* 44(11): 2591–2610.

Arruzza, C., N. Fraser, and T. Bhattacharya. (2019). *Feminism for the 99%: A Manifesto.* London: Verso.

Athanasiou, A. (2018). "States of Emergency, Modes of Emergence. Critical Enactments of 'The People' in Times of Crisis." In *Critical Times in Greece: Anthropological Engagements with the Crisis,* edited by D. Dalakoglou and G. Agelopoulos, 15–31. New York: Routledge.

Aureli, P. V., M. S. Giudici, and P. Issaias, P. (2012). "From Dom-ino to Polykatoikia." *Domus,* October 31, 2012. https://www.domusweb.it/en/architecture/2012/10/31/from-dom-ino-to-em-polykatoikia-em-.html.

Bartos, A. (2019). "Introduction: Stretching the Boundaries of Care." *Gender, Place & Culture,* 26(6): 767–777.

Berlant, L. (2016). "The Commons: Infrastructures for Troubling Times." *Environment and Planning D: Society and Space*, 34(3): 393–419.

Bhattacharya, T. (ed.). (2017). *Social Reproduction Theory. Remaping Class, Recentering Oppression*. London: Pluto.

Boano, C., and S. Gyftopoulou. (2016). "Crisis-Ridden Space, Politics, and the Social Imaginary: The Case of Athens." *Critical Planning*, 22(3): 67–97.

Brenner, N., P. Marcuse, and M. Mayer (eds.). (2012). *Cities for People, Not for Profit: Critical Urban Theory and the Right to the City*. London: Routledge.

Brenner, N., and N. Theodore. (2002). "Cities and the Geographies of Actually Existing Neoliberalism." *Antipode*, 34(3): 349–379.

Brenner, N., and N. Theodore (eds.). (2004). *Spaces of Neoliberalism: Urban Restructuring in Northern America and Western Europe*. Oxford: Blackwell.

Butler, J. (2015). *Senses of the Subject*. New York: Fordham University Press.

Butler, J., and A. Athanasoiu. (2013). "The Governmentality of 'Crisis' and Its Resistances." In *Dispossession: The Performative in the Political*. Malden, Mass.: Polity.

Cabot, H. (2016). "'Contagious' Solidarity: Rreconfiguring Care and Citizenship in Greece's Social Clinics." *Social Anthropology*, 24(2): 152–166.

Castoriadis, C. ([1975] 1987). *The Imaginary Institution of Society*. Translated by K. Blamey. Malden, Mass.: Polity.

Chalkias, C., P. Delladetsimas, and K. Sapountzaki. (2015). "Adjustments to the Financial Crisis: Redistributing Vulnerability and Producing New Long-Term Risks." *Athens Social Atlas*. https://www.athenssocialatlas.gr/en/article/natural-and-social-vulnerability/.

Chatzidakis A., J. Hakim, J. Littler, C. Rottenberg, and L. Segal. (2020). *The Care Manifesto: The Politics of Interdependence*. London: Verso.

Comité Invisible (2014). *A nuestros amigos*. Translated by V. E. Barbarroja and A. Barrera. Logroño: Pepitas de Calabaza.

Corsín-Jiménez, A. (2014). "The Right to Infrastructure: A Prototype for Open Source Urbanism." *Environment and Planning D: Society and Space*, 32(2): 342–362.

Corsín-Jiménez, A., T. Tiburcio Jiménez, and A. Cisneros. (2024). "Los ensamblajes comunitarios de la COVID-19 en Madrid." *Cuadernos de Trabajo Social*, 37(2): 253–264.

Dalakoglou, D. (2013). "The Crisis before 'The Crisis': Violence and Urban Neoliberalization in Athens." *Social Justice*, 39(1): 24–42.

Dalakoglou, D. (2016). "Infrastructural Gap." *City*, 20(6): 822–831.

Dalakoglou, D., G. Agelopoulos, and G. Poulimenakos. (2018). "*De te fabula narrator?* Ethnography of and during the Greek Crisis." In *Critical Times in Greece: Anthropological Engagements with the Crisis*, edited by G. Agelopoulos and D. Dalakoglou, 1–12. New York: Routledge.

Dalakoglou, D., and Y. Kallianos. (2018). "'Eating Mountains' and 'Eating Each Other': Disjunctive Modernization, Infrastructural Imaginaries and Crisis in Greece." *Politcal Geography*, 67: 76–87.

Dalla Costa, M., and S. James. (1975). *The Power of Women and the Subversion of the Community*. Bristol: Falling Wall.

De Angelis, M. (2017). *Omnia Sunt Communia: On the Commons and the Transformation to Postcapitalism*. London: Zed.

Dowling, E. (2021). *The Crisis of Care*. London: Verso.

D'Souza, R. (2018). *What's Wrong with Rights? Social Movements, Law and Liberal Imaginations*. London: Pluto.

Economou, C., D. Kaitelidou, M. Karanikolos, and A. Maresso. (2017). "Greece Health System Review." *Health Systems in Transition*, 19(5). http://www.euro.who.int/__data /assets/pdf_file/0006/373695/hit-greece-eng.pdf.

Espai en Blanc (2009). "Prólogo: La fuerza del anonimato." *Espai en Blanc*, 5–6. http://espaienblanc.net/?page_id=742.

Federici, S. (2012). *Revolution at Point Zero: Housework, Reproduction, and Feminist Struggle*. Oakland, Calif.: PM Press/Common Notions/Autonomedia.

Federici, S. (2019). *Re-enchanting the World: Feminism and the Politics of the Commons*. Oakland, Calif.: PM Press/Kairos.

Fernández-Savater, A. (2012). "Política literal y política literaria (Sobre ficciones políticas y 15-M." *Interferencias eldiario.es*, December 30, 2012. https://www.eldiario .es/interferencias/ficcion-politica-15-M_6_71452864.html.

Fernández-Savater, A. (2018). "Políticas del deseo: Retomar la intuición del 68." *Interferencias eldiario.es*, May 11, 2018. https://www.eldiario.es/interferencias/mayo -del-68-deseo-lyotard_132_2124280.html.

Fernández-Savater, A. (2020). *Habitar y gobernar: Inspiraciones para una nueva concepción política*. Barcelona: NED Ediciones.

Ferrara, F. (2003). *Más allá del corte de rutas: La lucha por una nueva subjetividad*. Buenos Aires: La Rosa Blindada.

Foucault, M. ([1969] 2002). *The Archaeology of Knowledge*. Translated by A. M. Sheridan Smith. London: Routledge.

Foucault, M. (2008). *The Birth of Biopolitics: Lectures at the Collège de France, 1978–1979*. Edited by M. Senellart. Translated by G. Burchell. New York: Palgrave Macmillan.

Foucault, M. (2017). *Subjectivity and Truth: Lectures at the Collège de France, 1980–1981*. Edited by F. Gros. Translated by Burchell, G. London: Palgrave Macmillan.

Fraser, N. (2013). *Fortunes of Feminism: From State-Managed Capitalism to Neoliberal Crisis*. London: Verso.

Garcés, M. (2013). *Un mundo común*. Barcelona: Bellaterra.

Gibson-Graham, J. K. (2006). *A Postcapitalist Politics*. Minneapolis: University of Minnesota Press.

Gibson-Graham, J. K., J. Cameron, and S. Healy. (2013). *Take Back the Economy: An Ethical Guide for Transforming Our Communities*. Minneapolis: University of Minnesota Press.

Gilligan, C. (1982). *In a Different Voice: Psychological Theory and Women's Development*. Cambridge, Mass.: Harvard University Press.

Graham, S., and C. McFarlane. (2015). "Introduction." In *Infrastructural Lives: Urban Infrastructure in Context*, edited by S. Graham and C. McFarlane, 1–14. New York: Routledge.

Guattari, F. (2015). *Psychoanalysis and Transversality: Text and Interviews, 1955–1971*. Translated by A. Hodges. Los Angeles: Semiotext(e).

Gutiérrez Aguilar, R. (2017). *Horizontes comunitario-populares: Producción de lo común más allá de las políticas estado-céntricas*. Madrid: Traficantes de Sueños. Mapas.

Gutiérrez Aguilar, R. (2018). "Prefacio." In *Cuidado, comunidad y común: Experiencias cooperativas en el sostenimiento de la vida*, edited by C. Vega Solís, R. Martínez Buján, and M. Paredes Chauca, 11–13. Madrid: Traficantes de Sueños.

Hadjimichalis, C. (2015). "Seizing Public Land in Attica." *Athens Social Atlas*. https://www.athenssocialatlas.gr/en/article/seizing-public-land/.

Haiven, M., and A. Khasnabish. (2014). *The Radical Imagination: Social Movement Research in the Age of Austerity*. London: Zed.

Harvey, D. (2000). *Spaces of Hope*. Edinburgh: Edinburgh University Press.

Harvey, D. (2004). "The 'New' Imperialism: Accumulation by Dispossession." *Socialist Register*, 40: 63–87.

Harvey, D. (2007). *A Brief History of Neoliberalism*. Oxford: Oxford University Press.

Harvey, D. (2008). "The Right to the City." *New Left Review*, 53: 23–40.

Harvey, D. (2012). *Rebel Cities: From the Right to the City to the Urban Revolution*. London: Verso.

Hiernaux, D., and A. Lindón. (2012). "Renovadas intersecciones: La espacialidad y lo imaginario." In *Geografías de lo imaginario*, edited by D. Hiernaux and A. Lindón, 9–28. Barcelona: Anthropos.

Hirschon, R. (1989). *Heirs of the Greek Catastrophe: The Social Life of Asia Minor Refugees in Piraeus*. Oxford: Clarendon Press.

Hochschild, A. (2000). "Global Care Chains and Emotional Surplus Value." In *On the Edge: Living with Global Capitalism*, edited by A. Giddens and D. Hutton, 130–146. London: Vintage.

Holston, J. (1998). "Spaces of Insurgent Citizenship." In *Cities and Citizenship*, edited by J. Holston, 155–173. Durham, NC: Duke University Press.

Horelli, L., and K. Vepsä. (1994). "In Search of Supportive Structures for Everyday Life." In *Women and the Environment*, edited by I. Altman and A. Churchman, 201–206. New York: Plenum.

Isin, E. (2009). "Citizenship in Flux: The Figure of the Activist Citizen." *Subjectivity*, 29: 367–388.

Isin, E. (2012). *Citizens Without Frontiers*. London: Bloomsbury.

Isin, E. (2014). "Acts." In *Migration: A COMPAS Anthology*, edited B. Anderson and M. Keith, 162–164. Oxford: COMPAS.

Isin, E. (2017). "Performative Citizenship." In *The Oxford Handbook of Citizenship*, edited by A. Shachar, R. Bauböck, I. Bloemraad, and M. Vink, 500–523. Oxford: Oxford University Press.

Isin, E., and G. Nielsen. (2008). "Introduction: Acts of Citizenship." In *Acts of Citizenship*, edited by E. Isin and G. Nielsen, 1–12. London: Zed.

James, S. (1952). "A Woman's Place." *Correspondence*, February.

Kalandides, A., and D. Vaiou. (2015). "Practices of Collective Action and Solidarity: Reconfigurations of the Public Space in Crisis-Ridden Athens, Greece." *Journal of Housing and the Built Environment*, 31(3): 457–470.

Kalantzis, K. (2016). "Introduction—Uncertain Visions: Crisis, Ambiguity, and Visual Culture in Greece." *Visual Anthropology Review*, 32(1): 5–11.

Kaltsa, M., and T. Maloutas. (2015). "The Project 'Reactivate Athens—101 Ideas': Athens in Crisis and the Social Dimension of Urban Design." *Athens Social Atlas.* https://www.athenssocialatlas.gr/en/article/reactivate-athens/.

Kapsali, M. (2020). "Political Infrastructures of Care: Collective Home Making in Refugee Solidarity Squats." *Radical Housing Journal,* 2(2): 13–34.

Komporozos-Athanasiou, A. (2015). "Alternative Futures Emerging from the Debt Crisis: The Sociological Imagination of the Greek 'OXI.'" *Sociological Review,* July 25, 2015. https://thesociologicalreview.org/collections/greece-debt-and-europe-in-crisis/alternative-futures-emerging-from-the-debt-crisis-the-sociological-imagination-of-the-greek-oxi/.

Koutrolikou, P. (2016). "Governmentalities of Urban Crises in Inner-City Athens, Greece." *Antipode,* 48(1): 172–192.

Lafazani, O. (2018). "Κριση and Μετανάστευση in Greece: From Illegal Migrants to Refugees." *Sociology,* 52(3): 619–625.

Lawhon, M., D. Nilsson, J. Silver, H. Ernstson, and S. Lwasa. (2018). "Thinking through Heterogeneous Infrastructure Configurations." *Urban Studies,* 55(4): 720–732.

Lawson, V. (2007). Geographies of Care and Responsibility." *Annals of the Association of American Geographers,* 97(1): 1–11.

Lefebvre, H. ([1974] 1992). *The Production of Space.* Translated by D. Nicholson-Smith. Malden, Mass.: Wiley-Blackwell.

Lefebvre, H. ([1992] 2004). *Rhythmanalysis: Space, Time and Everyday Life.* Translated by G. Moore and S. Elden. London: Bloomsbury Academic.

Lindón, A. (2012). "¿Geografías de lo imaginario o la dimension imaginaria de las geografías del Lebenswelt." In *Geografías de lo imaginario,* edited by D. Hiernaux and A. Lindón, 65–86. Barcelona: Anthropos.

Lister, R. (2003). *Citizenship: Feminist Perspectives.* 2nd ed. New York: Palgrave Macmillan.

Maloutas, T., and S. N. Spyrellis. (2016). "Vertical Segregation: Mapping the Vertical Social Stratification of Residents in Athenian Apartment Buildings." *Méditerranée,* 127: 27–36.

Manrique, P. (2020). *Lo común sentido como sentido común: Políticas, poléticas y políricas contra el credo neoliberal.* Santander: La Vorágine.

Marshall, T. H. (1950). *Citizenship and Social Class and Other Essays.* New York: Cambridge University Press.

Massey, D. (2005). *For Space.* London: SAGE.

McEwan, C., and M. Goodman. (2010). "Place Geography and the Ethics of Care: Introductory Remarks on the Geographies of Ethics, Responsibility and Care." *Ethics, Place and Environment,* 13(2): 103–112.

McFarlane, C., and J. Silver. (2017). "Navigating the City: Dialectics of Everyday Urbanism." *Transactions of the Institute of British Geographers,* 42(3): 458–471.

Milligan, C., and J. Wiles. (2010). "Landscapes of Care." *Progress in Human Geography,* 34(6): 736–754.

Mitchell, K., S. Marston, and C. Katz. (2004). *Life's Work: Geographies of Social Reproduction.* Malden, Mass.: Blackwell.

Morado Castresana, C. (2021). "Urbanisms for Life Sustenance: An Ethnographic Approach to Collective Methods of City Making from the Periphery of Bogota." PhD diss., Universidad Politécnica de Madrid.

Papadopoulos, T., and A. Roumpakis. (2012). "The Greek Welfare State in the Age of Austerity: Anti-social Policy and the Politico-Economic Crisis." In *Social Policy Review 24: Analysis and Debate in Social Policy, 2012*, edited by M. Kilkey, G. Ramia, and K. Farnsworth, 203–227. Bristol: Policy Press.

Papadopoulos, T., and A. Roumpakis. (2013). "Familistic Welfare Capitalism in Crisis: Social Reproduction and Anti-social Policy in Greece." *Journal of International and Comparative Policy*, 29(3): 204–224.

Pérez Orozco, A. (2014). *Subversión feminista de la economía. Aportes para un debate sobre el conflcito capital-vida.* Madrid: Traficantes de Sueños. Mapas.

Petropoulou, C. (2008). "'Non/de/re/regulation' and Athens' Urban Development (1834—2008)." Translated by P. Koutrolikou, D. Siatitsa, and A. Mermigas. Athens: INURA08 International Congress. https://inura08.files.wordpress.com/2008/10/introductiontoathens.pdf.

Pinson, G., and C. Morel Journel. (2016). "The Neoliberal City: Theory, Evidence, Debates." *Territory, Politics, Governance*, 4(2): 137–153.

Power, E. R., I. Wiesel, E. Mitchell, and K. J. Mee. (2022). "Shadow Care Infrastructures: Sustaining Life in Post-Welfare Cities." *Progress in Human Geography*, 46(5): 1165–1184.

Puig de la Bellacasa, M. (2017). *Matters of Care: Speculative Ethics in More than Human Worlds.* Minneapolis: University of Minnesota Press.

Rakopoulos, T. (2015). "'Solidarity' Tensions. Informality, Sociality, and the Greek Crisis." *Social Analysis*, 59(3): 85–104.

Rivera Cusicanqui, S. (2018). *Un Mundo Chíxi es posible: Ensayos desde un presente en crisis.* Buenos Aires: Tinta Limón Ediciones.

Roitman, J. (2013). *Anti-Crisis.* Durham, NC: Duke University Press.

Sánchez de Madariaga, I. (2004). "Infraestructuras para la vida cotidiana y calidad de vida." *Ciudades: Revista del Instituto Universitario de Urbanística de la Universidad de Valladolid*, 8: 101–133.

Siatitsa, D. (2016). "Changes in Housing and Property under the Austerity Regime in Greece: Challenges for Movements and the Left." In *Urban Austerity: Impacts of the Global Financial Crisis on Cities in Europe*, edited by B. Schönig and S. Schipper, 145–160. Berlin: Theater der Zeit.

Simone, A. (2004). "People as Infrastructure: Intersecting Fragments in Johannesburg." *Public Culture*, 16(3): 407–429.

Simone, A. (2015). "Relational Infrastructures in Postcolonial Urban Worlds." In *Infrastructural Lives: Urban Infrastructure in Context*, edited by S. Graham and C. McFarlane, 1–14. New York: Routledge.

Simone, A. (2018). *Improvised Lives: Rhythms of Endurance in an Urban South.* Cambridge, Mass.: Polity.

Soudias, D. (2023). *Paradoxes of Emancipation: Radical Imagination in Neoliberal Greece.* Syracuse, New York: Syracuse University Press.

Spade, D. (2020). *Mutual Aid: Building Solidarity during This Crisis (and the Next)*. London: Verso.

Stavrides, S. (2016). *Common Space: The City as Commons*. London: Zed.

Theocharopoulou, I. (2017). *Builders, Housewives and the Construction of Modern Athens*. London: Artifice.

Tonkiss, F. (2015). "Afterword: Economies of infrastructure." *City*, 19(2–3): 384–391.

Tronto, J. (1993). *Moral Boundaries: A Political Argument for an Ethic of Care*. New York: Routledge.

Tronto, J. (2015). *Who Cares? How to Reshape a Democratic Politics*. New York: Cornell University Press.

Tronto, J., and B. Fisher. (1990). "Toward a Feminist Theory of Caring." In *Circles of Care: Work and Identity in Women's Lives*, edited by E. K. Abel and M. K. Nelson, 35–62. Albany: SUNY Press.

Tsilimpounidi, M. (2017). *Sociology of Crisis: Visualising Urban Austerity*. New York: Routledge.

Vega Solís, C., R. Martínez Buján, and M. Paredes Chauca. (2018). "Introducción. Experiencias, ámbitos y vínculos cooperativos para el sostenimiento de la vida." In *Cuidado, comunidad y común. Experiencias cooperativas en el sostenimiento de la vida*, edited by C. Vega Solís, R. Martínez Buján, and M. Paredes Chauca, 15–50. Madrid: Traficantes de Sueños.

Venkatesan, S., L. Bear, P. Harvey, S Lazar, L. Rival, and A. Simone. (2018). "Attention to Infrastructure Offers a Welcome Reconfiguration of Anthropological Approaches to the Political." *Critique of Anthropology*, 38(1): 3–52.

Vogel, L. ([1983] 2013). *Marxism and the Oppression of Women: Toward a Unitary Theory*. Leiden: Brill.

Wilkinson, S. (1997). "Feminist Psychology." In *Critical Psychology: An Introduction*, edited by D. Fox and I. Prilleltensky, 247–264. London: Sage.

Zechner, M. (2021). *Commoning Care and Collective Power: Childcare Commons and the Micropolitics of Municipalism in Barcelona*. Vienna: Transversal Texts.

ARTWORKS AND FILMS

Aikinis, T., M. Twenhoeven, F. Lonardi, and L. Serra, City Plaza, and Solidarity2refugees. (2016). *Welcome to the Self-Organised Kitchen of City Plaza Squat*. 3 min., 10 sec.https://www.facebook.com/sol2refugeesen/videos/2026399187652414/.

City Plaza. (2018). *2 Χρόνια*. https://www.facebook.com/sol2refugeesen/videos /2053680748257591/.

Domoney, R., D. Dalakoglou, and C. Filippidis (2013). *Landscapes of Emergency*. Crisis -scape.net. 11 min., 52 sec. https://vimeo.com/69824235.

Filippidis, C., A. Vradis, D. Dalakoglou, R. Domoney, and J. K. Brekke. (2014). *Future Suspended: Athens from Olympic Spectacle to the Dawn of the Authoritarian-Financial Complex*. Crisis-scape.net. 35 min. 26 sec. https://vimeo.com/86682631.

Ogboh, E. (2017). *The Way Earthly Things Are Going*. Documenta 14, Athens Conservatoire (Odeion), Athens, June 13, 2017.

Oikonomakis, L., and J. Roos. (2012). *Utopia on the Horizon: Documentary on the Greek Debt Crisis.* Roar Magazine, November 17, 2012, YouTube, 27 mins., 53 sec. https://www.youtube.com/watch?v=OAnGxynPxL4.

REPORTS

FEANTSA (2017). "Homelessness in Greece." European Federation of National Organisations Working with the Homeless. https://www.feantsa.org/download/greece-20172928673074328238317.pdf.

FIDH/HLHR (2014). "Downgrading Rights: The Costs of Austerity in Greece." Hellenic League for Human Rights. https://www.fidh.org/IMG/pdf/grece646a2014-2.pdf.

Konstantinou, A., and A. Georgopoulou, A. (2018). "Country Report: Greece." Asylum Information Database (AIDA), Greek Council for Refugees, European Council on Refugees and Exiles (ECRE). https://asylumineurope.org/wp-content/uploads/2019/03/report-download_aida_gr_2018update.pdf.

Organisation for Economic Co-operation and Development (2019). "Country Statistical Profile: Greece 2019/2. Key tables from OECD." https://www.oecdilibrary.org/economics/country-statistical-profile-greece-2019-2_g2g9e4f2-en.

Paraskevis, D., G. Nikolopoulos, C. Tsiara, D. Paraskeva, A. Antoniadou, M. Lazanas, P. Gargalianos, et al. (2011). "HIV-1 Outbreak among Injecting Drug Users in Greece, 2011: A Preliminary Report." *Euro Surveillance*, 16(36): pii=19962. http://www.eurosurveillance.org/ViewArticle.aspx?ArticleId=19962.

Solidarity for All. (2014–2015). "Building Hope against Fear and Devastation." Solidarity4all.gr. https://issuu.com/solidarityforall/docs/report_2014.

WEBSITES

Athens Community Polyclinic and Pharmacy website. http://www.kifa-athina.gr/?fbclid=IwAR3fGwKrKEfHDoKQm_5ACCpl-esECk43sQsMetEW1Gxa6mgc6qVTIC_roZk.

European Council on Refugees and Exiles (ECRE). Asylum Information Database (AIDA). http://www.asylumineurope.org/.

Hellenic Republic, Ministry of Migration and Asylum. Asylum Service. https://migration.gov.gr/en/gas/.

Hellenic Statistical Authority. https://www.statistics.gr/en/home/.

Index Mundi. "Greece: Education Expenditure." https://www.indexmundi.com/facts/greece/education-expenditure.

Khora Athens website. https://khoracollective.org/.

Khora Athens Facebook site. https://www.facebook.com/KhoraAthens/.

Κοινωνικό Ιατρείο-Φαρμακείο Αθήνας (Solidarity Social Clinic of Athens) Facebook site. https://www.facebook.com/KoinonikoIatreioPharmakeioAthinas/.

Ο Αλλοσ Ανθρωποσ (O Allos Anthropos). "Ο Αλλοσ Ανθρωποσ Κοινωνικη Κουζινα Δωρεαν Φαγητο για Ολουσ" (Other man social kitchen free food for all). http://oallosanthropos.blogspot.com/.

Refugee Accommodation and Solidarity Space City Plaza Facebook site. https://www
.facebook.com/sol2refugeesen/.

tiki-toki.com. "Athens and the Crisis Timeline." http://www.tiki-toki.com/timeline
/entry/128759/Athens-and-the-Crisis/#vars!date=2012-04-18_00:08:25!.

UK Research and Innovation. "The City at a Time of Crisis: Transformations of Public
Spaces in Athens, Greece." University of Sussex, School of Global Studies. https://gtr
.ukri.org/projects?ref=ES%2FK001663%2F1.

PRESS NEWS

Amnesty International. (2014). "Impunity, Excessive Force and Links to Extremist
Golden Dawn Blight Greek Police." *Amnesty International*, April 3, 2014. https://
www.amnesty.org/en/latest/news/2014/04/impunity-excessive-force-and-links
-extremist-golden-dawn-blight-greek-police/.

Brozak, S. (2015). "Greece Is on the Verge of a Health Catastrophe." *Forbes*, July 15, 2015.
https://www.forbes.com/sites/stephenbrozak/2015/07/15/greece-medical-collapse/.

Estepa, H. (2015). "Drogas, depresiones y prostitución: Los efectos de un lustro de crisis
en Grecia" (Drugs, depressions and prostitution: The effects of a lustrum of crisis in
Greece). *El Confidencial*, January 22, 2015. https://www.elconfidencial.com/mundo
/2015-01-22/droga-y-prostitucion-se-multiplican-en-la-grecia-deprimida-por-la
-crisis_627176/.

Human Rights Watch. (2012). "Greece: Hate on the Streets." *Human Rights Watch*, July 5,
2012. https://www.hrw.org/video-photos/interactive/2012/07/05/greece-hate-streets.

Human Rights Watch. (2013). "Greece: Abusive Crackdown on Migrants." *Human
Rights Watch*, June 12, 2013. https://www.hrw.org/news/2013/06/12/greece-abusive
-crackdown-migrants.

Human Rights Watch. (2016). "Greece: Humanitarian Crisis at Athens Port." *Human
Rights Watch*, March 24, 2016. https://www.hrw.org/news/2016/03/24/greece
-humanitarian-crisis-athens-port.

Katsounaki, M. (2010). "Επικίνδυνα σημάδια γκετοποίησης στην Αθήνα" (Dangerous
ghetto signs in Athens). *Kathimerini*, September 5, 2010. https://www.kathimerini.gr
/society/403891/epikindyna-simadia-gketopoiisis-stin-athina/.

Kitsantonis, N. (2011). "Violent Crime Soars in Athens." *New York Times*, June 14, 2011.
https://www.nytimes.com/2011/06/15/world/europe/15iht-greece15.html.

Kotseta, R. (2012). "Σαμαράς εφ' όλης της ύλης και με σημαία το μεταναστευτικό"
(Samaras for all intents and purposes and with the immigration flag). *Newsbomb*,
March 29, 2012. https://www.newsbomb.gr/politikh/story/174738/samaras-ef-olis-tis
-ylis-kai-me-simaia-to-metanasteytiko?fbclid
=IwAR31m4HvROIOOEcMoFf054oqS5Fj5_r2vd3VdodonOzxACaIrX6VhZ6eGqQ.

Lampropoulos, V. G. (2010). "Αθήνα, η μητρόπολη των παρανόμων" (Athens, the
metropolis of the illegal). *To Vima*, January 31, 2010. https://www.tovima.gr/2010/01
/31/society/athina-i-mitropoli-twn-paranomwn/?fbclid=IwAR05oScDK8fMiFbgShC
oVE4oLT7qWhfQScAzvUtNDh5SK_Cb8WcL8pR4W6Q.

Leontaridis, K. (2011). "The Right to Fear." *Kathimerini*, May 25, 2011. https://www
.kathimerini.gr/opinion/725306/to-dikaioma-ston-fovo/.

Markaris, P. (2013). "La incurable enfermedad de Atenas" (The incurable illness of Athens). *El País*, October 27, 2013. https://elpais.com/elpais/2013/10/23/opinion /1382530173_733758.html.

Médicins du Monde. (2010). "Athens, a City in Humanitarian Crisis." *Médicins du Monde Greece*, November 7, 2010. https://old.mdmgreece.gr/en/athina-mia-poli-se -anthropistiki-krisi/.

Politaki, A. (2013). "Greece Is Facing a Humanitarian Crisis." *The Guardian*, February 11, 2013. https://www.theguardian.com/commentisfree/2013/feb/11/greece -humanitarian-crisis-eu.

Pouliopoulos, G. (2011). "Faces and Tragedies in the Centre of Fear." *To Vima*, May 15, 2011. https://www.tovima.gr/2011/05/15/society/proswpa-kai-tragwdies-sto-kentro -toy-foboy/.

UNHCR. (2016). "UNHCR Warns of Imminent Humanitarian Crisis in Greece amid Disarray in Europe over Asylum." UNHCR, March 1, 2016. https://www.unhcr.org /uk/news/briefing/2016/3/56d564ed6/unhcr-warns-imminent-humanitarian-crisis -greece-amid-disarray-europe-asylum.html.

Vithoulkas, D. (2010). "Σύσκεψη Χρυσοχοΐδη με Δημάρχους: 'Μηδενική ανοχή και κοινωνική συνοχή'" (Consultation between Chrisochoidis and mayors: Zero tolerance and social cohesion). *To Vima*, January 9, 2010. https://www.tovima.gr /2010/01/09/politics/b-syskepsi-xrysoxoidi-me-dimarxoys-b-br-mideniki-anoxi-kai -koinwniki-synoxi/.

INDEX

Academic Asylum, 133

Acharnon Street, 53

ACP&P: ethical, political, and disciplinary considerations, 37–42

ACP&P. *See* Athens Community Polyclinic and Pharmacy

active politics, 98–99

Agamben, Giorgio, 143n14

Aguilar, Raquel Gutiérrez, 17–18, 40, 72, 85, 94, 111, 124, 126

AIDA. *See* Asylum Information Database

alliances, weaving. *See* political possibility, weaving geographies of

Amerikis Square, x53

Amnesty International, 147n17

Angelis, M. De, 72

Angelo, Hillarie, 25, 27

anomie, concept, 50

anonymity: achieving, 30–31; collectiveness and, 112–14; force of, 124

antiausterity movement. *See* Movement of the Squares

antiparochi, method of, 44–45

Anti-Racist Festival, 82

Anti-Racist Parade, 82

Antonis Samaras (ND), 50

Arab Spring, 149n33

Arampatzi, A., 81, 83

assemblies, 35–36, 82, 95, 113, 126; challenging urban processes, 85–88; complaints about sexual misbehaviors in, 108; doctors taking part in, 78; nature of, 101–2; NGO professionals taking part in, 84; structures, dispositives, codes, and pacts, 99–100; Syntagama Square, 62–64; types of, 97–99

Asylum Information Database (AIDA), 149n32

Asylum Service, 148n30

Athanasiou, A., 54

Athens, emergence of ICCs in, 130–35; dispossessions, 55–60; exclusions, 55–60; infrastructural imaginations of care for life sustenance, 88–91; Movement of the Squares, 60–64; production/management of crisis through urban, 48–55; setting up ICCs, 64–68; striving to care otherwise, 74–80; urban development, 43–48; weaving geographies of political possibility, 80–85

Athens Community Polyclinic and Pharmacy (ACP&P), 130–35, 150n8; becoming anonymous collectively, 112–14; case study overview, 33–34; challenging urban processes, 85–88; gender perspective, 107–9; infrastructural imaginations of care for life sustenance, 88–91; methodology, 35–37; self-recalibration in, 114–19; setting up ICCs, 65–66; smooth space in, 119–21; spatiotemporalities, 102–7; striving to care otherwise, 74–80; structures, dispositives, codes, and pacts, 95–102; weaving geographies of political possibility, 80–85

Athens Conservatoire, 1, 141n3

Athens in crisis, constructing, 10, 37, 85, 88–89, 130; area redevelopment, 54; and crisis governmentality," 52; increase in police presence, 52–53; legitimizing social control, 52; naming and configuring specific groups, 53–54; overview, 54–55

Athens Metropolitan Plan, 46

Aureli, P. V, 45

GEOGRAPHIES OF JUSTICE AND SOCIAL TRANSFORMATION

www.ingramcontent.com/pod-product-compliance
Lightning Source LLC
Chambersburg PA
CBHW031356181125
35463CB00090B/2294